The What, Why & How of Instructional Technique

for Driving Instructors

Stuart Kelley

Edited by Hazel Jones

Contents

Forward

There are many books on various aspects of driving instruction on the market today. So what, you may ask, is different about this book?

The aim of this book is to teach you to deliver Effective Instructional Technique. To do this, I have tried to avoid too much general discussion and theory. Instead, this book uses teaching scenarios between instructor and pupil with lessons on all the subjects contained in the current instructional ability examination for driving instructors.

As you read each lesson, it is as if you are sitting in the back of a driving instructor's car listening to a real lesson.

This manual is about what to say, when to say it and how to say it. It contains full briefings, talkthrough routines, carefully constructed questions and fault assessment on all the main examination subjects. It is aimed at potential driving instructors working towards passing their instructional ability test and also approved driving instructors preparing for their check test.

If you are one of the growing number of candidates for the instructional ability test and check test where English is a second language, then you will find this manual particularly valuable.

There are also separate sections covering in detail the core competencies (fault assessment) - the identification, analysis and rectification (remedy) of faults - which is an area that so many potential and approved driving instructors find the most difficult, question and answer technique, and check test preparation.

About the Author and Editor

Stuart Kelley and Hazel Jones are both practicing DSA Approved Driving Instructors (cars). They are also on the DSA Official Register of Driving Instructor Training (ORDIT) and have an impressive reputation for instructor training of the highest quality.

Stuart Kelley runs InstructorDoctors, a successful instructor training organisation based in Uxbridge, West London, which not only provides full instructor training courses, but also specialises in part 3 rescue courses helping potential driving instructors who are having difficulty in passing the qualifying examinations.

Hazel Jones has over 22 years of experience of successfully training driving instructors and has been on the voluntary DSA register of driving instructor trainers since its inception. Having run her own driving school for many years, Hazel now works with Stuart providing their unique blend of expertise and one to one in-car training.

As grade 6 (the highest grade awarded) instructors, Stuart and Hazel also spend a lot of their time helping approved driving instructors to prepare for their periodic check test.

Further information can be found by visiting the website:
www.instructordoctors.co.uk

Acknowledgements

I would firstly like to thank Terry Springle and Hazel Jones for all the help and advice they have given me in the production of this publication and for access to Terry's original instructional techniques manual. Without their valuable on-going support, this project would never have been completed.

Next, I would like to acknowledge all our students, both those still under training with us and those who are now enjoying successful careers as DSA Approved Driving Instructors. Working closely with all these people is what inspired the writing of this book.

Next, I would like to thank the examiners who undertake the instructor examination in our area, for their skill and expertise during the examination and valuable feedback afterwards. Also, for their sound and unbiased advice in response to my questions from time to time.

Lastly, to Rob Jennings and Laura Harvey at Fraction, who have, through their expertise, turned my many pages of original manuscript into this easy to use and expertly designed manual. Also to my wife Maryse, who's proof reading skills were certainly needed to improve the grammar and punctuation of the final draft.

Stuart Kelley

How to use this manual

This manual is aimed principally at potential driving instructors studying for the instructional ability test and for approved driving instructors looking for advice and guidance when preparing for the periodic check tests. Just as importantly however, the instructional techniques you will learn will improve your ability to teach pupils on a daily basis.

Throughout this manual, dialogue between the driving instructor and pupil are used. In order to ensure full understanding by the reader, a descriptive style has been necessary, especially with some of the replies by the pupil to the instructor's questions or comments. This needs to be taken in the context within which it is written, as in real life the pupil's replies may not be so complete.

Parts I and 2 cover all the subjects used in the current instructional ability examination and part 3 contains detailed explanations for all the instructional techniques that you will need to demonstrate. Part 4 deals specifically with check test preparation. The appendix at the end contains other useful advice and guidance as well as explanations of terms used in this manual.

Potential Driving Instructors
Preparing for the instructional ability examination.

Section 1: Beginner and partly trained pupils
Your first task is to work through each lesson in this section.

Recap and Briefing
Learn the recap questions and briefings for each lesson and be able to recite them almost verbatim from the manual wording. This will obviously take some time until you can do this confidently. I suggest that for all the briefings, once you have learnt the basic text, you then try to give the briefing using an appropriate lesson plan and diagram, as this will simulate how you will do this when teaching a real pupil. Once you can do this then record yourself, so that you can listen for any errors or points missed and then practice again until you are happy that all the key points are covered. This method of rote learning is useful to ensure you cover all the areas on the appropriate examination sheet and that you can give a concise, thorough and fluent description of what you will ask the pupil to do in practice after the briefing. Try to time the briefings so that, apart from the Controls lesson (this briefing should take about 30 minutes from start to finish), they can be completed within 6–10 minutes.

Talkthrough routines
For all the partly trained subjects (except the Controls lesson), you will find that a 'talkthrough' follows the briefing. These too need to be learnt by heart and are used to control the pupil as they carry out this exercise for the first time. You will find that, to gain fluency, it is helpful to practice the talkthroughs as you are driving the exercise yourself. For example, once you have learned the talkthrough for moving off and stopping, go out in your car and practice talking yourself through in detail. You will find that this is more difficult than it appears because, as drivers, we do things automatically without really thinking about how we achieve the result. You will find that you have to slow down your actions to give yourself time to say everything. Once you have learnt the basic talkthrough routines then these can be adapted to various traffic conditions that may apply.

Prompting

Once a pupil can perform an exercise under talkthrough, you need to reduce your instruction using prompting. Each lesson in section 1 gives examples of how this can be achieved (also see section on question and answer technique).

The Core Competencies

For each lesson in section 1 the core competencies are dealt with separately, but during the examination, faults will occur throughout the lesson. Fault assessment is the most important part of the instructional ability test and you need to study and develop your understanding and delivery of the identification, analysis and remedial action which make up the core competencies. A separate section is also devoted to fault assessment.

Section 2: Trained pupils and Full Licence Holders

After completing section 1, study the section 2 lessons carefully.

You are now dealing with pupils who have previous knowledge and experience of the lesson subject chosen. This section will develop your question and answer technique to enable you, firstly to try to find out the extent of the pupil's current knowledge and secondly expose the gaps and weaknesses.

Recap

The questions for each lesson are based around the key points from the relevant marking sheet. Study their construction carefully.

Pro-active Q&A and Fault Assessment

In section 2, pro-active Q&A technique and fault assessment are grouped together as they would be in the examination. Study the structure of the questions for each lesson, which are designed to expose gaps in the pupil's knowledge and lead to an analysis of why a fault has occurred. Also see Section 3 where question and answer technique and fault assessment are covered in more detail.

Section 3: Instructional Techniques and the Core Competencies

This section should be studied in conjunction with sections 1 & 2.

In this section, the instructional ability test marking sheet is explained in detail and useful background information is included on the various instructional techniques.

There are separate sections on question and answer technique and the core competencies and these should be studied carefully.

Approved Driving Instructors

Part 4: Check Test Preparation:

This section is for approved driving instructors who are preparing for their periodic test of continued ability and fitness to give instruction - check test.

Firstly, study section 4. Once you have chosen your pupil and subject for your check test then study the relevant lesson in either section 1 or 2. I also recommend that you read the chapters on question and answer technique and the core competencies.

The instructional techniques used throughout this manual are just as relevant for the check test as they are for those studying for the instructional ability test. It is recommended that you study this manual and use it to compare your current teaching methods with those used here and then incorporate those which you feel will enhance and improve these.

> Instructor note: This manual concentrates on the subjects covered in the current instructional ability test and so does not have separate lessons on subjects such as roundabouts or the pass plus syllabus. Also this manual does not cover fleet check tests.

> Author's note: Throughout the scenarios in this manual, any names used are purely imaginary and bear no relation whatsoever to any person bearing those names. Furthermore, I have tried to make sure that the content of this book applies equally to both sexes and if the reader prefers, names or gender can be changed for the various scenarios as appropriate.

Key

Recap		Fault identification	
Objective		Fault analysis	
Briefing		Fault rectification	
Cock pit drill & move off		Driver development	
Talkthrough		Summary	
Prompting		Lesson timing	
Fault assessment		Lesson number	

Instructional ability test examination requirements

On the day of the examination, make sure you arrive at the test centre in good time. However, there will normally be learner driver tests taking place throughout the day, so follow the instructions on your DSA appointment letter.

When meeting the examiner, make sure you have the following documents:
- Your letter of appointment
- Your photo driving licence and paper counterpart
- If you still have the old style licence, you will also need an acceptable form of identification such as a passport.

You should check your appointment letter for any further instructions regarding required documents.

The examiner will ask you to confirm that your vehicle is insured for him to drive for the purposes of the test and will then ask you to sign the declaration at the beginning of the ADI 26 Instructional Test part 3 form.

If you hold a trainee licence, you will be asked for a completed Instructor Training Declaration form ADI 21AT, or a letter confirming additional training received if it is a second or third test. If you do not have this with you the test will normally still be conducted.

Vehicle requirements
Your vehicle should be fitted with 'L' plates which must comply with Regulation 16 of the Motor Vehicles Regulations of 1999.

Insurance
You should check with your insurance company that your vehicle has valid insurance for the part 3 test. As mentioned earlier, the examiner will be driving. The DSA will not normally name an examiner so insurance cover should be for any examiner. Examiners for this test are normally over 25. For any further information you should contact the DSA. You should note that some hire cars are not suitably insured for the examination.

The other requirements for the vehicle used for the examination are as follows:
- Properly taxed and vaild MOT (if required)
- Saloon/estate or hatchback car with rigid roof (with or without a sliding panel)
- Be in a roadworthy condition with seat belts in working order
- Manual transmission and right hand drive with readily adjustable forward facing driver and passenger seats both with head restraints and an internal rear view mirror. Rear head restraints should be working and remain in position (an additional examiner may sit in the back of your vehicle to assess the examiner conducting the examination)
- It should not be fitted with a space saver tyre.

Dual Controls

Your vehicle does not have to have dual controls fitted for the part 3 examination.

Role Play

The examiner will try to adopt and remain in the character of the pupil he/she is playing during each exercise of the test. When you meet a real pupil for the first time, your first task is to check both parts of the driving licence and also carry out an eyesight check by getting them to read a number plate from the required distance. However, for the examination, you can normally assume this has already been carried out. Examiners will try to ensure that any scene set is realistic and relevant in order to try to hide the fact that you are actually teaching a DSA official.

The examiner will test you by committing faults appropriate to the learner driver they are portraying and these will be based around the key points listed at the start of each chapter. The examiner will assess your ability to identify, analyse and remedy these faults.

Although the faults are realistic, the examiner will not place the vehicle, you or other road users in jeopardy because of his/her actions.

Part 3 test requirements

Throughout the part three test the examiner, acting as the pupil, will drive and respond as appropriate to the instruction given. You will be assessed on the method, clarity, adequacy and correctness of your instruction, the observation and correction of driving errors, compliance with the core competencies and your general manner. You will be expected to maintain control of the lesson, display a professional approach by being patient and tactful, and give feedback and encouragement to the pupil when needed. The level of instruction will need to be matched to that of the pupil's ability level portrayed. Whilst the use of diagrams or photographs is an accepted form of training aid, PDIs should not read verbatim from literature or notes.

With the consent of the trainee, Trainers/Tutors may accompany their trainees on test.

The Pre-Set Tests (PST's)

There are two 30 minute phases of the part 3 test and the examiner assumes two roles: first, as either a beginner or a partly trained pupil and finally one who is at about driving test standard (trained) or a full licence holder (FLH). For each of these two phases, the PDI will be asked to give instruction from one of the 12 subjects which are included in the 10 Pre-Set Tests (PSTs). These are as follows:

PST	Phase 1	Phase 2
1	**Controls** - Beginner	**Crossroads** - Trained or Full Licence Holder
2	**Moving off and stopping** - Beginner	**Meeting, crossing, overtaking other traffic, allowing adequate clearance and anticipation** - Trained or Full Licence Holder
3	**Turn in the road** - Partly Trained	**Approaching junctions to turn either right or left** - Trained
4	**Reversing** - Partly Trained	**T junctions, Emerging** - Trained
5	**Emergency stop and use of mirrors** - Partly trained	**Progress, Hesitancy and Normal Positioning** - Trained or Full Licence Holder
6	**Pedestrian crossings and use of signals** - Partly Trained	**Reverse parking** - Trained or Full Licence Holder
7	**Approaching junctions to turn either right or left** - Partly Trained	**Pedestrian crossings and use of signals** - Trained or Full Licence Holder
8	**T junctions, Emerging** - Partly Trained	**Meeting, crossing, overtaking other traffic, allowing adequate clearance and anticipation** - Trained or Full Licence Holder
9	**Crossroads** - Partly Trained	**Pedestrain Crossings and use of signals** - Trained or Full Licence Holder
10	**Meeting, crossing, overtaking other traffic, allowing adequate clearance and anticipation** - Partly Trained	**Progress, Hesitancy and Normal Positioning** - Trained or Full Licence Holder

A more detailed explanation of the beginner, partly trained, trained or full licence holder scenarios are given in the introductions to part 1 and 2.

Part 1

Beginner / Partly Trained Pupil

Introduction to Part 1

The objective of the part 3 test is to assess the value of the instruction that you give, and your ability to impart knowledge to pupils. To do this, the examiner sits in the driving seat and acts the roles of two pupils.

For the first part of the test, the examiner will portray either a beginner or partly trained pupil. Examples of how the examiner will introduce themselves as a pupil are given at the beginning of each lesson.

Beginner Pre-set test (PST) 1 - This is the Controls lesson and the examiner should explain that, as a pupil, he/she has never sat in the driving seat of a car before.

Beginner Pre-set test (PST) 2 - This is the Moving off and Stopping lesson and the examiner should explain that as a pupil, he/she has had a lesson during which the controls were fully explained but they did not get round to moving off.

Partly Trained - The examiner should explain that as a pupil, he/she has had some tuition with another instructor and is at the partly trained stage. The number of hours of tuition already received would not normally be quoted and if asked to state the number of lessons, the 'pupil' would usually say he/she cannot remember exactly how many.

As all phase 1 lessons start from the driving test centre, the examiner will also normally add that all their previous driving lessons have started from there. This is an important point, as each test centre will have particular junctions and hazards to negotiate during the first few minutes after moving off. This may have implications for the lesson you are teaching and you should fully familiarize yourself with the test centre and surrounding area where you intend to take the examination.

The examiner chooses the route for the test and will give you directions (whilst still in role). If they are sat in the driving seat then you need to repeat these directions back to them as you would for a real pupil.

With Pre-set tests 1 and 2, it is often not feasible to conduct these from the test centre. The examiner will advise you that as a pupil, to assume (for example) you have picked them up from their place of work and that it is necessary to drive them for a short distance to a suitable area. They will still be in role, so you should treat them as a pupil. As with all Pre-set tests, they will give you directions.

The examiner will try to stay in role as a pupil throughout phase 1. When he/she wants this phase to end, the examiner will usually say "Would you ask me to pull up in a place that you think is convenient please". He/she will then come out of role and terminate this phase of the test.

At the end of a driving lesson, it is customary to give a summary of the lesson. However at phase 1, because it is the examiner who decides when the lesson will end, he/she is usually out of role before you would have an opportunity of doing this. For this reason summaries are not included in the phase 1 lessons but it is recommended that a summary is offered. For examples of summaries, you should refer to the phase 2 lessons.

Once the examiner has ended phase 1, he/she will usually inform you of the subject for phase 2 to give you a few minutes to prepare yourself.

Controls

Level: Beginner

Lesson Plan

Recap
Objective

Briefing/Practice on Controls
Starting the Engine
Moving Off (if time allows)
Stopping (if time allows)
Summary

Key Points

Doors
Seat/Head restraint
Seat belt
Mirrors
Accelerator
Footbrake
Clutch
Handbrake
Gears
Steering
Indicators
Starting

Precautions before moving off
Normal Stop Position
Normal Stop Use of MSM
Normal Stop Control

This exercise may be introduced to the PDI by the examiner saying:

'I would like you to assume that I am a complete beginner and instruct me on the safety aspects on entering the car for the first time, explain the important controls, and, if time permits, instruct me in moving off and stopping. You can assume that my provisional driving license is valid and that my eyesight has been previously checked. Please correct any faults that may occur. You can call me John.'

> Instructor notes: It is important to note that the examiner will normally start by sitting in the passenger seat of your car at the test centre. The examiner will then go into role (become a pupil) and ask you to drive to a suitable location (examiner will give directions). It is important to remember that the lesson starts as soon as the examiner goes into role and you should treat him/ her as a pupil from this point on.

Instructor:

'Hello John. I understand that you are a complete beginner and that this is your first ever driving lesson. In a moment I am going to drive to a suitable location to carry out today's lesson, but before I do, I would firstly like to ask you: have you put a seat belt on before? *(examiner will normally answer yes)*. Good. Please check that your door is shut securely and then put your seat belt on. Please ensure you do not put your feet on the dual control pedals.

Do you have any questions before we start?'

Recap

Instructor (suggested questions):

'Before I explain the lesson, I would like to ask you a few questions to establish your previous knowledge and experience:

- Have you ever driven any other form of motorised vehicle such as a motorcycle or farm vehicle?
- Have you started studying for your theory test yet and if so do you have the publication "Driving the Essential Skills?"
- What are your reasons for wanting to learn to drive?
- Have you ever been shown how to put a seat belt on properly?'

Note: Depending on the examiner's replies, you may wish to ask follow up or other relevant questions.

Objective

Instructor:

'Our objective today is to be able to locate, identify and operate the main controls of the car .'

Initial Drive

> Instructor notes: During the initial drive it is important that you start to build a relationship with the pupil. The recap questions on the previous page can be asked either whilst at the test centre or during the initial drive. It is also a good idea to highlight some of the basic driving procedures which the pupil will be learning about during the lesson. Some examples are given on the next page.

Instructor:

'Before moving off, you will notice that I have to depress the left hand pedal and put the car into 1st gear using what we call the palming method. You will be learning how to do this today. Now I am looking in my mirrors and also checking two areas known as blind spots. We have different mirrors and I will be explaining these in detail to you. Whilst I am steering you will notice that I do not cross my hands. This is known as the pull, push method of steering and we will be looking at how and why we use this method.'

Instructor:

Precautions before entering and leaving a car

In a moment I am going to ask you to swap places with me. Before you do this, I want you to check your exterior door mirror and over your shoulder, plus look ahead to ensure there are no pedestrians or cyclists about to walk or ride past the vehicle.
Once you open the door, hold it with your left hand in case there is any wind that could blow the door open, which could damage the hinges.
Once you are on the pavement shut the door and then walk round the rear of the vehicle. Whilst you are doing this visually check that the rear passenger and tail gate doors are shut properly by making sure they are flush with the body work. Before walking out into the road towards the drivers door, check up and down the road for any oncoming vehicles.
Wait on the pavement if traffic is approaching closely. Once you have entered the car shut the door securely and sit comfortably but do not touch any of the controls at the moment. Let us do this now.'
(When you swap places with the pupil, remember to take the key with you.)

Cockpit Drill

Cockpit Drill

'Once you are seated you need to carry out a cockpit drill. This includes checking that the doors are shut properly, your seat is correctly adjusted, you can reach the steering wheel comfortably, your seat belt is fastened securely and your mirrors are correctly adjusted. An easy way to remember this is DSSSM (Doors, Seat, Steering, Seat belt and Mirrors).'

Doors

'You checked the rear passenger and tailgate doors as you walked round the vehicle. Now we just need to check the drivers and front passenger doors are shut securely.'

Seat

'Firstly lets look at the bottom part of the seat. This needs to be adjusted so that you can reach the pedals comfortably. Press down the left hand pedal fully with your left foot. When it is fully pressed your leg should be slightly bent so you are not stretching. As you lift your foot off the pedal ensure that no part of your leg comes into contact with the steering wheel. You adjust the seat backwards and forwards as follows: hold the steering wheel with one hand and with the other, reach under your seat and raise the lever. 'Move yourself forwards or backwards as necessary. Once you have found the correct position, release the lever, place both feet on the floor and hold the steering wheel with both hands and then try to move the seat. This will ensure it is locked securely into position.'

Seat/Steering

'Next we need to adjust the rake or back of the seat so you can reach the steering wheel without stretching. To correctly position your hands on the steering wheel, you need to imagine it is a clock face and you should place your hands in the ten to two position - we will discuss how to use the steering wheel later in the lesson.'

'On the left hand side of your seat you will find a lever *(or dial depending on the vehicle)*. Support your body weight by holding the steering wheel with your right hand and raise the lever. This will allow you to move the rake either forwards or backwards. Then release the lever and make sure that, once again, it has locked into place.

To find the correct position, put your arms straight out in front of you with your palms facing downwards just above the top of the steering wheel. Adjust the rake until the top of the steering wheel touches your wrist. Now place your hands back at the ten to two position on the steering wheel and you will find your arms are slightly bent and you have unrestricted movement. You should grip the steering wheel lightly as if you were squeezing a tube of toothpaste or holding a small child's hand.

Lastly, we need to ensure that the head restraint is in the correct position to ensure maximum protection from a rear end collision and to prevent whiplash. Generally, the top of the head restraint should be level with the top of your head. Also, if you turn your head towards the head restraint, the middle of the head restraint should be in line with your eyes and the top of your ears.'

Seat Belt

'Now let us look at the correct procedure for putting on your seat belt. Take the buckle in your left hand and pull the seat belt towards the top of the steering wheel, place your right hand through the 'V' which the seat belt has made and then pull the buckle to the anchor point which is situated to the left of your seat. Push the buckle into the locking mechanism and make sure it is secure by giving the buckle a tug. Now, using the thumb and forefinger of your right hand, remove any twists and ensure that the upper belt fits comfortably across your right shoulder and the lower belt across your hips.

To release the belt, hold the buckle in your right hand whilst pressing the release button with your left. Now transfer the buckle to your left hand and return the belt to its resting position by the door pillar. With inertia seat belts, the return spring is quite strong and can do damage if it is not controlled. On the door pillar, there is an extra adjustment to move the top of the seat belt up or down for extra comfort.

Before driving, you must ensure that your seat belt is securely fitted. It is against the law to drive without a seat belt on unless you have a medical exemption certificate. Adult passengers and children over 14 years must use a seat belt or child restraint where fitted and you must ensure that children under 14 years of age wear seat belts or sit in an approved child restraint where required.'

Mirrors

'We have two types of mirrors on this vehicle. Firstly our interior mirror which is made of flat glass and gives us a true image of what is behind. Secondly, we have two exterior door mirrors which are made of convex glass. This gives a wider field of vision to the sides but makes things look smaller than they actually are. You should be aware that when using the exterior mirrors, vehicles will actually be closer than they appear. There are two areas that the mirrors do not cover and these are called the main blind spots.

To adjust the interior mirror, hold the edge of the mirror between the thumb and forefinger of your left hand ensuring that you do not smudge the glass. Swivel the mirror until you can see fully out of the rear window. The top of the window should run across the top of the mirror and you should be able to see about a thumbs width of the drivers head restraint in the right hand corner.

Try to make the adjustments whilst sitting in your normal driving position. To adjust the exterior mirrors, which are electronically operated, we firstly have to turn on the ignition. I will be explaining this in detail later in the lesson, but for now I would like you to follow my instructions.

On the right hand side of the steering column you will find the steering lock. Please insert the key in this now but do not turn it yet. With your left hand pull up the handbrake to ensure it is secure. Also with your left hand hold the top of the gear lever and move from side to side to ensure it is in neutral.

Now I would like you to turn the key forwards toward the front of the car until you hear two clicks and you see lights appear on the dashboard. Most of these will soon disappear. We can now adjust the mirrors. You may need to release the steering lock by moving the steering wheel.

(The following explanation may need to be adapted depending on the vehicle used)
On the drivers door you will see a small joystick button. Firstly click this to the right. This will allow you to adjust the right exterior door mirror. The mirror is adjusted by moving the joystick forwards, backwards, left and right.

When the mirror is correctly positioned you should be able to see about a thumbs width of the car bodywork on the side of the mirror nearest to the door and the horizon of where the road meets the houses and trees etc. should run horizontally across the centre of the mirror to give you a clear view to the side of the vehicle. To adjust the left exterior door mirror, click the joystick button to the left position. Now adjust this mirror in a similar fashion but this time the pavement should meet the houses and trees etc. horizontally across the centre of the mirror. Once again you should have a clear view to the side of the vehicle.

That completes the cockpit drill. Do you have any questions before we move onto the rest of the controls?

Foot Pedals

Now lets move onto the foot pedals. We have three pedals which, working from right to left are the accelerator, brake and clutch. A way to remember this is ABC. The accelerator and the brake are used with the right foot only and the clutch is used with the left foot only.

Let us firstly correctly position your feet. Place your right foot over the brake pedal so that the top of the pedal is in line with the end of your toes and the bottom of the pedal is near to the ball of your foot. Rest your heel on the floor behind the brake pedal and use your heal as a pivot, so you can swivel your right foot across and down onto the gas pedal and back to the brake.

Now place your left foot over the clutch pedal with once again the top of the pedal near the end of your toes and your heel either close to or on the floor. When you are not using the clutch pedal your foot can move to the foot rest which is to the left of the clutch pedal (or rest on the floor). I will deal with the accelerator first.

Accelerator (Gas)

'I will call the accelerator the gas as it is easier to say when I am giving you commands. When you press the gas, it supplies a mixture of fuel and air to the engine which makes it run faster. As you remove your foot from the gas, the engine will run slower. The gas pedal is very sensitive and so you should only press it gently. The commands I will use are:

- *Cover the gas* - put your right foot over the pedal (it can be touching it but not pressing it)
- *Set the gas* - squeeze the gas pedal down about the depth of a pound coin until we get a gentle hum on the engine
- *More gas* - squeeze the gas gently until the required speed is reached
- *Off the gas* - release the gas pedal.'

Brake Pedal

'This pedal operates the brakes on all four wheels and when it is pressed the brake lights illuminate at the rear of the car to warn other drivers that you are slowing down. We use a form of braking called 'progressive braking'. Apply light pressure as the brake begins to act, increase the pressure and then, just before the car stops, ease off the brake slightly but not completely. This will ensure a smooth stop. We should never stamp on the brake as this can cause a skid. The commands I will use are: *(you should get the pupil to practice carrying out the commands as you explain them).*

- *Cover the brake* - put your right foot over the pedal (it can be touching it but not pressing it)
- *Gently brake* - Squeeze the brake pedal until the car starts to slow down
- *More brake* - apply more pressure
- *Off the brake* - release the brake pedal.'

Clutch Pedal

'The clutch pedal is used with the left foot only. The clutch is the link between the power of the engine and the driven wheels and consists of two plates, one attached to the engine, which is rotating all the time the engine is running, and one attached to the road wheels via the gear box. When the clutch pedal is fully down, these plates are apart, which enables you to select different gears, and when the clutch pedal is up the plates are together. The point where the two plates meet is called the bite point.

It doesn't matter how quickly the clutch pedal is put down, but you must bring the pedal up smoothly. This is because the clutch plates bind together by friction and if you bring up the clutch pedal too quickly it will cause the car to stall or jump forwards out of control. My commands will be as follows:
(you should get the pupil to practice carrying out the commands as you explain them)

- *Cover the clutch* - put your left foot over the pedal (it can be touching it but not pressing it)
- *Clutch down* - raise your heel slightly off the floor, bend your toes and push the pedal down fully
- *Clutch gently up to the bite point* - to do this properly, we need the engine running and first gear selected, but for now gently raise the pedal up by sliding your heal back to about half way
- *Clutch up until the car starts to move* - again we will simulate this by raising your clutch up about the depth of a pound coin
- *Off the Clutch* - gently raise your foot until the clutch is fully up.

You may find you have more control if you place your heel on the floor once you have found the bite point.

This completes the foot pedals, do you have any questions regarding these?'

Handbrake

'The lever between the two seats is called the handbrake or parking brake. This operates on the rear wheels only. The handbrake should only be applied once the vehicle has stopped. If it is applied when the car is moving, it can lock up the rear wheels and cause a skid. The purpose of the handbrake is to secure the car when parked or when the vehicle is stationary such as at junctions and traffic lights. When the engine is running, most vehicles will have a red warning light on the dashboard to tell you when the handbrake is on or not fully released. The commands I will use are as follows:

(you should get the pupil to practice carrying out the commands as you explain them)

- *Prepare the handbrake* - place your left hand on the handbrake with your thumb over the button. Pull the handbrake up slightly and as you do this press the button in
- *Release the handbrake* - hold the button in and push the handbrake down fully until you feel it reach the floor
- *Apply the handbrake* - press the button in and hold it in while you lift up the handbrake as far as it will go. When it will not lift any further, release the button.

It is important that we keep the button depressed when applying the handbrake, otherwise it will wear the locking mechanism which keeps the handbrake in place.'

Gears

'The gear lever is situated in front of the handbrake and is operated with your left hand. The purpose of the gears is to match the power of the engine to the appropriate road speed. On most vehicles there are five forward gears and one reverse gear.

The first gear is the most powerful gear and is used when moving off and manoeuvring at low speed. As the vehicle gets faster, you need to change up through the gears, resulting in less engine power but more road speed.

Fifth gear should be regarded as a cruising gear for economic driving at speeds of around 40 mph and above. Reverse gear should only be selected when the car is stationary and will cause white lights to be illuminated at the rear of the car. This serves a double purpose of informing other drivers of your intentions and to help you see behind you at night when reversing.

When the vehicle is parked, the gear lever should be in the neutral position, where no gear is selected. You can check this by moving the gear lever from side to side. You will notice that when doing this, the lever always springs back to the same position, which if you look at the diagram on the gear lever, is at the junction between third and fourth gear.

This means that to select first gear, we firstly need to push the gear lever over to the left. To do this safely, we use what is called the palming method. We are now going to practice selecting the various gears, but whilst you do this you should not look at the gear lever but try to keep your eyes on the road ahead.

Place your left hand on the gear lever knob with your palm on the right hand side and wrap your fingers gently around the gear lever knob. Firstly push the clutch down with your left foot and then push gear lever over to the left until you feel it hit an imaginary wall and then push it forwards along the wall. This is 1st gear and is used for speeds up to about 10 mph.

Keeping your hand in this position, pull the gear lever backwards along the wall as far as it will go. This is 2nd gear and is used for speeds up to around 20 mph. To select 3rd gear move your hand so that your palm is now on the left side of the gear lever knob. As you push the gear lever forward out of 2nd gear you will feel it spring over towards the right which will bring it opposite 3rd gear. Now just push it forwards. Do not try to push it further to the right as you do this, as this would be 5th gear. Third gear is normally used for speeds up to around 30 mph.

To select 4th gear just pull the gear lever towards the rear of the car without pulling it to the left or right. To select 5th gear, push the gear lever forwards until it reaches the neutral area and then push it over to the right as far as it will go and then forwards. Now put the gear lever back to the neutral position and we will look at how to select reverse.

The reverse gear position varies with different vehicles *(the briefing will need to be adapted depending on the vehicle)*. For this vehicle it is positioned to the left of first gear. To ensure it cannot be selected accidentally, it has a special safety mechanism. Under the gear lever knob is a safety collar. Place your forefinger and index finger each side of this collar and lift it up. Now move the gear lever over to the left as far as it will go and then push it forwards. To get back to neutral, just pull the gear lever out of the reverse position. You can now release the clutch pedal with your left foot.

Do you have any questions regarding the gears?'

Steering
'For the best control of the steering wheel we use a method called 'Pull - Push'. Most modern vehicles are fitted with a safety air bag situated beneath the trim in the centre of the steering wheel. The air bag is designed to protect our face and head in the event of an accident, so we should avoid crossing our arms over this area whilst steering.

Whilst carrying out the cockpit drill you learnt how to place your hands on the steering wheel in the ten to two or quarter to three position. To steer left you need to firstly slide your left hand up to the 12 o'clock position, then grip the wheel with your left hand and pull down, whilst at the same time sliding your right hand down the outside of the wheel so that both hands meet near the bottom of the steering wheel. Next grip with your right hand and push up whilst sliding your left hand up so that both hands meet near the top of the steering wheel. To turn right, you reverse the procedure.

You should try to keep both hands on the steering wheel when the vehicle is moving, except when operating another control such as changing gear. Never try to turn the steering wheel whilst the vehicle is stationary as this can wear the tyres and cause damage to the steering mechanism. Never let the wheel slip through your fingers.'

Indicators, Switches and Dials

'The indicator lever is situated just behind the steering wheel on the left (or right) hand side. It is situated in this position so that it can be operated by flicking the lever down for left or up for right with your fingers whilst still keeping your hand on the steering wheel. When operated, the indicator lever illuminates flashing amber lights at the front and rear of the vehicle to inform other road users of the direction we intend to travel.

There are often additional smaller indicator lights situated adjacent to the front driver and passenger doors. There is also a flashing indicator light on the dashboard to remind you which direction you have chosen and an audible clicking sound whilst the indicator is operating.' (Also, see following instructor note)

Dual Controls

'On my side of the car, I have a dual clutch and foot brake. If I need to use them I will tell you and I will explain the reasons why I have used them. Once I have taken control, it is most important that you remove your feet from these pedals and wait until I return the controls to you.'

Starting the Engine

'Before starting an engine we should carry out the following safety precautions. Make sure the hand brake is fully applied and that the gear lever is in the neutral position. The ignition switch is situated behind and to the right of the steering wheel and operated by a key.

Insert the key into the ignition switch. Firstly we need to release the steering wheel lock. To do this turn the key forwards one click whilst shaking the wheel slightly with your left hand. Now turn the key forward one more click to turn on the car electrics, which will illuminate all the dashboard lights. Most of these will go out again to show that the vehicle is ready for starting. Now turn the key one more click. Once the engine starts release the key, otherwise you could cause damage to the starter mechanism. The engine is now started.

Do you have any questions regarding safety precautions or starting the car?'

Instructor notes: Depending on the vehicle used, additional information may need to be included to various sections of the briefing. For example:

- Doors - self locking etc.
- Seat - height adjustment
- Switches and dials - take the pupil through the main ones that he/she is likely to use such as windscreen wipers, hazard warning lights, rear screen heater and electronic window switches etc.
  Also explain which is the speedometer and rev-counter (if fitted) and what the main warning lights mean.

The examiner will stop the lesson after 30 minutes and in practice, this is often when you have just finished explaining the gears and steering. If time allows, continue the lesson with explanations of the dual controls and starting the engine.

Instructor notes: Under the key points included at the beginning of this chapter, you will see that there is a line after starting the engine and then the key points continue with precautions before moving off, normal stop position, normal stop use of MSM and normal stop control. The reason for this is that there is a possibility that the pupil could have driven another type of motor vehicle such as a farm tractor or other off road vehicle and so may have some prior knowledge and experience, which would mean that explanations of some of the earlier key points would not be required. These extra key points are covered fully in the next chapter under moving off and stopping.

**Fault
ssessment**

When getting into the drivers seat, the pupil does not shut the door correctly.

Instructor:
'Your door is not shut securely.'

'This is because you are holding the door opening lever whilst shutting it. If you were to drive off like this, the door could fly open.'

'Check your exterior mirror and over your right shoulder and road ahead then open the door again. Hold the arm rest handle with your left hand and release the opening lever. Now close the door firmly. Shake the door to make sure it is locked securely and look in your exterior mirror to see that the door is flush with the bodywork of the car.'

Pupil twists seat belt when putting it on.

Instructor:
'Your seatbelt is twisted.'

'If you had to stop suddenly this twist could cause bruising. Also the twist could work its way up to the top of the seat belt and jam the inertia mechanism.'

'Once you have locked the buckle in securely, run your thumb and forefinger along the diagonal and lap part of the belt to check for any twists.'

Pupil leans forward when adjusting the internal mirror.

Instructor:
'You are leaning forward when adjusting the mirror.'

'When you lean back into your seat your view in the mirror will be too low.'

'Make sure you are sitting in the normal driving position when adjusting the mirrors.'

Pupil places foot too high when using the clutch.

Instructor:
'Your foot is too high on the clutch pedal.'

'When you bring the pedal up your foot may get caught under the steering column.'

'Place your foot so that the top of the pedal is at the top of your shoe and the bottom is near the ball of your foot.'

Pupil does not release handbrake fully.

Instructor:
'The handbrake is not fully released.'

'If you were to move away like this, the brakes would still be partially applied.'

'When releasing the handbrake, hold the button in until you feel the handbrake lever hit the floor. When the engine is running you will also have a handbrake warning light which will go out when the handbrake is fully released.'

When moving the gear lever from 2nd to 3rd the pupil selects 5th.

Instructor:
'You have selected 5th gear instead of 3rd.'

'This is because you have pushed the gear lever too far to the right.'

'Remember that when moving the gear lever from 2nd, the lever will spring across towards 3rd. Do not pull it further to the right at this point: just push it forwards to select the correct gear.'

Pupil leaves the key turned forward too long once engine has started.

Instructor:
'Release the key. You are holding the starter on too long.'

'If you do this once the engine has started, it will damage the starter mechanism.'

'Once you hear the engine start, release the key immediately.'

Moving Off & Stopping

Level: Beginner

Lesson Plan

Recap
Objective

Briefing
Full Talkthrough
Prompting (less instruction with Q&A)
Independence
Summary

Key Points

Briefing
Mirrors, vision and use
Mirrors, direction,
overtaking & stopping
Mirror, Signal, Manoeuvre
Precautions before moving off
Co-ordination of controls
Normal stop position
Normal stop control

This exercise may be introduced to the PDI by the examiner saying:

'I would like you to assume I am a beginner and that you instruct me in moving off and making normal stops. I had one lesson last week in a car similar to yours and the instructor explained the controls. We did not get round to moving off and I am not too sure about when to use the mirrors. Please correct any faults which may occur. You can call me John.'

Instructor notes: It is important to note that the examiner will normally start by sitting in the passenger seat of your car at the test centre. The examiner will then go into role (become a pupil) and ask you to drive to a suitable location (examiner will give directions). It is important to remember that the lesson starts as soon as the examiner goes into role and you should treat him/her as a pupil from this point on.

Instructor:

'Hello John, I understand that you have had one previous lesson in which the controls were explained to you and that today you require a lesson in moving off and making normal stops. In a moment, I am going to drive to a suitable location to carry out today's lesson, but before I do please check that your door is shut securely and then put your seat belt on. Please do not put your feet on the dual control pedals.

Do you have any questions before we start?'

Recap

Instructor (suggested questions):

'Before I explain the lesson, I would like to ask you a few questions to establish your previous knowledge and experience.

- Name me the three foot pedals from right to left?
- What does progressive braking mean?
- Show me where are your main blind spots on this vehicle?
- Did you get as far as starting the engine in your last lesson? *(if the pupil answers yes ask the following question)*
- What are the safety precautions you need to carry out before starting a car?'

Note: Depending on the examiner's reply, you may wish to ask follow up or other relevant questions.

Objective

Instructor:

'Our objective today is to move away safely, steer to a normal driving position and then select and stop in a safe position.'

Initial Drive

> Instructor notes: During the initial drive, it is important that you start to build a relationship with the pupil. The recap questions on this page can be asked either whilst at the test centre or during the initial drive. It is also a good idea to highlight some of the basic driving procedures which the pupil will be learning about during the lesson. Some examples are given on the next page.

Instructor:

'Before moving off, you will notice that I firstly get the car ready to move in first gear. Now I am checking all round for vehicles and pedestrians before moving off. You will be learning how to do this today. When driving down a road where there are no parked vehicles or other hazards, we should keep to our normal driving position and we will be learning how to keep a safe distance from the kerb. You will notice that whenever I change direction to the left or right, I always check at least two mirrors. This is called mirror - signal - manoeuvre and I shall be explaining this in more detail during the lesson.'

Instructor notes: Once you have reached the location for the main part of the lesson, you need to swap seats so that the pupil is sitting in the driving seat. Remember that the examiner is in role so watch in case he makes any faults as he changes places. *Also, remember to remove the key and take it with you.*

For the purposes of this manual, the fault assessment is given separately. In the examination, the examiner will be making faults throughout the lesson and these should be dealt with as they occur. This briefing assumes that during the recap questions, it was established that the pupil had started the engine in his/her previous lesson. See the controls lesson for a briefing on starting the engine.

Briefing Plan:

Section 1:
Moving off (Preparation - Observation - Manoeuvre), Indicating, Normal Driving Position, Pulling in and parking, Safe, legal and convenient place to park (SCALP).

Section 2:
Mirrors - vision and use; Mirrors - direction, overtaking and stopping; MSM.

Section 3:
Clutch control; progressive braking; pull push steering.

Briefing: Section 1

'After starting the engine, to move off safely, you are going to use a routine called preparation, observation and manoeuvre (POM). To prepare the car to move, I will ask you to firstly place both hands on the steering wheel at the ten to two position.

Next cover the clutch with your left foot and put the clutch down fully. Place your left hand on the gear lever, palm towards me. Push the lever to the left and forward to select first gear, then put your left hand back on the steering wheel.

Now you need to set the gas by squeezing the gas pedal with your right foot about the depth of a pound coin until you obtain a gentle hum on the engine. Gently raise the clutch until you hear the engine note drop slightly: this is what we call the bite point. Now keep both feet still. Try to keep the heel of your left foot on the floor once you have found the bite point, as this will help you to keep the pedal still. The car is now prepared to move.

Next you need to make effective all round observations. To do this, you are going to use a six point check working round the car from left to right. Firstly check your left blind spot by looking over your left shoulder out through the rear side window, next check your left exterior mirror, then your interior mirror. Now check forward through the front windscreen, then your right exterior door mirror and finally over your right shoulder out through the rear side window.

You are checking for any pedestrians who may be about to cross the road near your vehicle and any approaching motor vehicles or cyclists. When moving off you should not cause another vehicle to change speed or direction. You are also checking to see if you need to indicate.

The rule for moving off is that you indicate if this would be of use to another road user. For today however you will be indicating right to move off and left before stopping so that you can practice using the indicators. So, if the road is clear, indicate up right, carry out a final check in your interior, right mirror and right blind spot then release the handbrake.

Now lift your clutch up about the depth of a pound coin until the car starts to move slowly and then keep your feet still. If you lift the clutch fully up at this point the car will move off too fast or may stall.

Now you need to steer to your normal driving position or safety line. This is normally about a metre from the kerb and to help maintain this, you can check the position of the kerb stones as they appear along the bottom of the windscreen and also check your left exterior mirror. On narrower roads, it is best to position the car in the centre of your side of the road. To do this you steer a quarter of a turn to the right. Then once the car is about a metre from the kerb, steer half a turn to the left. Once the car is parallel with the kerb, straighten the wheels by turning back to the right a quarter of a turn. If you need to pass parked vehicles you leave a safety line to your left of about a car doors width.

Once you have reached the safety line, you need to check your mirrors again for any overtaking vehicles and then lift the clutch up fully and gently apply the gas. This completes the manoeuvre part of the POM routine.

Next I will ask you to pull in and park on the left. Firstly you need to use the Mirror, Signal, Manoeuvre routine by checking your interior and left exterior mirrors and then signal down left. Depending on your speed, I may ask you to release the gas at this point. Then you steer a quarter of a turn to the left and then when the front wheels are about half a drains width from the kerb, steer half a turn to the right. When the car is parallel with the kerb, steer back to the left a quarter of a turn to straighten the wheel. Now cover the brake and clutch, gently brake and just before the car stops push the clutch fully down. Keep both feet still whilst you apply the handbrake and put the gear into neutral. Finally, cancel the indicator if it is still on and release the pedals.

When choosing a place to pull in and park, I want you to remember SCALP. This stands for Safe, Convenient and Legal Position. Safe means that you should not park within 10 metres of a junction, near a sharp bend or brow of a hill. Convenient means that you should avoid blocking driveways or parking where opening the nearside doors could be blocked by lampposts or telegraph poles. Legal includes not parking on double yellow lines or within the zigzag lines of a pedestrian crossing.

To ensure that the wheels do not hit or mount the kerb when parking, you can use the reference point of where the kerbstones appear along the bottom of the front windscreen at the moment and also by checking your left exterior mirror to leave a space of about 6 inches (15 cm) between the nearside wheels and the kerbstones.'

Briefing: Section 2

'You may remember from your controls lesson that there are two types of mirrors on this vehicle. The interior mirror which is made of flat glass gives you a true picture of what is directly behind you and the exterior mirrors which are convex to give a wider field of vision to the side but make things appear smaller than they actually are. In addition to this, as mentioned earlier, we have two main blind spot areas which are not covered by the mirrors that we need to check at certain times especially for pedestrians or motorcyclists for example.

You should check your mirrors before indicating, changing speed and changing direction. You need to do this well before these actions to give you time to act on what you see.

Today we will start to use the Mirror, Signal, Manoeuvre or MSM routine. This is the most frequently used routine when driving and whenever using, it we should always check at least two Mirrors - firstly the interior mirror then the exterior mirror of the direction you intend to travel.'

Briefing: Section 3

'It is very important that you use the clutch pedal correctly. If you bring the clutch up too quickly the car will either stall or jerk forward out of control. Remember to keep your feet still once you have found the bite point and then to only bring the clutch up enough to get the car moving slowly until you have reached your normal driving position. It is equally important to push the clutch down fully just before the car stops and then keep your feet still until the handbrake is on and the gear lever is in neutral.

You should use the brakes progressively. Start by applying the brakes early and use increasing pressure as you bring the car to a stop then just before stopping ease off the brakes slightly, but not completely. This will ensure a smooth stop. You should never stamp on the brakes at any time as this could cause a skid.

You should be aware of the pull-push method of steering from your controls lesson. To move away from the kerb to our safety line I want you to steer as follows: Imagine that your steering wheel is a clock face. Place your right hand at 12 o'clock and pull down a quarter of a turn until your right hand is at 3 o'clock. Once the front of the car is about a metre from the kerb, place your left hand to 12 o'clock and pull the wheel down half a turn until your left hand is at 6 o'clock. Then once the car is parallel with the kerb-line, steer back to the right a quarter of a turn to straighten the road wheels by placing your right hand at 12 o'clock and pulling down to 3 o'clock (also see following instructor note). When pulling in and parking you steer the same amount but this time you start with the left hand.

Do you have any questions?'

Instructor notes: The example given about how much to steer when moving off is one method. Another is to get the pupil to hold the steering wheel at the 10 minutes to 2 position and, whilst gripping the wheel with both hands, steer to the right until the left hand is at the 12 o'clock position.
Then once the car is about a metre from the kerb steer left until the right hand is at the 12 o'clock position. Then once the car is parallel with the kerb line, steer right until the hands are back in the 10 minutes to 2 position and the steering wheel is straight.

Instructor:
'Before we move off I would like you to carry out your cockpit drill please.'
Watch carefully for any faults and correct as necessary. Check mirrors are correctly adjusted.

Instructor:
'Sit in your normal driving position and describe to me what you can see in your interior and exterior mirrors.'

Pupil:
'In my interior mirror, I can see fully out of the rear window. The top of the mirror is level with the top of the rear window and I can see about a thumbs width of my head restraint in the right hand corner. In the right exterior mirror, I can see fully down the road and pavement with about a thumbs width of the car in the corner.'

Instructor:
'Good. We will firstly practice this exercise once or twice under my control by talkthrough. This is where I will tell you all the actions you need to carry out with a series of commands. Then we will practice with less control from me.'

> Instructor notes: The examiner will try to choose a road where you can perform this manoeuvre several times. However, if space is limited or you run out of room, the examiner may come out of role and either turn the car round (so you can continue to use the same road) or turn into a new road.
>
> You should also be prepared to adapt your instruction to be able to steer round parked vehicles and/or park in between them. Try to conserve the road space by moving no further than necessary before parking again and try to predetermine the place you will park.

Moving Off

- Check mirrors, clutch, gently up, gently on gas

- Steer ¼ turn to right, ½ turn left, ¼ turn to right

- Clutch gently up until car starts to move, keep feet still

- Left hand back to steering wheel

- Release the handbrake

- Check interior, right mirror & right blind spot again

- Prepare the handbrake

- Indicate up right

- Check your left blind spot, left exterior mirror, interior mirror, forward, right exterior mirror & right blind spot

- Gently clutch up until engine note dips slightly, keep both feet still

- Set gas with your right; foot keep foot still

- Hand back on steering wheel

- Push lever left and forward to select 1st gear

- Left hand on gear lever, palm towards me

- Clutch down; hold it down

- Left foot cover clutch

- Both hands on steering wheel at 10–2 position

- Start the engine

- Check the handbrake is on and the gear lever is in neutral

Pulling In and Parking

- Rest your feet, cancel the indicator

- Handbrake on, gear lever into neutral

- Clutch down; keep feet still

- Gently brake

- Cover brake and clutch

- Steer ¼ turn left, ½ turn right, ¼ turn left

- Off the gas (optional)

- Signal down left

- Check interior mirror & left mirror

"On the left pull in and park please"

Important note: All talkthrough routines included in this manual are examples only and will need to be adapted to the size and type of road you are on. You will also need to take into account any hazards such as parked vehicles. The talkthrough routines should be read from bottom to top.

Prompting

Instructor notes: With only 30 minutes to complete this lesson in the examination, you may only have time for one or two full talkthroughs and then move the pupil towards independence using prompting. Prompting is where we use selective questions to remind the pupil of the actions they need to carry out. These questions should be based on the commands from talkthrough routines. Some examples are given below.

Moving Off

Instructor:
'When you are ready I would like you to prepare the car to move'
'Where should the clutch be once you have set the gas?'

Pupil:
'At the bite point.'

Instructor:
'Good. Now where do you need to look before moving off?'

Pupil:
'All round from left to right.'

Instructor:
'Well done. Is it safe to move off?'

Pupil:
'Yes the road is clear.'

Instructor:
'Excellent, carry on. Where is your normal driving position?'

Pupil:
'About a metre from the kerb.'

Instructor:
'Normally yes, but this road is a bit narrower so position in the centre of your lane.'

Pulling In & Parking

Instructor:
'On the left, pull in and park please.'
'What mirrors are you going to check?'

Pupil:
'Interior and left.'

Instructor:
'There is a car behind you. Do you think you need to indicate?'

Pupil:
'Oh yes, I need to indicate left.'

Instructor:
'Good. How do you check your position from the kerb when parking?'

Pupil:
'I use the reference point along the bottom of my front windscreen and check my left mirror.'

Instructor:
'Well done. Don't forget to cancel your indicator once you have stopped.'

Instructor notes: Prompting questions should elicit either a correct or incorrect response from the pupil. When an incorrect response is given, then use fault assessment and appropriate instruction to control the situation.

Your aim is that by the end of the lesson, the pupil has attempted the exercise at least once with little or no assistance from you.

**Fault
Assessment**

Pupil checks gear lever before handbrake when starting engine.

Instructor:
'You have carried out your safety checks in the wrong order.'

'If you were on a hill and the vehicle had been left in gear the vehicle could roll if the handbrake was not fully applied.'

'Always check the handbrake first then the gear lever.'

Pupil lifts clutch too high when finding bite point.

Instructor:
'Stop! Your clutch is too high.'

'If you release the handbrake the car could jump forward or stall.'

'As soon as you hear the hum of the engine drop slightly keep your feet still. If you feel the bonnet rise then squeeze the clutch down about the depth of a pound coin.'

Pupil doesn't check right blind spot when carrying out observations.

Instructor:
'You haven't checked your right blind spot.'

'There could have been a vehicle reversing out of a driveway or a pedestrian crossing the road on your right.'

'Look over your right shoulder out through the rear passenger (or driver) door window.'

Pupil moves off too fast.

Instructor:
'You are too fast. Off the gas!'

'You have brought the clutch all the way up and you won't have time to steer correctly.'

'Only bring the clutch up about the depth of a pound coin until the car starts to move slowly and then keep your feet still.'

Pupil doesn't check mirrors before pulling in and parking.

Instructor:
'You haven't checked your mirrors.'

'You need to know what is behind you before you move and whether to indicate left.'

'Remember MSM and check interior and left mirror.'

Pupil puts clutch down before braking when parking.

Instructor:
'You have put the clutch down too early. This is called coasting.'

'This disconnects the engine and we have less control.'

'Brake first and put the clutch down just before you stop.'

Pupil mounts a drop kerb when parking.

Instructor:
'You have mounted the kerb.'

'This can damage your nearside wheels and tyres and be dangerous to pedestrians.'

'Use the reference point along the bottom of the windscreen and check your left exterior mirror.'

Pupil stalls the car when stopping.

Instructor:
'You have stalled the car.'

'You released the pedals too early.'

'Keep your feet still until the handbrake is applied and the gear lever is in neutral.'

Turn In The Road

Level: Partly Trained

Key Points

Briefing
Co-ordination of Controls
Observation
Accuracy

Lesson Plan

Recap
Objective

Initial Drive
Briefing
Full Talkthrough
Prompting (less instruction with Q&A)
Independence
Summary

This exercise may be introduced to the PDI by the examiner saying:

'I would like you to assume I am a partly trained pupil and we haven't met before. You are filling in for my regular instructor. I have had a few lessons in a car similar to yours so I am familiar with the controls and their layout. I would like you to instruct me in turning the vehicle round in the road using forward and reverse gears and also correct any faults that may occur. You can call me Tom.'

Instructor notes: The examiner will start by sitting in the driving seat of the car, where he/she will go into role as a pupil. The Recap and objective should be given before moving off, but the briefing should only be given when you have arrived at a suitable location (chosen by the examiner). During the initial move off and drive, you should be looking for faults that are connected with what you are about to teach, namely clutch, steering and observation faults.

Instructor:

'Hello Tom, I understand you have had a few driving lessons in a car similar to this and that today you require a lesson on turning the vehicle round in the road using forward and reverse gears. After we have driven to a suitable location, I will fully explain the turn in the road and then we will practice the first one or two under my control by talkthrough. Then we shall practice with less control from me. Do you have any questions before we start?'

Recap

Instructor (suggested questions):

'Before we move off, I would like to ask you a few questions to establish your previous knowledge and experience.
- When looking for a place to pull in and park, what does safe, legal and convenient mean?
- Take me through the routine you would use when approaching a closed T-junction to turn right?
- Once reaching the junction, if your view of the new road was blocked by parked vehicles, explain to me how you would use clutch control to move the car forward slowly to get a better view?'

Note: Depending on the examiner's replies, you may wish to ask follow up or other relevant questions.

Objective

Instructor:

'Our objective today is to be able to turn the vehicle round to face in the opposite direction and to be able to control the vehicle in a confined space, using clutch control, whilst being aware of other traffic and pedestrians.'

Cockpit Drill & Move Off

Instructor:

'Before we move off, I would like you to carry out your cockpit drill please.'
Watch carefully for any faults especially with regards to mirrors and correct as necessary.

'When you are ready I would like you to start the car and then move off please.'
Once again, watch carefully for faults and correct as necessary.

Fault
ssessment

Initial Drive

Pupil brings up clutch too high during preparation to move off

Instructor:
'Stop! Your clutch is too high.'

'If you release the handbrake the car will either jump forward out of control or stall.'

'Once you have set the gas, only bring the clutch up until you hear the engine note drop slightly. If the bonnet lifts up then this is a sign that the clutch is too high and you should squeeze the clutch back down about the depth of a pound coin.'

> Instructor notes: The clutch fault shown above concerns the pupil not being able to find the bite point correctly. This should not be confused with clutch control, which is the ability to move the car forward or backwards slowly using clutch, gas and brake. It is advisable to check the pupil's clutch control either in the test centre car park or at the location before starting the manoeuvre. Also, ask if the pupil has reversed before and if not, demonstrate how to select reverse gear.

Pupil uses short rapid movements when steering.

Instructor:
'You are not using enough of the steering wheel when turning.'

'You are only moving your hands from the 10 to 2 position to the quarter to three position which makes it more difficult to keep control of the car.'

'Try to use the whole of the steering wheel by moving your hands from the 10 to 2 to the 5 and 7 position.'

Pupil not observing effectively when passing parked vehicles.

Instructor:
'You are not scanning ahead and using your mirrors effectively.'

'You must always be aware of vehicles and other road users.'

'Make sure you are scanning all round every few seconds.'

> Instructor notes: Once you arrive at the location for carrying out the manoeuvre, make sure that any faults that occurred on the initial drive are fully rectified before starting the briefing.

Instructor:

'Before I start the briefing, I would like to ask you a couple of questions.

- Have you ever reversed a car in a straight line before?
- Have you been instructed on any of the other manoeuvres such as reversing into a limited opening or reverse parking?'

Briefing

'There are two main reasons why it is necessary to learn this manoeuvre. Firstly, because it is a safe way of turning the car round should you, for example, find yourself in a dead end road. Secondly, you may be asked to perform the manoeuvre in your driving test, so that the examiner can test your control, accuracy and observation skills.

Always try to choose a safe, convenient and legal position. Avoid carrying out the manoeuvre near to junctions or sharp bends and on very busy roads; try not to block driveways, so if possible find a space where there are raised kerbstones on both sides of the road; remember it is illegal to turn the car round in one-way streets.

The main skills needed to perform this manoeuvre successfully are co-ordination of the controls - using gas, clutch and brake to keep the car slow, full and brisk steering (slow car, quick wheel) and effective all round observation at all times.
Prepare the car to move in first gear and then check all round from left to right. This is known as the six point check. You are looking for vehicles approaching from either direction and pay particular attention to any pedestrians who may be on both pavements.

Once you have established it is safe to proceed, release the handbrake, lift the clutch up just until the car starts to move at a snails pace and then steer fully and briskly to the right, clockwise to full right lock, this is achieved when you cannot steer any more. Once the vehicle has passed over the centre of the road, cover the brake and gently brake squeezing the clutch slightly. When the front of the car is about 2 feet (½ metre) from the kerb, start steering back to the left about two turns. Your reference point for this is when the kerbstone you are approaching starts to appear under the right exterior door mirror. At the same time start to squeeze the clutch down gently and brake to a stop before you touch the kerb. This is usually when the kerb moves from under the right door mirror to between 9–12 inches (20–30cm) further up the drivers door window.

Once you have stopped, apply the handbrake, select reverse gear, set the gas and find the bite point. This time we look all round from right to left. This is called a seven point check and you need to finish up by looking over your left shoulder out through the rear window.

When it is safe to proceed, release the handbrake, clutch up just until car starts to move and then steer briskly to the left, anticlockwise to full left lock. As the vehicle passes over the centre of the road, turn your head to look over your right shoulder through the rear offside passenger window at the kerb and at the same time cover the brake and start to squeeze the clutch down slightly. When the rear of the car is about two feet from the kerb, start to steer right about two turns and stop the car before you touch the kerb (reference points will depend on car & height of pupil).

Once you have stopped, apply the handbrake, clutch fully down and select first gear, set the gas and find the bite point. As we are about to move forward, check all round from left to right.

When it is safe to proceed, release the handbrake, clutch up just until the car starts to move and then steer to the right until you reach your normal driving position. Next, you would normally straighten the car up, check your mirrors and drive on. However, today I will be asking you to pull in and park so that you can practice the manoeuvre again.

Let us consider the camber of the road. If you look at the road in front of you, you will notice that it is higher in the centre and lower at the sides. That is why you need to use gas and clutch up slightly until you pass over the centre of the road and then use the brake and squeeze the clutch as you go slightly down the dip.

Another point to consider is, that if on reaching the other side of the road a vehicle was to appear from either direction, you must wait to see what they are going to do. They will either try to go round you if there is room, or wait in which case you need to continue with the manoeuvre. Try to obtain eye contact with the driver to establish what they intend to do. For today's lesson, I may ask you to wait while I check that the road is clear and then call the waiting vehicle through. This will give you more time whilst you are still learning the manoeuvre.

As well as other vehicles, you need to be looking out for pedestrians. Think of the area in which you need to carry out this exercise as about 2–3 car lengths square. This is your danger area and if a pedestrian should enter this then you should stop and wait until he/she exits it again or you have established he/she is no longer a hazard.

To summarise, make sure you keep the vehicle slow by using good clutch control. The steering should be full and brisk and most importantly, you must observe fully and effectively to ensure it is safe to carry out the manoeuvre.

Do you have any questions?'

Position 1 to Position 2 -

- Clutch down, brake to a stop, handbrake on

- Steer left (2 feet/ ½ metre from kerb)

- Cover brake and clutch, gently brake & squeeze clutch

  (pupil crosses over centre of the road)

- Steer fully and briskly to the right full lock

- Clutch up until car starts to move, feet still

- Release handbrake

- Check all round from left to right

- Select first gear, set gas & find the bite point

" When you are ready, start the engine"

Position 2 to Position 3 -

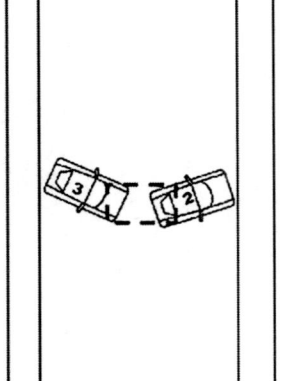

- Clutch down, brake to a stop, handbrake on

- Steer right (2 feet/ ½ metre from kerb)

- Cover brake and clutch, gently brake & squeeze clutch

- Look over right shoulder at kerb

  (pupil crosses over centre of the road)

- Steer fully and briskly to the left full lock

- Clutch up until car starts to move, feet still

- Release handbrake

- Check all round from right to left

- Select reverse gear, set gas & find the bite point

Position 3 to 4 -

- Drive on (or park on the left)

- Check mirrors

- Steer left to straighten the car

  (pupil reaches normal driving position)

- Steer briskly to the right

- Clutch up until car starts to move, feet still

- Release handbrake

- Check all round from left to right

- Select first gear, set gas & find the bite point

Important note: All talkthrough routines included in this manual are examples only and will need to be adapted. For example, if another vehicle approaches, you will need to control the pupil at this stage.

Prompting

Instructor:
'When you are ready I would like you to prepare the car to move off.'
'Where are you looking?'

Pupil:
'All round from left to right.'

Instructor:
'Good. How much are you going to lift the clutch up?'

Pupil:
'Just enough to get the car moving slowly.'

Instructor:
'Well done. How much are you going to steer?'

Pupil:
'Full right lock.'

Instructor:
'Excellent. What is your reference point for steering back to the left?'

Pupil:
'When the kerb appears under the right door mirror.'

Instructor:
'Yes, but remember to stop before you hit the kerb'

Instructor:
'Before reversing, which way do you need to look round?'

Pupil:
'Right to left so I finish up looking out of my rear windscreen .'

Instructor:
'Good. There is a vehicle approaching, what should you do?'

Pupil:
'Wait until I can see whether he is going to stop or try to go round me.'

Instructor:
'Well done, when should you start looking over your right shoulder?'

Pupil:
'Just after I pass over the centre of the road.'

Instructor:
'Yes, but remember to gently brake as you come down the camber'

Instructor:
'Why is it necessary to apply the handbrake once you have stopped?'

Pupil:
'Because I could roll back and hit the kerb whilst I prepare the car to move again.'

Instructor:
'When it is clear, I would like you to complete the manoeuvre and pull in and park on the other side of the road please.'

> Instructior notes: Prompting questions should elicit either a correct or incorrect response from the pupil. When an incorrect response is given, then use fault assessment and appropriate instruction to control the situation.

**Fault
Assessment**

The examiner will make faults at all stages of the examination. The faults committed will be mainly based around the key points listed at the beginning of this lesson. Each time a fault is committed, you should try to respond with an identification, analysis and rectification. The identification should always be given the moment a fault is committed. The analysis and rectification should be given as soon as it is safe to do so. As previously mentioned, the examiner/pupil is likely to commit faults based around clutch, steering and observation during the initial drive and these are dealt with at the beginning of the lesson.

Pupil carries out observations but fails to see pedestrian approaching on the near side.

Instructor:
'Stop. There is a pedestrian approaching on your left.'

'When checking your left blind spot and mirror, make sure you scan down the pavement.'

Remember, when a pedestrian enters the area, you need to carry out the manoeuvre stop and wait until you are sure it is safe to proceed.'

Pupil doesn't steer to full right lock.

Instructor:
'Steer more to the right, you are not at full lock.'

'If you don't achieve full lock the car will not move far enough to the right as you cross the road.'

Keep steering briskly to the right until you cannot steer the wheel any more.'

Pupil forgets to steer back to the left before stopping.

Instructor:
'You haven't steered back to the left.'

'This will mean that, when you reverse, the car will start to go back in the wrong direction.'

'As the kerb appears under your right exterior door mirror, steer back to the left about two turns before stopping.'

Pupil doesn't bring the clutch up to the bite point before trying to reverse.

Instructor:
'Stop. You are not at the bite point.'

'If you release the handbrake you will roll forward and hit the kerb.'

'Always make sure you find the bite point before releasing the handbrake.'

Uses mirrors instead of looking out of rear window when reversing.

Instructor:
'You are not looking out of the rear window.'

'If you try to use your mirrors you will have a restricted view.'

'When reversing look over your left shoulder out of the rear window until you pass over the centre of the road.'

Pupil Moves off too fast.

Instructor:
'Off the gas and squeeze the clutch, you are too fast.'

'You have brought the clutch up too far.'

'Only bring the clutch up enough to move the car forward slowly and then use clutch control to keep the car slow.'

Reversing - to the Left & Right

Level: Partly Trained

Lesson Plan

Recap
Objective

Initial Drive
Briefing
Full Talkthrough
Prompting (less instruction with Q&A)
Independence
Summary

Key Points

Briefing
Co-ordination of Controls
Observation
Accuracy

This exercise may be introduced to the PDI by the examiner saying:

'I would like you to assume I am a partly trained pupil and we haven't met before. You are filling in for my regular instructor. I have had a few lessons in a car similar to yours so I am familiar with the controls and their layout. I would like you to instruct me in reversing into a limited opening and also correct any faults that may occur. For this lesson you can call me Jenny.'

The examiner will start by sitting in the driving seat of the car, where he/she will go into role as a pupil. The RECAP and objective should be given before moving off, but the briefing should only be given when you have arrived at a suitable location (chosen by the examiner). At this stage the examiner may not commit himself/herself as to whether you should teach the left or right reverse, however this will become evident once you have arrived at the chosen location (depending on which side of the junction they park). During the initial move off and drive, you should be looking for faults that are connected with what you are about to teach, namely clutch, steering and observation faults.

Instructor:

'Hello Jenny, I understand you have had a few driving lessons in a car similar to this and that today you require a lesson on reversing into a limited opening, either to the right or to the left. After we have driven to a suitable location, I will fully explain the manoeuvre and then we will practice the first one or two under my control by talkthrough. Then we shall practice with less control from me. Do you have any questions before we start?'

Recap

Instructor (suggested questions):

'Before we move off, I would like to ask you a few questions to establish your previous knowledge and experience:
- When looking for a place to pull in and park, what does safe, legal and convenient mean?
- Take me through the routine you would use when approaching a closed T-junction to turn right
- Once reaching the junction, if your view of the new road was blocked by parked vehicles, explain to me how you would use clutch control to move the car forward slowly to get a better view?

Note: Depending on the examiner's replies, you may wish to ask follow up or other relevant questions.

Objective

Instructor:

'Our objective today is to be able to reverse the vehicle into a limited opening either to the right or left keeping reasonably close to the kerb using clutch control, whilst being aware of other traffic and pedestrians.'

Cockpit Drill & Move Off

Instructor:

'Before we move off I would like you to carry out your cockpit drill please.'
Watch carefully for any faults especially with regards to mirrors and correct as necessary.

'When you are ready I would like you to start the car and then move off please.'
Once again, watch carefully for faults and correct as necessary.

**Fault
ssessment**

Initial Drive

Pupil uses brake and clutch only when preparing the car to move.

Instructor:
'Stop! Your clutch is too high.'

'If you keep the right foot pressing the brake you will not be able to feel the bite point and the clutch will be too high.'

'Once you have selected first gear, set the gas and only bring the clutch up until you hear the engine note drop slightly.'

Instructor:
'As you had a problem finding the bite point, I would like to check your clutch control. Please move the car forward two car lengths at a snails pace.'

Pupil keeps pushing clutch to the floor in his/her attempt to keep the car slow.

Instructor:
'You are pushing the clutch down too far when trying to keep the car slow.'

'This then results in you bringing the clutch up too high when trying to move the car forward slowly.'

'Once you have found the bite point if the vehicle starts to move too fast only depress the clutch down past the bite point, about the depth of a pound coin and gently brake. To get the car to move slowly, bring it up past the bite point the depth of a pound coin and apply a little gas.'

> Instructor note: The example above shows a fault for both finding the bite point and using clutch control which is the ability to move the car forward slowly using all three pedals.

Pupil uses short rapid movements when steering.

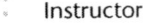

Instructor:
'You are not using enough of the steering wheel when turning.'

'You are only moving your hands from the 10 to 2 position to the quarter to three position, which makes it more difficult to keep control of the car.'

'Try to use the whole of the steering wheel by moving your hands from the 10 to 2 to the 5 to 7 position.'

Pupil not observing effectively when passing parked vehicles.

Instructor:
'You are not scanning ahead and using your mirrors effectively.'

'You must always be aware of vehicles and other road users.'

'Make sure you are scanning all round every few seconds.'

> Instructor notes: Once you arrive at the location for carrying out the manoeuvre make sure that any faults that occurred on the initial drive are fully rectified before starting the briefing.

Instructor:

'Before I start the briefing, I would like to ask you a couple of questions.

- Have you ever reversed a car in a straight line before?
- Have you been instructed on any of the other manoeuvres such as the turn in the road or reverse parking?'

Left Reverse

> Instructor note: The following briefing presumes that the examiner/pupil has stopped a safe distance before a minor road on the left and that the whole of the briefing is given from this position.

'There are two main reasons why it is necessary to learn this manoeuvre. Firstly, because it is a safe method should you need to turn the car round if, for example, you have gone past your destination. Secondly you may be asked to perform the manoeuvre in your driving test, so that the examiner can test your control, accuracy and observation skills.

Always try to choose a safe, convenient and legal position to carry out this manoeuvre. For example, avoid busy main roads where you would be inconveniencing other traffic and do not reverse into one-way streets. Never reverse from a minor road into a major road, never reverse towards on-coming vehicles and never reverse towards pedestrians.

The main skills needed to perform this manoeuvre successfully are co-ordination of the controls - using gas, clutch and brake to keep the car slow, full and accurate steering and effective all round observation at all times.

The road on the left that you can see in front of you, is the one that you are going to reverse into. At this point it is a good idea to try to assess the sharpness of the bend as this will help you determine how much you need to steer. As a general rule, you can assume there are three types of bend - sharp, medium or gradual.

First of all, you need to move off, drive past the junction and then gently stop again a safe distance from the junction.

To do this, you will need to prepare the car to move in first gear, check all round from left to right and then move off in the normal way. Next you need to carry out your MSM routine in preparation for pulling in and parking, so check your interior and left mirrors and also scan the junction and ahead for vehicles and pedestrians to assess if a left indicator signal is necessary. The timing of this signal is very important as, if you signal too early other road users could think you are intending to turn left into the junction, so signal once you are about half way across the junction. It is also useful to assess the sharpness of the bend at this stage and also check there are no obstructions such as parked vehicles which would stop you carrying out the manoeuvre.

You now need to pull in and stop about two to three car lengths past the junction, parallel with the kerb, wheels straight and about a drains width (a little less than half a metre) away. You can check this by looking into your left exterior mirror. Also if you have a normal parking reference point of where the kerbstones appear along the bottom of the front windscreen, move this about a palms width to the left. Once you have stopped, apply the handbrake and put the gear lever into neutral.

The next part of the manoeuvre will be to move the car back to what is called the point of turn. To help you achieve this, I am going to point out two reference points which we will call point A and point B. Point A is where the straight part of the kerb, which at the moment you can see in front of you, becomes curved and point B, which is further into the minor road, is where the curved part of the kerb becomes straight again.

Before you start reversing you need to ensure that you can see comfortably through the rear windscreen but still be able to operate the controls. To do this, you will need to turn slightly in your seat. It is permissible to remove the seat belt whilst reversing, but it is much safer to leave it on especially as this vehicle is fitted with inertia seat belts, which allow you normal movement.

Next select reverse gear and prepare the car to move. Check all round from right to left so that you end up looking out the rear window, in the direction you intend to travel. At this point you should be able to see point A through the rear windscreen.

You now need to reverse the vehicle slowly until Point A disappears. Check all round at this point as you will shortly need to steer left. You should still be able to see the curved kerb stones through the rear windscreen. Continue to reverse a little further until the point where they disappear and then look through the left hand rear side window where you should now be able to see point B. Finally, check your left exterior mirror and you should be able to see that the rear of your car is now at point A. This is your point of turn and I will ask you to pause the vehicle at this point.

When you start to steer left, the front of the vehicle will swing out into the road, so before doing this you need to check forward for any oncoming vehicles and over your right shoulder for any vehicles approaching from behind or any pedestrians that may be about to cross the road.'

'As you negotiate the bend, you need to keep about a drains width from the kerb.

Depending on whether you have assessed that this is either a sharp, medium or gradual bend, you need to start by steering anti-clockwise to the left, either a whole turn, three quarters of a turn or half a turn respectively. Your main observation as you negotiate the bend should be out of the rear window, in the direction you are travelling, but you should also make frequent glances into your left exterior mirror to check your distance from the kerb. When checking this mirror, you should be able to see that the vehicle is still a drains width from the kerb. If however, all you can see is road and no pavement then the vehicle is too wide and you need to add about another quarter of a turn to the left to correct this. On the other hand if, when glancing into the left exterior mirror, all you can see is pavement and no road, then you are too close and you need to steer about a quarter of a turn clockwise to the right to ensure the back wheels do not hit the kerb.

About half way round the bend, you should be looking all round again for any closely approaching vehicles or pedestrians.

As the rear of the vehicle reaches the end of the bend, the straight kerbstones of the new road will appear in the rear window. Continue a little further until the vehicle becomes almost parallel with these straight kerbstones. You can check this by once again looking into your left exterior mirror and also by looking forward where you will see that the vehicle has turned into the road approximately 90°. At this point you need to steer back to the right the same amount that you steered left to straighten the wheels.

Once the steering wheel is straight, place your hands at the quarter to three position with your thumbs around the wheel so that you can feel that the wheel is straight whilst looking out of the rear window.

You now need to reverse back into the road a safe distance which is approximately 3–4 car lengths. As you do this, check that the vehicle is still a drains width from the kerb by ensuring that the straight kerbstones are near to the centre of the bottom of the back window and by once again checking the left exterior mirror. If you find that you are too wide then steer left a quarter of a turn until your right hand is at twelve and your left hand is at six. Once you are back to a drains width then steer right half a turn until your left hand is at twelve and your right hand is at six. When the car becomes parallel with the kerb then steer left a quarter of a turn until your hands are back at the quarter to three position. If you find, on the other hand, you are too close to the kerb then you reverse this procedure, taking care that the front wheels do not hit the kerb.

Whilst you are reversing into the new road, a vehicle could approach from behind. When this happens you should be prepared to drive forward and start the manoeuvre again so that you do not encourage the vehicle onto the wrong side of the road near the junction. However, usually the vehicle will try to pass you and if this happens you should stop and wait and once the road is clear again you can proceed with the manoeuvre. Occasionally a vehicle will come up close behind you. When this happens then you need to abort the manoeuvre, move off safely, turn left at the junction and stop on the left ready to start this part of the manoeuvre again.

To sum up, total control of the vehicle is essential throughout this manoeuvre. The speed of the vehicle is controlled by good clutch control. Reasonable accuracy is achieved by effective use of the steering. Finally, good all round observation is essential before and during the manoeuvre. Do you have any questions?

Right Reverse

'There are two main reasons why it is necessary to learn this manoeuvre. Firstly, because it is a safe method should you need to turn the car round if, for example, you have gone past your destination, or if you are driving a van or close sided vehicle with limited side vision, as you should not reverse left. Secondly, you may be asked to perform the manoeuvre in your driving test, so that the examiner can test your control, accuracy and observation skills.

Always try to choose a safe, convenient and legal position to carry out this manoeuvre. For example, avoid busy main roads where you would be inconveniencing other traffic and do not reverse into one-way streets. Never reverse from a minor road into a major road, never reverse towards on-coming vehicles and never reverse towards pedestrians.

The main skills needed to perform this manoeuvre successfully are co-ordination of the controls - using gas, clutch and brake to keep the car slow, full and accurate steering and effective all round observation at all times.

The road on the right that you can see in front of you is the one that you are going to reverse into. At this point, it is a good idea to try to assess the sharpness of the bend as this will help you determine how much you need to steer. As a general rule, you can assume there are three types of bend - sharp, medium or gradual.

First of all you need to move off, drive past the junction and then gently stop again a safe distance from the junction on the right hand side of the road.

To do this, you will need to prepare the car to move in first gear, check all round from left to right and then move off in the normal way. Next you need to check your interior and right exterior mirrors and position the car just left of the centre line. Now check these mirrors again in preparation for pulling in and stopping and also scan the junction and ahead for vehicles and pedestrians to assess if a right indicator signal is necessary. The timing of this signal is very important as, if you signal too early, other road users could think you are intending to turn right into the junction. So signal once you are about half way across the junction. It is also useful to assess the sharpness of the bend at this stage and also check there are no obstructions such as parked vehicles which would stop you carrying out the manoeuvre. Once you have passed the junction, assess the road ahead for oncoming vehicles and when safe, steer right across the road gently stop, about two to three car lengths past the junction, parallel with the kerb, wheels straight and about a drains width (a little less than half a metre) away from the kerb. You can check this by looking into your right exterior mirror and also by looking out or your drivers door window where you can see the kerb. Once you have stopped, apply the handbrake and put the gear lever into neutral.

The next part of the manoeuvre will be to move the car back to what is called the point of turn. To help you achieve this, I am going to point out two reference points which we will call point A and point B. Point A is where the straight part of the kerb, which at the moment you can see in front of you, becomes curved and point B, which is further into the minor road, is where the curved part of the kerb becomes straight again.

Before you start reversing, you need to ensure that you can see comfortably through the rear windscreen but still be able to operate the controls. To do this you may need to turn slightly in your seat. It is permissible to remove the seat belt whilst reversing, but it is much safer to leave it on, especially as this vehicle is fitted with inertia seat belts which allow you normal movement.

Next, select reverse gear and prepare the car to move. Check all round from right to left so that you end up looking out the rear window in the direction you intend to travel. At this point you may be able to see point A through the rear windscreen, but if not you will see this in your right exterior mirror.

You now need to reverse until the rear of your vehicle is level with point A. This is your point of turn. Whilst doing this, your main observation should be over your left shoulder out of the rear window, but you will need frequent glances into your right exterior mirror and over your right shoulder to check your position from the kerb. Whilst doing this check all round for oncoming vehicles or pedestrians. Once you have reached the point of turn, I will ask you to pause the vehicle at this point.

When you start to steer right, the front of the vehicle will swing out into the road, so before doing this you need to check forward for any oncoming vehicles and over your left shoulder for any vehicles approaching from behind or any pedestrians that may be about to cross the road.

As you negotiate the bend, you need to keep about a drains width from the kerb.

Depending on whether you have assessed that this is either a sharp, medium or gradual bend, you need to start by steering clockwise to the right, either a whole turn, three quarters of a turn or half a turn respectively. Your main observation as you negotiate the bend should be out of the drivers and/or passenger door window on your right where you can see the kerb, and you should also make frequent glances into your right exterior mirror to check your distance from the kerb. If the rear of the vehicle starts to move away from the kerb, then you need to add about a quarter of a turn clockwise to the right. If on the other hand the rear of the vehicle starts to move closer the kerb, then you need to steer anti-clockwise to the left about a quarter of a turn.

About half way round the bend, you should be looking all round again for any approaching vehicles or pedestrians. Keep reversing until the vehicle is almost parallel with the straight kerbstones of the new road. At this point, point B should be visible by looking over your right shoulder into the bottom right hand corner of your drivers door window. You can also check this by, once again, looking into your right exterior mirror and also by looking forward where you will see that the vehicle has turned into the road approximately 90°. At this point you need to steer back to the left the same amount that you steered right to straighten the wheels. Once the steering wheel is straight, place your hands at the quarter to three position with your thumbs around the wheel so that you can feel that the wheel is straight whilst looking out of the rear window.

You now need to reverse back into the road a safe distance which is approximately 6–8 car lengths. Your main observations should now be over your left shoulder out through the rear window. However you will also need frequent glances over your right shoulder and into your right exterior mirror to check that the vehicle is still a drains width from the kerb. If you find that you are too wide, then steer right a quarter of a turn until your left hand is at twelve and your right hand is at six.
Once you are back to a drains width, then steer left half a turn until your right hand is at twelve and your left hand is at six. When the car becomes parallel with the kerb then steer right a quarter of a turn until your hands are back at the quarter to three position. If you find, on the other hand, that you are too close to the kerb then you reverse this procedure, taking care that the front wheels do not hit the kerb.

Whilst carrying out this manoeuvre you need to remember you are on right side of the road facing any oncoming traffic so frequent forward observations are essential. If a vehicle turns into the road you should stop and wait. Usually the vehicle will try to pass you and once the road is clear again you can proceed with the manoeuvre. However, occasionally a vehicle will come up close in front of you. When this happens then you need to check it is safe and then reverse further into the new road so that the vehicle can pass you safely.

To sum up, total control of the vehicle is essential throughout this manoeuvre. The speed of the vehicle is controlled by good clutch control. Reasonable accuracy is achieved by effective use of the steering. Finally, good all round observation is essential before and during the manoeuvre. Do you have any questions?'

Important note: All talkthrough routines included in this manual are examples only and will need to be adapted to the pupil you are teaching and the situation. For example, with all manoeuvres, reference points may need to be moved or changed depending on the perception of the pupil and what he/she can see.

Left Reverse: Position 1 to Position 2 -

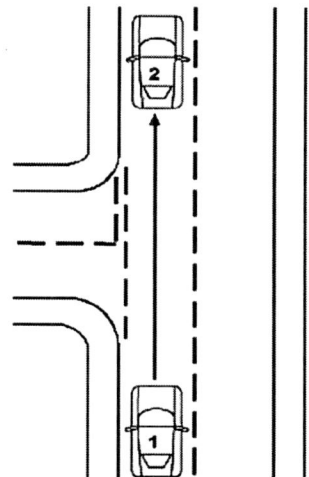

- Gently brake to a stop, handbrake on and into neutral

- Position a drains width from the kerb

- Signal left (if needed)

- Check interior & left mirror

- Look into junction

- Move off slowly when safe

- Check all round from left to right

- Prepare the car to move in first gear

" When you are ready, start the engine"

Position 2 to Position 3 -

- Check forward and into your right blind spot

- Check in left exterior mirror that rear of vehicle is level with point A

- Check point B is visible in nearside passenger door window

- Continue reversing until curved kerbstones disappear from rear window then pause

- When point A disappears from rear window - check all round

- Hands at ¼ to 3, keep wheel straight

- Release handbrake, clutch up until car starts to move slowly, then feet still

- Check all round from right to left

  (main observation through rear window)

- Select reverse gear & prepare the car to move

  (At this point it is advisable to get the pupil to turn slightly in their seat to improve their rear observation)

Additional note: After each attempt at the manoeuvre, you will need to direct the pupil to move off and turn left at the junction so that the manoeuvre can be carried out again.

Position 3 to 4 -

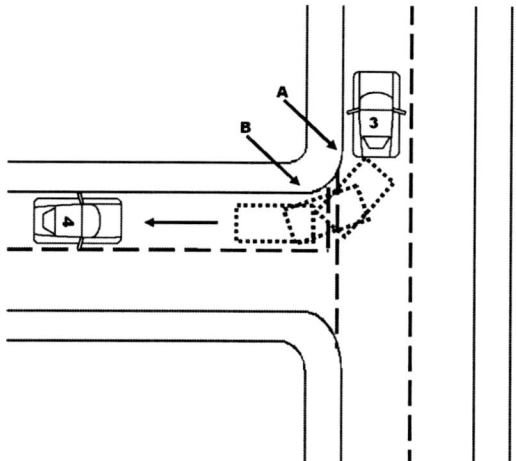

- Brake to a stop. Handbrake on, gear lever into neutral

- Reverse slowly 3–4 car lengths, keeping a drains width from the kerb

- Keep checking out of your rear window

- Hands at ¼ to 3, keep wheel straight

- As you start to move steer back to the right the same amount you steered left to straighten the wheel

- Check forward - you can see you have turned 90°

- Check your left exterior mirror - you can see the vehicle is almost parallel with the kerb

- Check through your rear window - you can now see the straight kerbstones of the new road - pause *(optional)* the vehicle

- Check all round for vehicles & pedestrians

- Check your left exterior mirror, you are too wide -
  steer ¼ turn to the left *(example)*

- Keep checking out of your rear window

- As you start to move steer ¾ (1 or ½) turn to the left

Right Reverse: Position 1 to Position 2 -

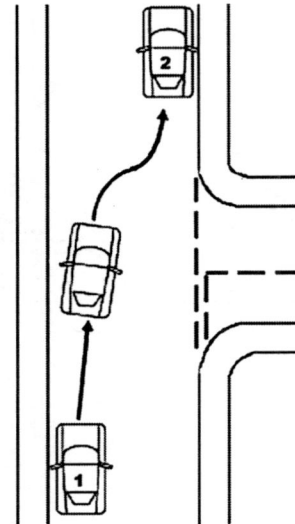

- Gently brake to a stop, hand brake on and into neutral

- Position a drains width from the kerb, wheels straight

- Steer right, across the road

- Signal right *(recommended)*

- Check interior & right mirror again

- Look into junction

- Position just left of centre line

- Check interior & right mirrors

- Move off slowly when safe

- Check all round from left to right

- Prepare the car to move in first gear

" When you are ready, start the engine"

Position 2 to Position 3 -

- Look into right exterior mirror & side windows *(main observation through right side windows and right mirror whilst negotiating bend)*

- Pause, check forward and over left shoulder blind spot

- Check all round & continue reversing until rear of vehicle is at point A

- Check right exterior mirror and over right shoulder for point A

- Hands at ¼ to 3, keep wheel straight

- Release handbrake clutch up until car starts to move slowly then feet still

- Check all round from right to left *(main observation through rear window until point of turn)*

- Select reverse gear & prepare the car to move

Additional note: After each attempt at the manoeuvre, you will need to direct the pupil to move off and turn right at the junction (ensuring correct positioning) so that the manoeuvre can be carried out again.

Position 3 to 4 -

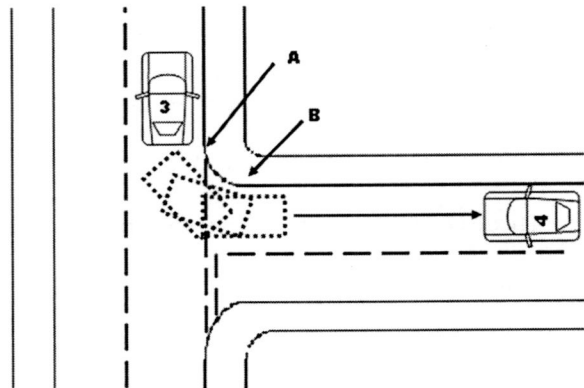

- Brake to a stop. Handbrake on, gear lever into neutral.

- Reverse slowly 6 to 7car lengths keeping a drains width from the kerb

- Look over left shoulder out of your rear window
  (main observations for straight reversing).

- Hands at ¼ to 3, keep wheel straight.

- As you start to move steer back to the left the same amount you steered right, to straighten the wheel

- Check forward - you can see you have turned 90°

- Check your right exterior mirror - you can see the vehicle is almost parallel with the kerb

- Check through your side window - you can now see point B in bottom right hand corner- pause *(optional)* the vehicle

- Check all round for vehicles & pedestrians

- Check your right exterior mirror, you are too close - steer ¼ turn to the left *(example)*

- Keep checking out of your rear window

- As you start to move steer ¾ (1 or ½) turn to the right

Instructor notes: Once you have talked the pupil through the manoeuvre, you need to move the pupil towards independence. In the examination, with only 30 minutes to complete the lesson, this will be after only one or two attempts. Prompting is where we use selective questions to remind the pupil of the actions he/she needs to carry out. These questions should be based on the commands from the talkthrough routine. Some examples are given below for the left reverse. Similar questions should be constructed for the right reverse.

Left Reverse

Instructor:
'When you are ready I would like you to move off please'.
'Where are you looking as you pass the junction?'

Pupil:
'In my mirrors to see if I need to signal and into the junction for any obstructions.'

Instructor:
'Good. How far from the kerb should you park?'

Pupil:
'About a drains width.'

Instructor:
'Well done. Which way do you look round when reversing?'

Pupil:
'From right to left.'

Instructor:
'Excellent. And where should your main observations be?'

Pupil:
'Over my left shoulder through the rear window.'

Instructor:
'Good. What reference points are you looking for to check you are at the point of turn?'

Pupil:
'The kerb should disappear from the rear window and I should see point B in the side window .'

Instructor:
'Well done. Before turning where do you need to look?'

Pupil:
'Ahead for oncoming vehicles and over my right shoulder for approaching vehicles and pedestrians.'

Instructor:
'How much are you going to steer left?'

Pupil:
'About ¾ of a turn.'

Instructor:
'Yes, but remember to glance in your left mirror to check your distance from the kerb.'

Instructor:
'When do you need to straighten the car up?'

Pupil:
'When the car is almost parallel with the straight kerbstones in the new road.'

Instructor:
'Well done. Now reverse back a safe distance before stopping.'

Instructor:
'That was a good attempt. I would now like you to move off, turn left at the junction and then pull in and park so that we can do the manoeuvre again.'

> Instructor notes: Prompting questions should elicit either a correct or incorrect response from the pupil. When an incorrect response is given, then use fault assessment and appropriate instruction to control the situation.

**Fault
ssessment**

The examiner will make faults at all stages of the examination. The faults committed will be mainly based around the key points listed at the beginning of this lesson. Each time a fault is committed you should try to respond with an identification, analysis and rectification. The identification should always be given the moment a fault is committed. The analysis and rectification should be given as soon as it is safe to do so. As previously mentioned, the examiner/pupil is likely to commit faults based around clutch, steering and observation during the initial drive and these are dealt with at the beginning of the lesson.

Some examples are given below for the left reverse. Fault assessment for the right reverse should be carried out in similar fashion.

Left Reverse

Pupil signals too early after moving off.

Instructor:
'Cancel your indicator. You have signalled too early.'

'The vehicle waiting to emerge may think you are turning and pull out in front of you.'

'Make sure you are at least half way across the junction before signalling left.'

Pupil parks too close to the kerb.

Instructor:
'You are too close to the kerb for this manoeuvre.'

'We need extra room for negotiating round the corner.'

'Move forward slightly until you are a drains width away from the kerb. Check this in your left exterior mirror.'

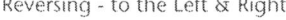

Pupil stops too early for point of turn.

Instructor:
'You have stopped too early.'

'If you start to steer now you will hit the kerb.'

'Look in your left exterior mirror and make sure that the back of the vehicle is level
with point A.'

Pupil doesn't check right blind spot before steering left.

Instructor:
'Stop. You have not checked your right blind spot.'

'Remember when you steer, the front of your vehicle will swing out into the road.'

'Always check for approaching vehicles and pedestrians before steering.'

Pupil steers too slowly.

Instructor:
'You are steering too slowly.'

'The vehicle will end up too wide from the kerb.'

'Once you have checked it is safe, steer briskly ¾ *(example)* of a turn to the left.'

Pupil not looking through rear window after straightening vehicle.

Instructor:
'You are not looking through the rear window.'

'If there was a vehicle approaching from behind you would not see it.'

'Remember your main observation whilst reversing should be over your left shoulder
out through the rear window.'

Emergency Stop & Use of Mirrors

Level: Partly Trained

Lesson Plan

Recap
Objective

Briefing/Q&A on Mirrors
Initial Drive: Mirrors
Briefing: Emergency Stop
Practice: Emergency Stop
Summary

Key Points

Briefing on emergency
Stop/Mirrors
Quick reaction
Use of footbrake/clutch
Skidding
Mirrors vision and use
Mirrors, direction, overtaking
and stopping
Mirror-signal-manoeuvre

This exercise may be introduced to the PDI by the examiner saying:

'I would like you to assume I am a partly trained pupil and we haven't met before. You are filling in for my regular instructor. I have had a few lessons in a car similar to yours so I am familiar with the controls and their layout. I would like you to give me some practical instruction on the use of the rear view mirrors and also to instruct me in how to make an emergency stop - that part should include a briefing followed by practice. Also correct any faults that may occur. You can call me John.'

It is important to remember that there are two elements to this PST and that both should be covered fully. The examiner will select a suitable location for the Emergency Stop and for this reason you should deal with mirrors on the initial drive. Therefore the brief for Mirrors should be covered at the test centre and the Emergency Stop should be given when you arrive at the chosen location. This PST shows the importance of listening carefully to the examiner's introduction and you will notice in this example the words 'practical instruction' on the use of mirrors. Once the examiner is in role, then this can be clarified (see recap questions).

Instructor:

'Hello John, I understand you have had a few driving lessons in a car similar to this and that today you require a lesson on the use of mirrors and the emergency stop. We will start by looking at the effective use of mirrors and then I will explain the emergency stop. We will then practice this several times until you can perform the manoeuvre correctly. Do you have any questions before we start?'

Recap

Instructor (suggested questions):

'Before I explain the lesson, I would like to ask you a few questions to establish your previous knowledge and experience.
- Imagine you are driving down a road and you see a parked vehicle on the left. What routine would you use on approach?
- Before signalling right or left, what are you looking for in your mirrors?
- Where are your two main blind spots?
- What does progressive braking mean?
- Why should we never stamp on the brake?

Note: Depending on the examiner's replies, you may wish to ask follow up or other relevant questions.

Objective

Instructor:

'Our objective today is to be able to be able to use the mirrors effectively using a reliable system and to stop the vehicle safely as if in an emergency.'

Briefing

Briefing Plan:
Use of mirrors: Type of mirror, areas covered, blind spots. When to use mirrors, Timing, MSM, Acting on what you see.

Emergency stop: Quick reactions, Brake-pause-clutch, Steering, Other controls. Moving off again. The instructor's command and signal. Skidding - causes & types. ABS

Instructor notes: You can assume that as the pupil has had a few previous lessons, he would have been using mirrors within the context of these lessons. The mirrors part of the briefing below shows an example of how to use Q&A when it has been established that the pupil has some previous experience of the subject. To give a full briefing in this case would be over instruction. However, we do need to establish their previous knowledge of the main points and cover any areas that the pupil is not familiar with.

Instructor:
'Let us deal with mirrors first. You said that you require some practical instruction on this aspect. Have you received a briefing on mirrors from your previous instructor?'

Pupil:
'Yes, I had a briefing on mirrors towards the end of my last lesson.'

Instructor:
'Did you receive any talkthrough on the effective use of mirrors?'

Pupil:
'No, there wasn't time before the end of the lesson.'

Instructor:
'OK, that's fine. Tell me the difference between the two types of mirrors we have on this car and the areas they cover.

Pupil:
'The interior mirror is made of flat glass and gives a true image of what is behind. The exterior mirrors are made of convex glass to give a wider field of vision to the sides, but they make things look smaller than they actually are.'

Instructor:
'Good. When moving off what are you looking for in your main blind spots?'

Pupil:
'On the left I am looking for any pedestrians and on the right any vehicles or cyclists and any pedestrians crossing the road.'

Instructor:
'Well done. Give me some examples of when you would check your mirrors before carrying out an action.'

Pupil:
'Before moving off, before signalling and before stopping again.'

Instructor:
'Yes. We need to check our mirrors well before signalling, changing speed, direction and overtaking. This is important so that we have time to act on what we see. What does MSM mean?'

Pupil:
'Mirror Signal Manoeuvre.'

Instructor:
'Good. Whenever we use MSM remember we must check at least two mirrors, the interior first followed by the exterior of the direction we need to travel.'

Instructor:
'Well John, you seem to have a good basic knowledge of mirrors. Now we are going to deal with them on the move. I will start with some talkthroughs of when and what mirrors to check and emphasise what you see in them and what action you should take. I will then reduce my instruction.'

**Cockpit Drill
& Move Off**

Instructor:
'Before we move off, I would like you to carry out your cockpit drill please.'
See fault assessment on following page.

'When you are ready I would like you to start the car and then move off please.'
Once again, watch carefully for faults and correct as necessary.

> Instructor notes: As with all the various PSTs, the examiner will choose the route and give you directions which you then repeat. The initial drive is likely to last only a few minutes during which time you need to cover mirrors fully using a mixture of instruction, Q&A and fault assessment, as appropriate. Some examples are given below. The examiner will then stop on a road suitable for the emergency stop and will expect you to move onto the briefing for this part of the lesson.

Prompting

Instructor:
'When you are ready prepare the car to move off please."
'Where do you need to look before you move off?'

Pupil:
'All round for any pedestrians or other vehicles.'

Instructor:
'Good. We call this a six point check. From left to right we check both blind spots and all the mirrors as well as the road ahead. *At the end of the road turn right.* Check your interior mirror and right mirrors before signalling right. What vehicle is behind you?'

Pupil:
'A motorbike.'

Instructor:
'Yes. It is important that you know where he is as you reach the give-way line. Just before we emerge, check your right door mirror again. Where is the motorbike now?'

Pupil:
'He is just behind me.'

Instructor:
'Good. What is the first thing you do once you are safely into the new road?'

Pupil:
"Check my mirrors again.'

Instructor:
'Good. Where is the motorbike now?'

Pupil:
'He is starting to overtake me.'

Instructor:
'Well done. Parked vehicle on the left, what mirrors do you check before moving out?'

Pupil:
'Interior and right.'

Instructor:
'Yes. Now check your interior and left mirrors to make sure you are safely past the parked vehicle before moving back over. The road is clear now, why do you need to keep glancing in your mirrors?'

Pupil:
'I always need to know what is behind me in case I need to change speed or direction.'

Instructor:
'Well done. Now I am going to stop giving you instruction on mirrors but will help and guide you as necessary.'

Instructor notes: Prompting questions should elicit either a correct or incorrect response from the pupil. When an incorrect response is given then use fault assessment and appropriate instruction to control the situation.

**Fault
Assessment**

Mirrors

> The examiner will make faults at all stages of the examination. Each time a fault is committed you should try to respond with an identification, analysis and rectification. The identification should always be given the moment a fault is committed. As the pupil will have used mirrors before, sometimes Q&A would be appropriate for the analysis and rectification.

Cockpit Drill - Pupil leans forward when adjusting interior mirror.

Instructor:
'You are leaning forward when adjusting your interior mirror.'

'When you adopt your normal driving position the mirror will be too low.'

'Sit back in your seat when adjusting this mirror'

Turning left - Pupil checks mirrors and signals at the same time

Instructor:
'You have checked your mirrors and signalled at the same time.'

'You are not giving yourself time to act on what you see.'

'Count to three in seconds and at the same time check interior mirror (1) Exterior mirror (2) and then signal (3).'

Parked vehicle on left - Pupil checks wrong exterior mirror

Instructor:
'You have checked the wrong exterior mirror.'

'As we are moving to the right we need to check the right exterior mirror.'

'Next time check interior, right exterior mirror before moving out.'

Pupil not checking mirrors enough when driving down a clear road.

Instructor:
(Puts hand over interior mirror). 'What colour is the car behind?'

Pupil:
'I don't know.'

Instructor:
'You are not checking mirrors enough during general driving.'

'You must always be aware of what is behind and to the sides.'

'Glance in your mirrors every few seconds on a straight road.'

Briefing

Emergency Stop (part 1)

'During your driving lessons, you will be learning how to avoid emergency situations. This is called defensive driving and is designed to help you plan ahead, develop your anticipation skills of what you can see and what you can't see and to teach you how to always drive at a safe speed. As part of this, regular mirror checks are vital so that you always know what is behind and to the sides of you.

However, occasionally an emergency situation may occur such as a child, who you could not see, running out in front of you from behind a parked vehicle. When this happens you need a quick reaction, as we need to stop the car quickly. It is unlikely that you will have time to check the mirrors before doing this.

We need to brake firmly but progressively. Do not stamp on the brake as this is likely to cause a skid. Only put the clutch down just before you stop so that engine braking can assist us to slow down quicker. To help you remember this, we will use a routine called "Brake - Pause - Clutch."
Keep both hands on the steering wheel with a firm grip and the wheels straight. Leave all the other controls alone until the vehicle has stopped. Then apply the handbrake and put the gear lever into neutral.

When moving off again, remember to check all round first, especially to your left and right blind spots to ensure the road is clear of other hazards.

Do you have any questions so far?

Emergency Stop (part 2)

'Now I would like to talk to you briefly about skidding. All skids are caused by driver error. It is the driver's responsibility to drive at a safe speed, avoid harsh braking and not to over or under steer. It is the driver's responsibility to ensure that their car always has first class brakes and tyres and it is the driver's responsibility to adapt their driving to take into account any road and weather conditions that prevail at the time.

There are various types of skid: The braking skid is where the brakes have been applied too harshly and the road wheels have locked up. If your car is not fitted with an anti-lock braking system (ABS) then, if the car skids, you need to use Cadence Braking.' This is where we release and re-apply the brakes rapidly several times until the tyres grip the road surface again. If your car is fitted with an anti-lock braking system then you should keep your foot firmly on the brake pedal. If this system 'kicks in' you will normally feel a slight juddering or vibration in the front wheels. You should also refer to the manufacturer's guide for whatever vehicle you are driving, for any special instructions during an emergency stop such as applying brake and clutch at the same time.

Next we have an acceleration skid. This is where too much gas has been applied and the driven wheels are spinning. If this happens simply come off the gas pedal immediately and re-apply it more gently.

Lastly, we have the steering skid. Occasionally, such as on wet or icy roads, when braking towards a sharp left hand bend for example, the weight of the car is shifted from the rear to the front and can cause the back of the car to skid to the right. If this happens, immediately come off the gas and/or off the brake and steer right into the skid. However, make sure you do not over-steer as this could cause a skid in the opposite direction. Then re-apply the brakes once the skid is under control.

Do you have any questions about skidding?'

Emergency Stop (part 3)

'The signal I will use to simulate the emergency stop is as follows: I will raise my right hand towards the windscreen and say 'Stop!' quite firmly. *(Instructor should demonstrate this to the pupil).*
Before I give the signal I will be checking behind to make sure the road is safe for carrying out the manoeuvre. *(Instructor should look over right shoulder out through rear windscreen).*

When I give the signal I want you to stop as quickly as you can under control as if a child has just run out into the road in front of you.

Before we do this I would like to practice the routine whilst stationary so that you can get used to the signal and practice the Brake - Pause - Clutch routine.'

Instructor note: It is a good idea, whilst the car is parked at the side of the road, to get the pupil to practice the routine a couple of times. Whilst he/she does this he/she should say the Brake-Pause-Clutch routine out loud.

Instructor notes: The examiner would have chosen a road suitable for this manoeuvre when you parked after the mirrors part of the PST. A talkthrough on the move for the emergency stop is not practicable. The examiner will expect you to decide when to give the stop signal. If you are unable to carry out the manoeuvre due to traffic or you run out of room, the examiner will direct you to another suitable road.

**Fault
Assessment**

Emergency Stop

> Instructor notes: You should identify each fault clearly as it occurs so you
> need to be looking at the pupil at the moment when you give the stop signal.
> Then it is advisable to park safely at the side of the road before giving the
> analysis and rectification. Some examples are given below.

Instructor:
'Stop!' *(gives signal after checking behind).*

Pupil doesn't apply brakes quick enough.

Instructor:
'You are braking too late.'

'If you do not react quicker you will not stop early enough.'

'As soon as I give the signal your right foot must immediately
move from the gas to the brake as quickly as possible.'

Instructor:
'Stop!' *(gives signal after checking behind).*

Pupil applies brake and clutch at the same time.

Instructor:
'You have put both feet down at the same time. *Please pull in and park on the left.'*

'By putting the clutch down just before you stop it allows us to use some engine
braking as well.'

'Next time remember Brake-Pause-Clutch down.'

Instructor:
'Stop!' *(gives signal after checking behind).*

Pupil puts clutch down before braking.

Instructor:
'You put the clutch down before braking. *Please pull in and park on the left'*

'This causes coasting and gives less control of the vehicle.'

'Next time remember Brake-Pause-Clutch down.'

Instructor:
'Stop!' *(gives signal after checking behind).*

Pupil applies handbrake just before stopping.

Instructor:
'You have applied the handbrake too early. *Please pull in and park on the left'.*

'This can cause the back wheels to lock up and skid.'

'Keep your hands firmly on the wheel until the car has stopped.'

Instructor:
'Stop!' *(gives signal after checking behind. Pupil carries out emergency stop correctly)*

Pupil then tries to move off after emergency stop without looking all round.

Instructor:
'Stop! You have not checked all round. *Please pull in and park on the left.'*

'You must make sure it is safe to move off.'

'Check all round from left to right including your blind spots.'

Pedestrian Crossings and use of signals

Level: Partly Trained

Lesson Plan

Recap
Objective

Briefing
Full Talkthrough (first few crossings)
Prompting (less instruction with Q&A)
Independence
Summary

Key Points

Briefing
MSM
Speed on approach
Stop when necessary
Overtaking on approach
Inviting pedestrians to cross
Signals by indicator
Signals by arm
Signals - timing
Unnecessary signals

This exercise may be introduced to the PDI by the examiner saying:

'I would like you to assume I am a partly trained pupil and we haven't met before. You are filling in for my regular instructor. I have had a few lessons in a car similar to yours so I am familiar with the controls and their layout. I would like you to instruct me on dealing with pedestrian crossings, also instruct me on how to give all signals by indicator and by arm and correct any faults that may occur. You can call me Tom.'

> Instructor note: This lesson covers the teaching and practice of arm signals whilst stationary. However, you should also aim to cover arm signals on the move if you have a safe opportunity to do so. You should also be prepared that the examiner/pupil might carry out an arm signal, with or without the use of the indicator. See lessons 9A for scenarios of arm signals on the move. The main criteria for assessing the use of arm signals on the move are: Was the arm signal given correctly? Was any fault caused because of the use of the arm signal?

'Hello Tom, I understand you have had a few driving lessons in a car similar to this and that today you require a lesson on pedestrian crossings and use of signals. I will fully explain how to deal with pedestrian crossings and use of signals and then we will practice the first few pedestrian crossings under my control by talkthrough. Then we shall practice with less control from me. We will also deal with signalling situations as they occur. Do you have any questions before we start?'

Recap

Instructor:

'Before I explain the lesson, I would like to ask you a few questions to establish your previous knowledge and experience.
- Before pulling in and parking, what routine would you use?
- Do you always need to indicate when you move off?
- When waiting at a closed T-junction to turn left where are you looking and what are you looking for?
- If a pedestrian steps into the road who has priority?
- As a pedestrian you will be familiar with zebra crossings. As you approach ready to cross, what does the traffic usually do?
- When a vehicle lets you cross, where does it stop?'

Note: Depending on the examiner's replies, you may wish to ask follow up or other relevant questions.

Objective

Instructor:

'Our objective today is to approach and negotiate all types of pedestrian crossings safely and with due regard to other road users and to give and recognise correct signals.'

Briefing

> **Pedestrian Crossings:**
> Controlled/uncontrolled; Zebra Crossings; Identify-Approach-Negotiate, Stop when necessary. Single/Split Crossings, Move off routine. Pelican, Puffin, Toucan, School Crossings, zigzag lines, Inviting pedestrians to cross.
>
> **Signals by indicator:**
> Purpose, when to signal, types, timing, unnecessary signals, other drivers signals.
>
> **Signals by arm:**
> Turn right, turn left, slowing down and signals to traffic controllers.

'We can classify pedestrian crossings into two groups: uncontrolled and controlled. With uncontrolled crossings we have to assess whether we need to stop. At controlled crossings, signals such as traffic lights decide this for us. However, at any pedestrian crossing, a pedestrian that has stepped into the road has the priority so we need to approach all pedestrian crossings at a speed where we can stop safely. The routine we are going to use for this is: Identify, Approach & negotiate (IAN).

Let us start with Zebra Crossings. As you are driving you need to scan the road ahead and look for the yellow flashing beacons on black and white poles each side of the road and sometimes on a central reservation. Also look for the black and white lines across the road and where people seem to be crossing the road in the same place. Sometimes, when our view of the pedestrian crossing is obscured by a sharp bend or hill, we will also see a triangular warning sign.

As soon as you have identified there is a pedestrian crossing ahead, check your mirrors and then scan both sides of the road. You need to give way to anyone who is already on the crossing or has just stepped onto the crossing. By assessing this early, you can often reduce your speed so that by the time you reach the crossing all pedestrians are back on the pavement, and you can proceed without stopping. However, remember to check your mirrors and scan both pavements again before negotiating the crossing. Occasionally it may be of benefit to other road users to emphasise that we are slowing down by giving an arm signal. I will deal with this fully when explaining signals.

If anyone is waiting to cross at a zebra crossing then we should stop, unless it is not safe to do so. Stop so that the front of your car is just behind the broken white line before the crossing, apply your handbrake and prepare the car to move, but do not rev the engine.

If it is a single zebra crossing you must wait until all pedestrians are safely on the pavement before moving off. This is because sometimes pedestrians change their mind, turning round on the crossing and walking back the way they have just come. If the zebra crossing has a central reservation, this is classed as a split crossing and you can treat is as two separate crossings.

Once the crossing is clear check both main blind spots, as well as your mirrors before moving off. You are looking for any pedestrians who may be making a last minute dash to get across the crossing.

Now let us look at controlled crossings. The routine you use is exactly the same as I have just explained for zebra crossings, however now you need to respond to traffic lights or traffic controllers.

The three main types of traffic light controlled crossing are Pelican, Puffin and Toucan. The Puffin and Toucan have a normal traffic light sequence and we can move on a green light if the crossing is clear. The puffin crossing is controlled by cameras and so will hold the traffic lights on red depending on pedestrian activity. The Toucan crossing is the only crossing that cyclists can legally ride across. Look for cycle signs and cycle lanes on approach. However you need to be aware that cyclists are likely to ride across all types of crossing.

The pelican crossing has a flashing amber light after the red light. This means you should proceed if the crossing is clear. You need to scan carefully for any pedestrians who may try to cross during this flashing amber phase. Although pelican crossings are normally staggered and would be treated as two crossings, a pelican crossing that goes straight across the road is treated as one crossing, even if there is a central island.

Near schools look out for flashing amber signals and warning signs that a school crossing patrol is in operation. You must stop at a pedestrian crossing when a school crossing patrol shows a 'Stop for children' sign.

At all pedestrian crossings we should not wave pedestrians across. This is because we can never predict the actions of other road users and so could be calling the pedestrians into danger. Also, if you are in a queue of traffic remember never block the crossing by stopping on it.

The zigzag lines either side of a pedestrian crossing mean that we should not overtake the leading moving or stationary motor vehicle. They also mean that we should not park within this area. It is permissible to overtake a cyclist within the zigzag lines, but only if it is safe to do so.

In summary, look well ahead to identify pedestrian crossings early. Scan both sides of the road for pedestrians and always approach at a speed at which you can stop safely if needed.

Do you have any questions on pedestrian crossings before I move onto use of signals?

The purpose of signals is to tell all other road users of our intentions. We should always indicate before turning left or right into or out of a junction. At most other times we would indicate if it is of benefit to another road user. The types of signal we have include our indicators, brake lights, reversing lights and arm signals. Signalling is part of our MSM routine and we always check our mirrors first to ensure a signal is needed and it is properly timed. The position of our car can also be a signal of our intentions, especially as we negotiate around parked vehicles. Timing of signals is very important to ensure we do not mislead other road users. To avoid giving unnecessary signals, use all round observation to decide if any road user will benefit.

Let us briefly consider other drivers signals. If another driver flashes his headlights at you as an indication for you to proceed, ask yourself two questions before moving: Is it for me? And is it safe? Remember that as good drivers we should only flash our headlights or sound the horn to warn another driver of our presence.

Now let us practice the main arm signals. Firstly open your drivers door window fully. Before putting your arm out of the window check your exterior mirror and your right blind spot to make sure it is safe.' *Teach the pupil the three main arm signals of turning right, turning left and slowing down.*

ckpit Drill
Move Off

Instructor:
'Before we move off I would like you to carry out your cockpit drill please.'
Watch carefully for any faults and correct as necessary. Check mirrors are correctly adjusted.

'When you are ready I would like you to start the car and then move off please.'
Once again, watch carefully for faults and correct as necessary.

> Instructor notes: As with all the various PSTs, the examiner will choose the route and give you directions which you then repeat. The examiner will not tell you where the pedestrian crossings are, so you will need to be scanning the road ahead so that you have time for your talkthrough routine. Remember that you are dealing with two subjects at the same time: pedestrian crossings and correct use of all types of signals.
>
> The pupil will have been using signals in his previous lessons so this part can be dealt with using more Q&A and fault assessment.

Talkthrough Routines

Zebra Crossing (no pedestrians)

- Check mirrors, on gas

- Continue scanning

  (pupil negotiates crossing)

- Crossing is clear, maintain this speed

  (pupil reaches safe speed)

- Off the gas, cover brake

- Scan both sides of the road

- Check your mirrors

" Zebra crossing ahead"

Zebra Crossing (pedestrian crossing)

- Check mirrors, on gas

- Continue scanning

  (pupil negotiates crossing)

- Crossing is clear, maintain this speed

  (pedestrian clears crossing)

  (pupil slows down)

- Off the gas, gently brake

- Scan both sides of the road

- Check your mirrors

" Zebra crossing ahead"

Zebra Crossing (pedestrian waiting)

- Move off

- Check mirrors and blind spots

  (pedestrian clears crossing)

- 1st gear, set gas find bite

- Handbrake on

- Stop at the give way line

- Off the gas, gently brake

- Scan both sides of the road

- Check your mirrors

" Zebra crossing ahead"

Pelican Crossing (red to flashing amber)

- Move off (crossing is clear)

- Scan both sides of the crossing

  (lights change to flashing amber)

- 1st gear, set gas, find bite

- Handbrake on

- Stop at the white stop line

- Off the gas, gently brake

  (red traffic lights ahead)

- Scan the road ahead

- Check your mirrors

" Pedestrian crossing ahead"

Prompting

Instructor notes: Once you have negotiated the first few pedestrian crossings under full talkthrough you now need to move the pupil towards independence. Prompting is where we use selective questions to remind the pupil of the actions they need to carry out. With this PST we also need to use prompting to check the pupil's knowledge of signals. On the move you need to deal with both subjects simultaneously. Some examples are given below.

Pupil about to move off

Instructor:
'When you are ready move off please.'
'Do you need to indicate?'

Pupil:
'No, I can't see any cars or pedestrians.'

Instructor:
'Good. Take the second road on the left. When should you indicate?'

Pupil:
'Just after I have passed the first one.'

Instructor:
'Well done. Zebra crossing ahead, what is the first thing you should do?'

Pupil:
'Scan both sides of the road.'

Instructor:
'No check your mirrors first, so you know what is behind you, then scan both sides of the road. There is a pedestrian waiting to cross, do you need to stop?'

Pupil:
'Yes, I should stop at the broken white line.'

Instructor:
'Yes, and remember to apply your handbrake and wait until all pedestrians are on the pavement before moving off again'

Instructor:
'At the next roundabout take the road ahead, second exit.'
  When should you signal?'

Pupil:
'Just as I pass the exit before the one I need.'

Instructor:
'Well done. Now scan the road ahead and tell me when you can see the next pedestrian crossing?'

Pupil:
'There are some red traffic lights ahead with people crossing the road.'

Instructor:
'Good. When should you start slowing down?'

Pupil:
'Now as then the lights may change back to green by the time I reach them.'

Instructor:
'Well done. But where should you look before negotiating the crossing?'

Pupil:
'Both sides of the road in case someone runs across at the last minute.'

Instructor:
'Excellent. You have learnt this subject well.'

Instructor notes:
Prompting questions should elicit either a correct or incorrect response from the pupil. When an incorrect response is given then use fault assessment and appropriate instruction to control the situation.

**Fault
Assessment**

The examiner will make faults at all stages of the examination. The faults committed will be mainly based around the key points listed at the beginning of this lesson. Each time a fault is committed you should try to respond with an identification, analysis and rectification. The identification should always be given the moment a fault is committed. The analysis and rectification should be given as soon as it is safe to do so. With this PST it is often difficult to find somewhere suitable to pull in and park, so most faults will need to be dealt with on the move. As you are dealing with two subjects at the same time, you will need to keep your fault assessment routines short and to the point. Some examples are given below.

Pupil signals unnecessarily when moving off.

Instructor:
'Cancel your signal, it is unnecessary.'

'There are no cars or pedestrians who will benefit.'

'When moving off ask yourself 'who am I signalling to?'

Pupil doesn't check mirrors on approach to pedestrian crossing.

Instructor:
'You haven't checked your mirrors.'

'You need to know how close the vehicles are behind as this may affect your braking and whether to give an arm signal for slowing down .'

'Check your mirrors first then scan both sides of the road.'

Pupil too fast on approach to zebra crossing.

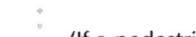

Instructor:
'Slow down, you are too fast.'

'If a pedestrian approached the crossing you couldn't stop safely.'

'Always approach at a speed at which you can stop safely if a pedestrian arrives at the crossing at the last minute.'

Pupil tries to move off too early after stopping at a single zebra crossing.

Instructor:
'Stop. The pedestrian has not finished crossing.'

'Pedestrians sometimes change their minds and turn back.'

'When at a single zebra crossing, wait until all pedestrians are on the pavement before moving off.'

Pupil tries to overtake a milk float within the zigzag line area.

Instructor:
'Hold back. Do not overtake until the zigzag lines finish.'

'Your view of the nearside of the crossing is obscured.'

'You must not overtake the leading motorised vehicle within the zigzag line area.'

Pupil stops at crossing and tries to wave pedestrian across road.

Instructor:
'Don't wave pedestrians across the road.'

'You could be calling the pedestrian into danger as we cannot predict the actions of other road users.'

'Wait patiently and let the pedestrian decide when to cross.'

Pupil signals too early when exiting a roundabout.

Instructor:
'Cancel your signal. You have signalled too early.'

'You are confusing the vehicle waiting to emerge who may pull out in front of you.'

'Wait until you have passed the exit before the one you want to take.'

Pupil gives wrong arm signal when demonstrating slowing down actions.

Instructor:
'You are giving the wrong arm signal. That is for turning left.'

'This would confuse the vehicle behind you.'

'The arm signal for slowing down is to move your hand and arm up and down.'

Pupil keeps indicating when moving out to pass parked vehicles.

Instructor:
'You are signalling unnecessarily.'

'This can cause confusion to other drivers.'

'If you move out early then the position of your car becomes a signal to other drivers.'

Approaching junctions to turn either right or left

7

Level: Partly Trained

Lesson Plan

Recap
Objective

Briefing
Full Talkthrough (first few junctions)
Prompting (less instruction with Q&A)
Independence
Summary

Key Points

Briefing
Mirrors
Signal
Brakes
Gears
Coasting
Too fast on approach
Too slow on approach
Position
Pedestrians
Cross Approaching Traffic
Right Corner Cut

This exercise may be introduced to the PDI by the examiner saying:

'I would like you to assume I am a partly trained pupil and we haven't met before. You are filling in for my regular instructor. I have had a few lessons in a car similar to yours so I am familiar with the controls and their layout. *(The examiner may add)* All my previous driving lessons started from here. I would like you to instruct me in approaching corners, concentrating particularly on turning right and left into side roads, that is major to minor, and correct any faults that may occur. You can call me Jill'

> Instructor notes: You should always listen very carefully to how the examiner introduces himself/herself as a pupil. For this lesson the examiner may say that all his/her previous driving lessons started from the test centre. This may indicate he/she has some limited experience of negotiating junctions other than turning left or right major to minor.

Instructor:

'Hello Jill, I understand you have had a few driving lessons in a car similar to this and that today you require a lesson on approaching junctions to turn either right or left from a major road to a minor road. I will fully explain the junction procedure and then we will practice the first few under my control by talkthrough. Then we shall practice with less control from me. Do you have any questions before we start?'

Recap

Instructor (suggested questions):

'Before I explain the lesson, I would like to ask you a few questions to establish your previous knowledge and experience.'

- Before pulling in and parking, what routine would you use?
- What does progressive braking mean?
- What gears have you used?
- What is your normal driving position or safety line from the kerb?

Note: Depending on the examiner's replies, you may wish to ask follow up or other relevant questions. Also due to the constraints of the examination, the location of the test centre may have a bearing on what the pupil may have done before. For example, if the first junction outside the test centre is a T-junction, then the pupil may have a limited experience of this and of the MSPSL routine. As the pupil (examiner) will be driving from the test centre, one or two questions should be asked to establish this. For example:

- Have you done T-junctions before?
- Can you tell me what MSPSL means?

Objective

Instructor:

'Our objective today is to approach and negoitate both left and right junctions safely from a major road to a minor road, with due regard for all other road users.'

Briefing Plan:

- **Introduction:** Identify (road signs & markings). MSM - PSL

- **Turning Left:** Use of MSPSL on approach, block gear changing, coasting, priorities, hazards, pedestrians & steering.

- **Turning Right:** Use of MSPSL on approach, safe gaps, point of turn, cutting corners

Briefing

'To be able to approach and negotiate left and right turns safely, you firstly need to assess the road ahead to identify where they are. Look for road signs such as warning triangles and markings such as hazard warning lines down the centre of the road which may indicate there is a junction ahead. In residential areas where there may not be road signs, look for gaps in houses, street name signs and vehicles emerging. On approach you need to use the Mirror, Signal Manoeuvre routine, but today you are going to divide the manoeuvre part into Position, Speed and Look so you now have a routine called MSPSL. As you progress we will break down the looking part into Assessing hazards, priorities and gaps and Deciding when it is safe to turn.

Let us look at turning left first. I want you to imagine you are driving down a main road at 30 mph in 4th gear and I ask you to take the next road on the left. The first thing you need to do is check your interior mirror and left mirrors for following traffic and then signal down left. The timing of the signal will depend on the junction you are approaching, but as a general rule, if you can see the junction clearly ahead, signal between six to eight car lengths before this. Next you need to check you are positioned on your safety line. This is usually about a metre from the kerb, but on narrower roads position in the centre of your lane. Now you need to slow down using progressive braking until by the time you are three to four car lengths from the junction, your speed is about 10–12 mph. At this point you select 2nd gear using block gear changing, as there is no need to use 3rd before 2nd, and bring the clutch up to avoid coasting. Your right foot should remain covering the brake. Next you need to check the road ahead for any oncoming traffic that may be turning right, you should have the priority but you should never assume this. Then check into the road you are turning into, firstly for any hazard such as parked vehicles close to the junction which could affect your positioning and secondly for any pedestrians who may be crossing the road. You also need to look at the sharpness of the corner as this will give us an indication of how much to steer. You should start to steer when the front of your car reaches the end of the last straight kerbstone before the corner and you need to conform to the shape of the kerb keeping to your safety line. About three quarters of the way round the corner you need to start straightening the wheel back to the right so that by the time you are parallel with the straight kerbstones in the new road your wheels are straight. Lastly you need to check your mirrors before applying gas and proceeding along the new road.

Now let us look at turning right. The main difference now is that you will be crossing a lane of traffic which has priority over you. This time check your interior mirror and right mirror and then signal right. Next you need to position the vehicle just left of the centre line. You can do this by keeping the white centre line visible in the bottom right hand corner of your front windscreen *(depends on vehicle)*. Start to brake so that once again by the time you are three to four car lengths from the junction your speed is about 10–12 mph, change into second gear and bring your clutch up whilst still covering the brake. This time you should look at the road ahead and road on the right. You are checking the road ahead for a safe gap in the oncoming traffic and into the new road for obstructions and pedestrians. You also need to look for your point of turn. When crossing traffic you should not cause another vehicle to change speed or direction by your action. To help us assess this we can use the 'walking rule'. If you have time to walk into the road then you have time to drive in.

If you have a safe gap, stay left of the centre line until you reach the point of turn. This is when your right exterior mirror is in line with the centre line of the new road. Steer right at this point, then start to straighten the road wheels about three quarters of the way into the new road. Once you are into the new road and the wheels are straight, check your mirrors and apply the gas.

It is important that you do not turn earlier than our point of turn as you will be cutting the corner and be in conflict with traffic in the new road that may be about to emerge.

If you do not have a safe gap then you need to stop at your point of turn, apply the handbrake, and prepare the car ready to move. Whilst waiting for a safe gap, keep checking into the new road for pedestrians and other vulnerable road users. If a pedestrian steps into the road they have priority over you. As you should never start a manoeuvre you cannot complete, you should wait at the point of turn until you can enter the new road safely.

To sum up, you firstly scan the road ahead to identify the junction early. Then use the MSPSL routine on approach so you can ensure a safe speed, correct gear selection and avoid coasting. Before negotiating the junctions look, assess, decide and act (LADA) on the effects of any hazard such as parked vehicles and pedestrians, learn how to choose safe gaps when crossing traffic and avoid cutting corners.

Do you have any questions?'

Instructor:

'Before we move off I would like you to carry out your cockpit drill please.'
Watch carefully for any faults and correct as necessary. Check mirrors are correctly adjusted.

'When you are ready I would like you to start the car and then move off please.'
Once again, watch carefully for faults and correct as necessary.

Instructor notes: As with all the various PSTs, the examiner will choose the route and give you directions which you then repeat. The location of the first major to minor junction will depend on the test centre where you take the examination so listen carefully for the words "Take the next road on the right/left" as this is your cue to start the first talkthrough routine. The constraints of the examination mean that the initial drive may include other junctions such as T-junctions, crossroads or roundabouts. This means that the pupil (examiner) will be able to negotiate these at a partly trained standard but will still require full instruction for the first few major to minor left/right turns.

The examiner will always try to give you directions early, to give you time to repeat them. Although it is recommended that talkthroughs should start early, so you have enough time to complete them, make sure you assess the junction before giving your words of command to ensure they are properly timed. For example, if the examiner says 'take the second road on the right' your talkthrough needs to be adapted to avoid a possible signal fault.

Turning Left

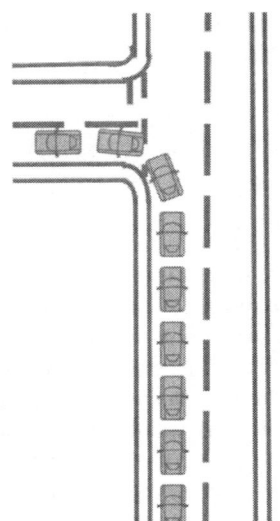

- Check mirrors, on gas

- Steer right

- Steer left

- Look road ahead, Look road on the left

- Clutch up

- Clutch down select 2nd Gear

- Gently brake to 10 mph

- Position on safety line

- Signal down left

- Check your interior mirror & left mirror

"Take the next road on the left"

Turning right (with gap)

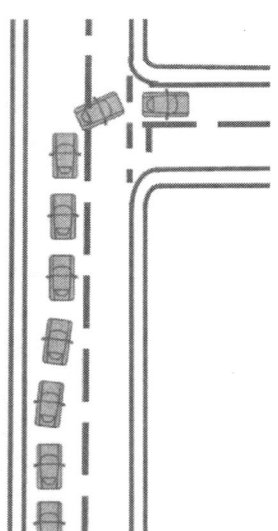

- Check mirrors, on gas

- Steer right, steer left

- Look road on the right

- Look road ahead (assess gap)

- Clutch up

- Clutch down select 2nd gear

- Gently brake to 10 mph

- Position just left of the centre line

- Signal up right

- Check your interior mirror & right mirror

"Take the next road on the right"

Turning Right (without gap)

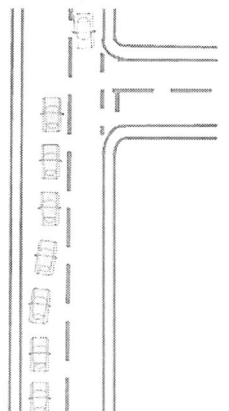

- Check mirrors, on gas

- Steer right, steer left

- Clutch gently up

- Release handbrake

- Clutch to bite point

- Handbrake on (wait for gap)

- Pause at your point of turn

- Clutch down select 1st gear

- More brake

- Look road on the right

- Look road ahead (assess gap)

- Clutch up

- Clutch down select 2nd gear

- Gently brake

- Position just left of the centre line

- Signal up right

- Check your interior mirror & right mirror

"Take the next road on the right."

Important note: All talkthrough routines included in this manual are examples only and will need to be adapted to each individual junction that is approached and negotiated. For example, when turning right, there may be bollards and a marked central area which would require different instructions.

You will also need to take into account any hazard such as parked vehicles and any particular road signs and markings etc.

Prompting

Major to Minor turning left

Instructor:
'Take the next road on the left please'.
'Which mirrors are you going to check?'

Pupil:
'Interior and left.'

Instructor:
'Good. Where are you going to position the car?'

Pupil:
'About a metre from the kerb.'

Instructor:
'Well done. What speed will you brake to?'

Pupil:
'About 10–12 miles per hour.'

Instructor:
'Excellent. What gear do you need?'

Pupil:
'Second gear.'

Instructor:
'Yes, but remember to bring your clutch all the way up to avoid coasting.'

Major to Minor turning right

Instructor:
'Take the next road on the right, please.'
What reference point are you going to use to position the car just left of the centre line?'

Pupil:
'I need to have the centre line in the bottom right hand corner of my windscreen.'

Instructor:
'Do you have a safe gap in the oncoming traffic?'

Pupil:
'No, I don't think so.'

Instructor:
'Good. Where are you going to wait?'

Pupil:
'At my point of turn.'

Instructor:
'Well done. What are you looking for in the new road?'

Pupil:
'Parked vehicles and pedestrians.'

Instructor:
'Yes. Tell me when you have a safe gap.'

Instructor notes: Prompting questions should elicit either a correct or incorrect response from the pupil. When an incorrect response is given then use fault assessment and appropriate instruction to control the situation.

**Fault
Assessment**

The examiner will make faults at all stages of the examination. The faults committed will be mainly based around the key points listed at the beginning of this lesson. Each time a fault is committed you should try to respond with an identification, analysis and rectification. The identification should always be given the moment a fault is committed. The analysis and rectification should be given as soon as it is safe to do so. With junction work this is often after the junction has been negotiated and if you cannot do this effectively on the move, then you may need to pull in and park in a safe place. Some examples are given below:

Pupil checks exterior mirror before interior mirror when turning left.

Instructor:
'You have checked the mirrors in the wrong order.'

'The interior mirror gives you the true image.'

'Check your interior mirror followed by your exterior mirror.'

Pupil positions too far to right when turning left.

Instructor:
'You are positioned too far to the right.'

'This is misleading to vehicles behind you.'

'Position a metre from the kerb' (use a reference point).

Pupil forgets to bring clutch up after changing gear.

Instructor:
'You are coasting. Bring your clutch up.'

'The engine is disconnected from the road wheels so we have less control of the car.'

'Remember, as soon as you have selected 2nd gear bring the clutch all the way up.'

Pupil doesn't look into the new road when turning left.

Instructor:
'You haven't checked the road on the left.'

'You need to check for parked vehicles and pedestrians.'

'Remember to look road ahead and road on the left before steering.'

Pupil positions too far to right when turning right.

Instructor:
'You are too far to the right. Position just left of the centre line.'

'You are in conflict with oncoming traffic.'

'Make sure the centre line is in the bottom right hand corner of your front windscreen'
(reference point depends on vehicle).

Pupil doesn't slow down early enough on approach to turn right.

Instructor:
'Slow down, you are too fast!'

'We need time to assess the junction and negotiate at a safe speed.'

'Brake to 10–12 mph by the time you are 3 to 4 car lengths from the junction.'

Pupil tries to turn right major to minor unsafely.

Instructor:
'Stop! You haven't got a safe gap in the oncoming traffic.'

'Remember, we must not cause a vehicle to change speed or direction when crossing
their path.'

'Use the walking rule (if you can walk into the junction you can drive in) to measure
the gap.'

Pupil stops too early when approaching point of turn major to minor turning right.

Instructor:
'You have stopped too early to turn right.'

'If you start to turn now you will cut the corner.'

'Line up your right exterior mirror with centre line of new road before steering right.'

T-junctions emerging

Level: Partly Trained

Lesson Plan

Recap
Objective

Briefing
Full Talkthrough (first few junctions)
Prompting (less instruction with Q&A)
Independence
Summary

Key Points

Briefing
MSM
Speed
Gears
Coasting
Observation
Emerging
Position Right
Position Left
Pedestrians

This exercise may be introduced to the PDI by the examiner saying:

'I would like you to assume I am a partly trained pupil and we haven't met before. You are filling in for my regular instructor. I have had a few lessons in a car similar to yours so I am familiar with the controls and their layout. I would like you to instruct me on how to deal with emerging at 'T' junctions, turning left and right from a minor road to major road and correct any faults that may occur. You can call me John.'

Instructor:

'Hello John, I understand you have had a few driving lessons in a car similar to this and that today you require a lesson on emerging at T-junctions. I will fully explain the procedure for emerging and then we will practice the first one or two under my control by talkthrough. Then we shall practice with less control from me. Do you have any questions before we start?'

Recap

Instructor:

'Before I explain T-junctions, I would like to ask you a few questions to establish your previous knowledge and experience.
- Imagine you are on a major road and I ask you to take the next road on the right, take me through the routine you would use on the approach.
- Before negotiating the junction, where are you looking and what are you looking for?
- What does coasting mean?
- How do you control the speed of the car at low speed using the clutch?
- What is the difference between an open and a closed junction?'

Note: Depending on the examiner's replies, you may wish to ask follow up or other relevant questions.

Objective

Instructor:

'Our objective today is to approach and emerge from T-junctions safely with due regard for all other road users.'

Briefing

Briefing Plan

> ***Introduction:*** Types, signs and markings, Open/closed, zones of vision, Traffic in new road has priority & effective observations.
>
> ***Emerging Left:*** Use of MSPSL on approach, positioning at give-way line, observations, choosing safe gaps. Pedestrians
>
> ***Emerging Right:*** Use of MSPSL on approach, positioning, observations, when to steer, parked vehicles in new road and clutch control to improve zone of vision

'The main types of T-junction are as follows: Unmarked, where no one has the priority and we need to take extra care before emerging; Give-way which has a double broken white line across our lane at the end of the road and sometimes a white inverted triangle on the road, and occasionally a Give-way sign on approach. Next we have Stop, which has a solid white line across our lane and a hexagonal stop sign - where we must stop and apply the handbrake as these are hazardous junctions; and finally traffic light controlled.

All T-junctions can be split into two groups: Open and Closed. An open junction allows us to see into the new road early whereas at a closed junction our view is blocked by houses, walls hedges and trees etc. This is called our zone of vision and is important as the traffic in the new road has the priority over us, so we need to assess when it is safe to emerge. We are going to use the MSPSL routine on approach. The most common T-junctions are Give-way so we will concentrate on these for the briefing. To identify a T-junction, in addition to signs and markings, scan the road ahead so you can see where it ends. You will often see houses, trees or hedges across the end of the road and vehicles passing right and left.

Let us firstly look at turning left, at an open junction. Check your interior mirror and your left mirror, indicate left, position on your safety line (metre from kerb or centre of lane depending on width of road) and gently brake. Bring your speed down to 10–12 miles an hour about 2–3 car lengths from the end of the road and change into second gear bringing your clutch all the way up whilst still covering the brake. Start to look right and left and if the road is clear continue by steering left when the kerb starts to bend to the left and conform to the line of the kerb until you are into the new road. Straighten the road wheels, check your mirrors and get back on the gas.

For a closed junction turning left, the mirrors, signal and position are the same, but you now need to slow the car down more as the zone of vision is blocked. I want you to brake so that by the time the front of the car reaches the end of the last straight kerb stone your speed is about 5 mph. When you are between one and half a car length from the junction, change back to 1st gear, steer to the left (conforming to the line of the kerb), bring your clutch back towards the bite-point and pause at the give way line. To ensure you are in the correct position, I want you to check that the give-way lines appear just under your right exterior door mirror and that you can see the left hand kerbstones in the bottom left hand corner of your front windscreen (except for sharp turn).

For the first few junctions, I will ask you to stop and apply the handbrake, so you can get used to the correct positioning and observations.

Next you need to look right, left and right again, as many times as it takes to ensure you have a safe gap in the traffic and you have assessed the effect of any hazards such as parked cars which may be in the new road. You also need to look for pedestrians crossing the road and other vulnerable road users such as cyclists. A safe gap when emerging is about the same as being able to walk across the road and back again. The reason for this is that you need time firstly to enter the new road and secondly to then get up to the speed of the traffic in the new road without causing it to slow down or change direction.

Whilst you are waiting, prepare the car to move and once you have a safe gap, release the handbrake and move into the new road taking into account any obstructions that may affect your positioning.

Now let's look at a closed junction turning right. This time check your interior and right mirrors and signal right. Then position your vehicle just left of the safety line. If the centre line stays straight, keep your wheels straight. If the centre line curves as you approach the junction then steer slightly left or right as appropriate. Once again, gently brake on approach until by the time you are half a car length from the give-way line your speed is about 5 mph. Change back to 1st gear, bring your clutch back towards the bite point and pause at the junction, once again checking that the give way line appears just behind your right exterior door mirror. Your observations are the same as for turning left and although you are now crossing one line of traffic and joining another, the gap can be measured in the same way. When emerging, it is important that you only start to steer right once your front wheels have passed over the give-way line, otherwise you will be in conflict with oncoming traffic. Sometimes however, if there are parked cars opposite you, you will need to steer a little earlier than this.

If your zone of vision is blocked by parked vehicles either side of the new road, you firstly need to pause at the give-way line so that you can scan across the pavements past the inside of the parked vehicles to the road beyond. This would also be where pedestrians may cross the road. Then you will need to move forward slowly until you reach a second imaginary give-way line where the front of your car is level with the outside of the parked vehicles. To do this safely, you will need to use clutch control, sometimes called 'peep and creep', and it will also help your zone of vision if you lean forward towards the steering wheel. Only when you can see clearly can you assess if it is safe to emerge into the new road.

To sum up, scan the road ahead to identify the junction early, use the MSPSL routine on approach so you can ensure a safe speed, correct gear selection and avoid coasting. Correct position at the junction is important and remember that the traffic in the new road has the priority, so you need to scan right and left to assess safe gaps and any hazard such as parked vehicles. Also look for vulnerable road users such as pedestrians and cyclists who are likely to cross the road near the give-way line.

Do you have any questions?'

**kpit Drill
Move Off**

Instructor:
'Before we move off I would like you to carry out your cockpit drill please.'
Watch carefully for any faults and correct as necessary. Check mirrors are correctly adjusted.

'When you are ready I would like you to start the car and then move off please.'
Once again, watch carefully for faults and correct as necessary.

Instructor notes: As with all the various PSTs, the examiner will choose the route and give you directions which you then repeat. The location of the first T-junction will depend on the test centre where you take the examination, so assess the road ahead to ensure you identify the first emerging situation and start the first talkthrough routine early enough.

The examiner will always try to give you directions early, to give you time to repeat them. Although it is recommended that talkthroughs should start early, so you have enough time to complete them, make sure you assess the junction before giving your words of command to ensure they are properly timed. For example, there may be a turning left or right before the end of the road and it would be better to start the talkthrough after passing this to avoid a possible signal fault.

Turning Left - Open Junction

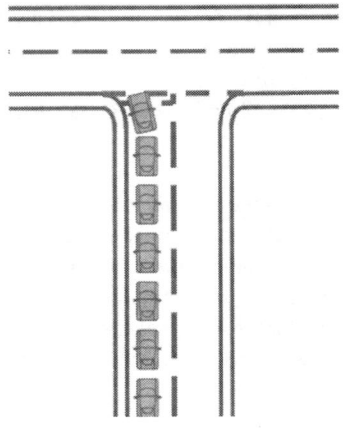

- Check mirrors, on gas
  (once into the new road)

- Steer right (to straighten wheels)

- Steer left *(at point of steer)*

- Look right, look left (repeat)

- Clutch gently up

- Select 2nd gear

- Clutch down

- Gently brake

- Position on safety line

- Signal Left

- Check your mirrors

"At the end of the road turn left"

Important note: All talkthrough routines included in this manual are examples only and will need to be adapted to each individual junction that is approached and negotiated. You will also need to take into account any hazards such as parked vehicles and any particular road signs and markings etc.

Turning Left - closed junction

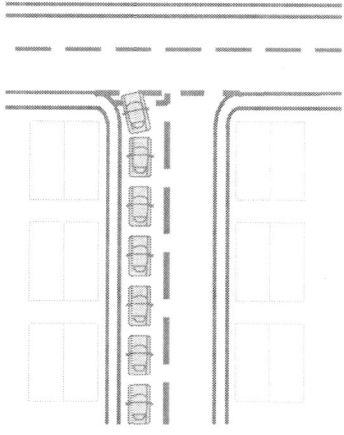

- Check mirrors, on gas

- Steer left, Steer right
  (to straighten wheels)

- Clutch gently up

- Release handbrake

- Look right, look left (repeat)

- Handbrake on

- Pause at the line

- Clutch up to bite

- Steer left *(at point of steer)*

- Select 1st gear

- Clutch down (1–1½ car
  length from give way line)

- Gently brake

- Position on safety line

- Signal Left

- Check your mirrors

"At the end of the road turn left"

Turning Right- closed junction

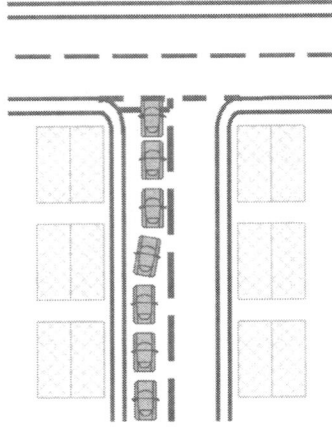

- Check mirrors, on gas

- Steer right, Steer left
  (to straighten wheels)

- Clutch gently up

- Release handbrake

- Look right, look left (repeat)

- Handbrake on

- Pause at the line

- Clutch up to bite

- Select 1st gear

- Clutch down (1–1½ car length
  from give way line)

- Keep wheels straight
  (If centre line straight)

- Gently brake

- Position just left of
  the centre line

- Signal right

- Check your mirrors

"At the end of the road turn right"

Instructor notes: Once you have negotiated the first few junctions under full talkthrough you now need to move the pupil towards independence. Prompting is where we use selective questions to remind the pupil of the actions they need to carry out. These questions should be based on the commands from the talkthrough routines. Some examples are given below.

Turning left - approach

Instructor:
'At the end of the road turn left'.
'What is the first thing you need to do?'

Pupil:
'Check my mirrors.'

Instructor:
'Good. There is a road on the left before the end of the road, when will you signal?'

Pupil:
'Just after I have passed that junction.'

Instructor:
'Well done. Where are you going to position as you approach the give-way line?'

Pupil:
'I need to steer left conforming to the line of the kerb.'

Turning left - emerging

Instructor:
'Where are you looking and what are you looking for?'

Pupil:
'I am looking right, left and right for a safe gap, any hazard and pedestrians.'

Instructor:
'Good. There are parked vehicles obscuring your view, what should you do next?'

Pupil:
'Creep forward using clutch control.'

Instructor:
'Yes, but lean forward to help your vision.'

Turning right- approach

Instructor:
'At the end of the road turn right'
'Where are you going to position the car?'

Pupil:
'Just left of the centre line.'

Instructor:
'Good. Closed junction, when are you going to change gear?'

Pupil:
'About half a car length from the junction.'

Instructor:
'Well done. What reference point will you use to stop at the give-way line?'

Pupil:
'I will check that the white line appears just behind my right exterior door mirror.'

Instructor:
'Well done. When will you start to steer right when emerging?'

Pupil:
'Just after my front wheels pass over the give-way line.'

> Instructor notes: Prompting questions should elicit either a correct or incorrect response from the pupil. When an incorrect response is given then use fault assessment and appropriate instruction to control the situation.

**Fault
sessment**

> The examiner will make faults at all stages of the examination. The faults committed will be mainly based around the key points listed at the beginning of this lesson. Each time a fault is committed you should try to respond with an identification, analysis and rectification. The identification should always be given the moment a fault is committed. The analysis and rectification should be given as soon as it is safe to do so. With junction work, this is often after the junction has been negotiated and if you cannot do this effectively on the move then you may need to pull in and park in a safe place. Some examples are given below.

Pupil changes gear too early on approach to a closed junction.

Instructor:
'You have changed gear too early.'

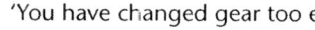

'This is causing you to coast up to the junction.'

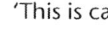

'We don't use first gear until we emerge so only select it half a car length from the junction.'

Pupil steers too late when approaching give-way line to turn left.

Instructor:
'You are positioned too far to the right because you steered too late.'

'When you emerge this will bring you too close to the centre of the new road.'

'Start to steer left when the front of your vehicle reaches the end of the last straight kerbstone.'

Pupil forgets to select first gear at the give-way line.

Instructor:
'You are in the wrong gear. Select 1st gear now.'

'If you try to move off in another gear the car will stall.'

'Remember, select 1st gear half a car length from the junction.'

Pupil stops too late at give-way line when turning right.

Instructor:
'You have stopped too late.'

'This puts you in conflict with traffic in the new road.'

'Remember to stop as soon as you see the give-way line appears behind your right exterior door mirror.'

Pupil doesn't look left when carrying out observations for emerging.

Instructor:
'You are not looking left, look left now.'

'You need to check for hazards such as parked cars and any pedestrian who may cross the road.'

'Remember to look right, left and right again.'

Pupil about to emerge unsafely.

Instructor:
'Wait! You don't have a safe gap.'

'You would have caused the oncoming vehicle to slow down.'

'Remember if you can walk across the road and back again then you have time to emerge safely.'

Pupil does not lean forward when emerging between parked vehicles.

Instructor:
'Lean forward towards the steering wheel.'

'Your zone of vision around the parked vehicles is restricted.'

'Leaning forward will give you improved vision round the parked vehicles.'

Pupil straightens up too late after entering new road turning right.

Instructor:
'You steered back to the left too late.'

'This brought you dangerously close to the centre line.'

'Start to straighten the car once you are three quarters of the way into the new road.'

Crossroads

9

Level: Partly Trained

Lesson Plan

Recap
Objective

Briefing
Full Talkthrough (first few junctions)
Prompting (less instruction with Q&A)
Independence
Summary

Key Points

Briefing
MSM
Speed
Gears
Coasting
Observation
Emerging
Position Right
Position Left
Pedestrians
Cross Approaching Traffic
Right Corner Cut

This exercise may be introduced to the PDI by the examiner saying:

'I would like you to assume I am a partly trained pupil and we haven't met before. You are filling in for my regular instructor. I have had a few lessons in a car similar to yours so I am familiar with the controls and their layout. I would like you to instruct me on how to deal with crossroads, that is all aspects to include proceeding ahead, turning right and turning left assuming that I am at the partly trained stage and correct any faults that may occur. You can call me Tom.'

Instructor:

'Hello Tom, I understand you have had a few driving lessons in a car similar to this and that today you require a lesson on Crossroads. I will fully explain the crossroads procedure and then we will practice the first one or two under my control by talkthrough. Then we shall practice with less control from me. Do you have any questions before we start?'

Recap

Instructor (question suggestions):

'Before I explain crossroads, I would like to ask you a few questions to establish your previous knowledge and experience.

- Imagine you were approaching a T-junction to turn right, take me through the routine you would use on approach.
- When you reach the give-way line where would you be looking and what would you be looking for?
- If your zone of vision was blocked by parked cars, explain to me how you would use clutch control to move the car forward slowly.
- Who has priority at an unmarked junction?
- What is the difference between an open and a closed junction and how does this affect your speed of approach?'

Note: Depending on the examiner's replies, you may wish to ask follow up or other relevant questions

Objective

Instructor:

'Our objective today is to be able to recognise, approach and negotiate crossroads safely with due regard for all other road users.'

Briefing Plan:

> ***Introduction:*** Accident blackspots, types including staggered and yellow box.
>
> ***Emerging:*** Observation of the road ahead and effects, eye contact, priority, observations at junction, turning left, going ahead, turning right.
>
> ***Approaching:*** Routines for going ahead, left and turning right. Offside and nearside (advantages and disadvantages), positioning, observations and how we choose which method to use.

'Crossroads are often accident blackspots so we need to take extra Care, make extra Observations because of the extra Danger (COD).

The types of crossroads are similar to T-junctions: unmarked, where no one has the priority, give way, stop and traffic light controlled. In addition to this, we have staggered crossroads where the road opposite you is offset to the right or left. Some major crossroads have a painted yellow box and diagonal lines across the centre of the junction which means we can only enter the box if our exit is clear and if this is the case, you can wait in the box when turning right.

Let us look at emerging first. We use our MSPSL routine on approach just as you would for a T-junction and normally our positioning at the junction would be the same as for T-junctions. However, as you can see into the road ahead on approach, we start to assess this as well. If, for example, there are parked vehicles close to the entrance of the road opposite or the junction is staggered to the right and you want to take the road ahead, it may be better to position your vehicle just left of the centre line than remain on our safety line. Also, if you can see that a vehicle facing you in the road opposite has been waiting for some time to emerge, then you can assume that the driver may be starting to become impatient. This brings us to the important point of eye contact with the driver opposite. We need to try to establish what they are going to do, so we need to look at the driver and vehicle: Is he/she signalling? Are his/her wheels turned to the right? Is he/she creeping forward? Are they looking at you? Is he/she flashing their lights at you or waving you out?

Our observations at the crossroads are similar to T-junctions but we also need to be looking at the road ahead, so we use a routine called RALAR –right, ahead, left, ahead, right. We are looking for safe gaps in the traffic and for any pedestrian and other vulnerable road users who may be crossing the road. You can choose a safe gap by assessing if you could walk across the road and back again. This will give you time to emerge and get up to the speed of the traffic in the new road if turning right or left. When going ahead across the main road, use the rule if you can walk across you can drive across.

The vehicle turning right normally has the least amount of priority, so if we are turning left and the vehicle opposite is turning right then we should have the priority. However, you should never assume priority and so rely on your eye contact to establish when it is safe to emerge. Remember the phrase 'Don't know, Don't go'.

When emerging across the main road, we need to do this slowly using clutch control so that we can continue our observations all round. We need to be able to stop safely if, for example, a pedestrian suddenly crossed the new road we are entering.

When turning right from a minor road and there is a vehicle opposite also turning right, usually one of us will emerge first so we need to use eye contact to establish this.

Now let us look at approaching crossroads on a major road. Look out for signs and markings and other indications such as gaps in houses and vehicles emerging across the road in front of you.

When approaching a crossroads to go road ahead, check your mirrors then scan both sides of the road (RALAR) for emerging vehicles and pedestrians crossing. You have the priority but always approach at a safe speed and be prepared to slow down, choose a lower gear or stop if necessary.

When turning left use MSPSL on approach and when you get to the looking part check the road on the right as well as ahead and left using the RALAR routine.

Turning right is a little more difficult as oncoming traffic may want to also turn right. To do this safely we use one of two methods, offside-to-offside or nearside to nearside. Do you know which is the offside and nearside of the car?

The important thing to remember is that not all oncoming vehicles will be turning right and we are still crossing this line of traffic, who have the priority over us.

Offside to offside is the safest method as it gives us a better view of the road ahead. However it does not help traffic flow as progress tends to be erratic. We position by driving past the oncoming vehicle and then turning right behind it. Our point of turn is usually a little later than usual.

Nearside to nearside is more hazardous as we now need to turn in front of the oncoming vehicle who is blocking our view of the road ahead. However, this method does help traffic flow and is often used at busy traffic light controlled crossroads. Our point of turn is usually slightly earlier than normal.

To choose which method to use, we firstly need to look for painted arrows on the road. We can also determine the method if the crossroads is staggered as this will require us to turn either before or after the oncoming vehicle. If there are no indications, then assume it is offside to offside but then use eye contact as you start to move to your point of turn. The oncoming driver will often determine which method you use as he will either turn in front of you or go round you.

To sum up, use the MSPSL routine on approach so you can ensure a safe speed, correct gear selection and avoid coasting. Use the RALAR routine to look for pedestrians and to choose safe gaps. When turning right across traffic, take extra care and avoid cutting corners.

Have you any questions?'

ckpit Drill
Move Off

Instructor:

'Before we move off, I would like you to carry out your cockpit drill please.'
Watch carefully for any faults and correct as necessary. Check mirrors are correctly adjusted.

'When you are ready I would like you to start the car and then move off please.'
Once again, watch carefully for faults and correct as necessary.

Instructor notes: Although the examiner will give you directions, he may not indicate where the crossroads are, especially if you are following the road ahead. For this reason it is vital that you are planning ahead so that you recognise any crossroads early enough to be able to deliver your instruction. Although the pupil will have previous experience of turning left and right, it is advisable to give a full talkthrough for the first few junctions. This will avoid confusing the pupil as to which parts of the routine he is supposed to do on his own and which you are going to control and will also enable you to have effective control during the early stages of the lesson.

Talkthrough Routines

Important note: All talkthrough routines included in this manual are examples only and will need to be adapted to each individual junction that is approached and negotiated. You will also need to take into account any hazards such as parked vehicles and any particular road signs and markings etc.

Crossroads, Emerging– Turning Left

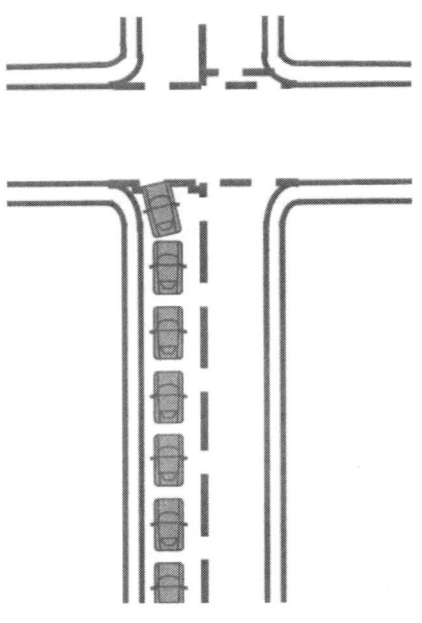

- Check mirrors, on gas

- Steer left, Steer right
  (to straighten wheels)

- Clutch gently up

- Release handbrake

- Look right ahead
  left ahead right (repeat)

- Handbrake on

- Pause at the line

- Clutch up to bite

- Steer left *(at point of steer)*

- Select 1st gear

- Clutch down *(1–1½ car length from give-way line)*

- Gently brake

- Position on safety line

- Signal Left

- Check your mirrors

"At the crossroads turn left"

Crossroads emerging- Turning Right

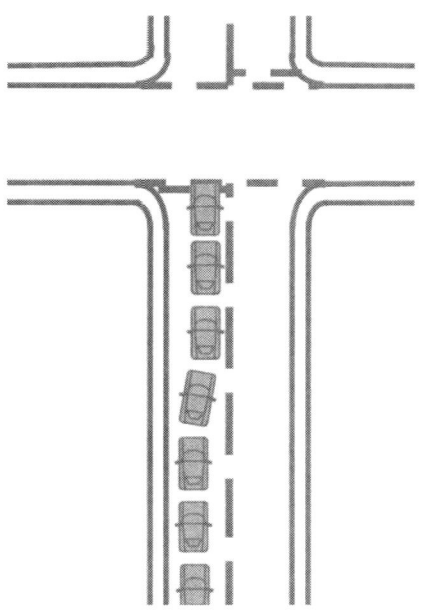

- Check mirrors, on gas

- Steer right, Steer left
  (to straighten wheels)

- Clutch gently up

- Release handbrake

- Look right, ahead, left,
  ahead, right *(repeat)*

- Handbrake on

- Pause at the line

- Clutch up to bite

- Select 1st gear

- Clutch down

- Keep wheels straight
  (If centre line straight)

- Gently brake

- Position just left of
  the centre line

- Signal Right

- Check your mirrors

"At the crossroads turn right"

Crossroads, emerging - Road Ahead

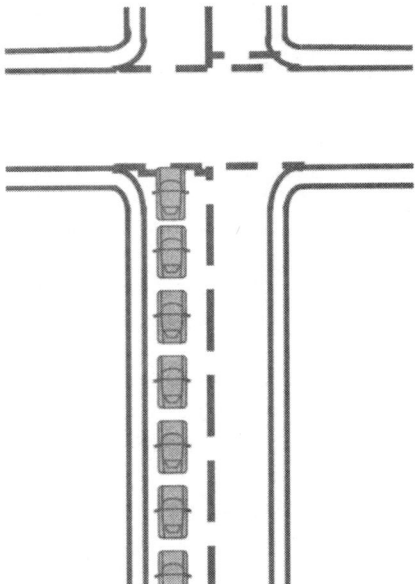

- Check mirrors, on gas

- Keep scanning

- Clutch gently up

- Release handbrake

- Look right, ahead, left, ahead, right. *(repeat)*

- Handbrake on

- Pause at the line

- Clutch up to bite

- Select 1st gear

- Clutch down

- Keep wheels straight

- Gently brake

- Position *(either)* on safety line *(or)* just left of centre line

- Scan the road ahead

- Check your mirrors

"At the crossroads take the road ahead"

Important note: All talkthrough routines included in this manual are examples only and will need to be adapted to each individual junction that is approached and negotiated. You will also need to take into account any hazards such as parked vehicles and any particular road signs and markings etc.

Crossroads, Approaching– Road Ahead

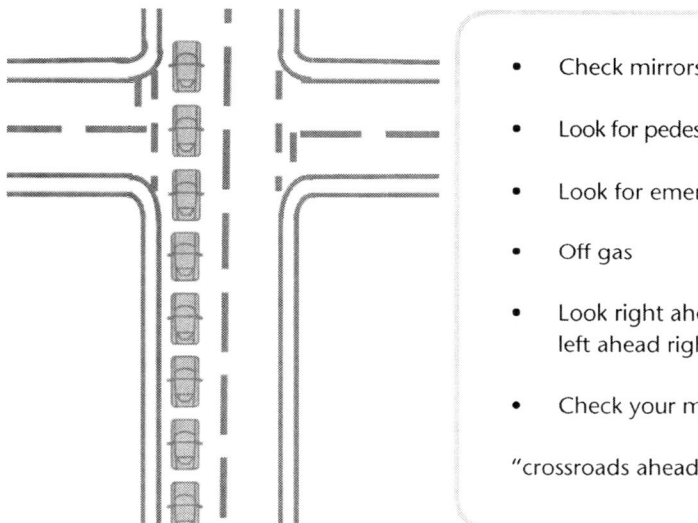

- Check mirrors, on gas

- Look for pedestrians crossing

- Look for emerging vehicles

- Off gas

- Look right ahead
  left ahead right

- Check your mirrors

"crossroads ahead"

Crossroads Approaching - Turning Left

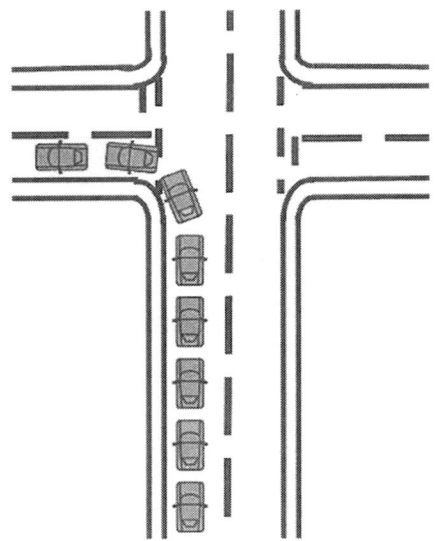

- Check mirrors, on gas

- Steer right

- Steer left

- Look right, ahead, left, ahead, right, (ahead)

- Clutch up, cover brake

- Clutch down select 2nd gear

- Gently brake

- Position on safety line

- Signal left

- Check your mirrors

"At the crossroads turn left"

Crossroads Approaching - Turning Right

- Check mirrors, on gas

- Steer right, steer left

- Clutch gently up

- Release handbrake

- Clutch to bite point

- Handbrake on

  (wait for gap)

- Pause at your point of turn

  (Point of turn will depend on nearside or offside)

- Clutch down select 1st gear

- More brake

- Look right, ahead, left, ahead, right

  (assess on-coming vehicle)

- Clutch up, cover brake

- Clutch down select 2nd gear

- Gently brake

- Position just left of the centre line

- Signal right

- Check your mirrors

"At the crossroads turn right"

Prompting

Instructor notes: Once you have negotiated the first few junctions under full talkthrough you now need to move the pupil towards independence. Prompting is where we use selective questions to remind the pupil of the actions they need to carry out. These questions should be based on the commands from the talkthrough routine.

Please refer to lessons 7 & 8 for examples of prompting questions during the approach to junctions.
Some further examples are given below.

Minor to Major

Instructor:
'At the end of the road follow the road ahead'.
'What is the first thing you need to do?'

Pupil:
'Check my mirrors.'

Instructor:
'Good. Scan the new road. Parked car near the junction, how will this affect your positioning on approach?'

Pupil:
'I will need to position just left of the centre line.'

Instructor:
'Well done. What observations will you carry out?'

Pupil:
'I will look right, ahead, left, ahead, right.'

Major to Minor (following road ahead)

Instructor:
'Crossroads ahead, what is the first thing you need to do?'

Pupil:
'Look right and left into the minor roads.'

Instructor:
'No. Check your mirrors first, then scan the minor roads.'

Instructor:
'Vehicle trying to emerge, how will this affect your speed of approach?'

Pupil:
'I need to come off the gas and be prepared to slow down.'

Instructor:
'Good. Cover the brake.'

Instructor notes: Prompting questions should elicit either a correct or incorrect response from the pupil. When an incorrect response is given then use fault assessment and appropriate instruction to control the situation.

Fault assessment

The examiner will make faults at all stages of the examination. The faults committed will be mainly based around the key points listed at the beginning of this lesson. Each time a fault is committed, you should try to respond with an identification, analysis and rectification. The identification should always be given the moment a fault is committed. The analysis and rectification should be given as soon as it is safe to do so. With junction work, this is often after the junction has been negotiated and if you cannot do this effectively on the move then you may need to pull in and park in a safe place.

Please refer to lessons 7 & 8 for examples of fault assessment during the approach to junctions.

Some further examples are given overleaf.

Pupil checks mirrors and signals right/left at the same time.

Instructor:

'You have checked your mirrors and signalled at the same time.'

'You need time to act on what you see before signalling.'

'Check your mirrors well before signalling. Count to three in seconds, 1 check interior mirror, 2 check exterior mirror, 3 signal.'

Pupil signals too early when on approach when emerging left.

Instructor:

'You have signalled too early.'

'There is another road on the left before the end of the road and this will mislead other vehicles.'

'Only signal once you have passed the first road on the left.'

Pupil changes gear on approach before braking.

Instructor:

'You have changed gear before braking.'

'The car behind you will not know you are slowing down as your brake lights will not come on.'

'Remember brake first then gear.'

Pupil doesn't look into road ahead when emerging to turn left.

Instructor:

'You haven't checked the road ahead.'

'You need to check for emerging vehicles and pedestrians.'

'Remember the RALAR routine (right, ahead, left, ahead, right).'

Pupil steers too early when approaching give-way line to turn right.

Instructor:
'You have steered too early.'

'If you steer too early when emerging, you will end up on the wrong side of the road.'

'Only start to steer right once your front wheels have passed over the give-way line.'

Pupil emerging to go road ahead, doesn't use eye contact with emerging vehicle opposite.

Instructor:
'Wait! You haven't assessed the emerging vehicle opposite.'

'The vehicle may try to emerge at the same time as you.'

'Use 'eye contact' to assess when it is safe to emerge.'

Pupil tries to turn right from a major road into a minor road unsafely.

Instructor:
'Stop! You haven't got a safe gap in the oncoming traffic.'

'Remember, we must not cause a vehicle to change speed or direction when crossing their path.'

'Use the walking rule (if you can walk into the junction you can drive in) to measure the gap.'

Pupil stops too early when approaching point of turn, from a major road to minor road, turning right.

Instructor:
'You have stopped too early to turn right.'

'If you start to turn now you will cut the corner.'

'Line up your right exterior mirror with centre line of new road.'

Meeting other traffic, crossing the path of other vehicles, overtaking other vehicles, allowing adequate clearance and anticipation of other road users

Level: Partly Trained

Lesson Plan

Recap
Objective

Briefing
Full Talkthrough (first few situations)
Prompting (less instruction with Q&A)
Independence
Summary

Key Points

Briefing
MSM
Meet approaching traffic
Cross other traffic
Overtaking other traffic
Keep a safe distance
Shaving other vehicles
Anticipation of pedestrians
Anticipation of cyclists
Anticipation of drivers

This exercise may be introduced to the PDI by the examiner saying:

'I would like you to assume I am a partly trained pupil and we haven't met before. You are filling in for my regular instructor. I have had a few lessons in a car similar to yours so I am familiar with the controls and their layout.'

- 'I would like you to instruct me on how to meet and cross the path of other vehicles and also in the anticipation of the actions of other road users.' Or:
- 'I would like you to instruct me on how to overtake other vehicles, in allowing adequate clearance to other road users including following behind other vehicles and also in anticipating the actions of other road users.' Or:
- 'I would like you to instruct me on how to meet approaching traffic and overtaking other vehicles and also in anticipating the actions of other road users.' Or:
- 'I would like you to instruct me on how to meet approaching traffic, in allowing adequate clearance to other road users including following behind other vehicles and also in anticipating the actions of other road users.' Or:
- 'I would like you to instruct me on how to cross the path of approaching traffic, overtake other vehicles and also in anticipating the actions of other road users.' Or:
- 'I would like you to instruct me on how to cross the path of approaching traffic, in allowing adequate clearance to other road users including following behind other vehicles and also in anticipating the actions of other road users.'

'You can call me John.'

Instructor:

'Hello John, I understand you have had a few driving lessons in a car similar to this and that today you require a lesson on ..../.............. and Anticipation (the first two elements will depend on the topics chosen). I will fully explain the procedures and then we will practice under my control. Then we shall practice with less control from me. Do you have any questions before we start?

Recap

Instructor (select only the questions that are relevant to the topics chosen)

'Before I explain the topics of today's lesson, I would like to ask you a few questions to establish your previous knowledge and experience.

- What is the normal speed limit in town? What hazards (*parked vehicles, road works etc.*) would make you drive slower than this?
- Before passing a hazard such as a parked vehicle on your left, which mirrors would you check?
- When turning right from a major road into a minor road, how do you choose a safe gap in the oncoming traffic?
- What is your normal driving position or safety line?
- Have you passed or are you studying for your hazard perception test? Can you tell me the difference between a potential and a developing hazard?'

Note: Depending on the examiner's replies, you may wish to ask follow up or other relevant questions.

Objective

Instructor:

'Our objective today is to recognise and deal with meeting situations, crossing traffic, overtaking, allowing adequate clearance and developing your anticipation skills.'
(Only include the topics chosen by the examiner).

Briefing Plan:

Meeting: Introduction, MSM, Basic routine for passing parked vehicles, priorities, assessing when to proceed & when to hold back, hold back position, assessing gaps on left and right - when to stay out, when to move over.

Crossing: Types of crossing situations, MSM, choosing safe gaps, positioning, importance of looking into new road, not starting a manoeuvre you cannot complete.

Overtaking: Safe, legal & necessary, overtaking routine (MSM), overtaking on left, overtaking cyclists & horse riders etc.

Adequate Clearance: MSM, clearance to sides, clearance in front & behind, shaving, clearance to cyclists etc.

Anticipation: MSM, potential and developing hazards - how to distinguish, looking for clues, other drivers, pedestrians & cyclists.

Meeting

When travelling on single carriage way roads, such as main roads where there is a centre line, as long as the road is clear then you should not come into conflict with oncoming traffic. However, when there are hazards such as parked vehicles, road works, narrow road, narrow bridge or traffic calming such as chicanes, then we are drawn towards the on coming traffic and we need routines to deal with these situations safely.

Let us deal firstly with a single parked vehicle on your left. Here the oncoming vehicle has priority so we need to assess whether it is safe to pass or if we need to hold back. As soon as you see the parked vehicle check your interior and right mirrors and then move to the right far enough for you to see ahead but not so far over that you would block any on coming traffic. This position is often just left of the centre line. By moving early the position of your vehicle is a signal to other drivers and also you will be able to assess the gap between you and any oncoming vehicles.

Next ask yourself two questions: Firstly, can you pass the parked vehicle and get back to your safety line without causing the oncoming vehicle to change speed or direction and secondly, is there enough space between the parked vehicle and the other side of the road for two vehicles to pass each other.

If the answer to these two questions is negative, then you need to hold back and let the oncoming vehicle through the gap. Your holdback position is ideally two car lengths back from the parked vehicle but still far enough out to be able to see without blocking the oncoming vehicle.

If there are only one or two oncoming vehicles, try to time your approach so that the vehicles have passed you by the time you reach the holdback position. In this way you will not have to keep stopping.

However, if there are several oncoming vehicles then you will need to stop at the holdback position. Apply your handbrake and prepare the car to move. Once the oncoming vehicles have passed, check all round before moving off. Don't forget to check your left blind spot for any cyclists and your right blind spot for any motorcyclists which may have approached from behind while you were waiting.

Ideally you should pass the parked vehicle leaving a gap on your left of a car door's width. It is essential that you check your interior and left mirrors to make sure that the back of your vehicle is at least a car length past the parked vehicle before steering back to your safety line. If you steered back any earlier than this, then you would be dangerously close to the parked vehicle - this is called shaving.

Next let us look at how to deal with a parked vehicle on the right hand side of the road. Use MSM on approach. You should have the priority over the oncoming vehicle. However, you should never assume priority but assess whether you think the oncoming vehicle is going to give way to you, so always approach at a safe speed. Occasionally it is courteous to give way to another vehicle such as an oncoming bus, when this may help the overall traffic situation.

Now let us look at a situation where there are several parked vehicles on both sides of the road. Once again use MSM on approach. Here no one has the priority and so you need to assess whether it is safe to proceed or hold back.

You need to be constantly assessing gaps between the parked vehicles on both the left and the right in case you need to either move into a gap on the left or let an oncoming vehicle into a gap on the right. If there are no oncoming vehicles then take up a safe position between the parked vehicles depending on the width of the road and try to pass all the parked vehicles before moving back to your safety line. If we weave in and out of gaps unnecessarily then this may mislead the vehicle behind us to think we are parking and result in this vehicle trying to overtake us.

If you do need to move into a gap on the left then you will often find that you need to position closer to the kerb and less than two car lengths from the parked vehicle in front. When moving off again, assess whether a right indicator signal would be of use.

Do you have any questions regarding meeting traffic?'

Crossing

'This part of the lesson is about crossing the path of other road users safely. There are various times when you will have to do this. The main ones are: Turning right from a major road into a minor road. Emerging right from a T-junction, Turning right at a crossroads and emerging from a crossroads to take the road ahead.

Firstly you need to assess the speed and proximity of oncoming vehicles to ensure that when crossing their path you do not cause them to change speed or direction. To do this you need to assess safe gaps in different situations. For example, when turning from a major road into a minor one, if you can walk into the new road then you can usually drive in safely. When emerging right from a T-junction this takes longer as you need time to drive into the new road and come up to the speed of the traffic in that road. This usually takes about the same amount of time as walking across the road and back again. Another way to measure a safe gap is to ask yourself, if you stalled the car whilst trying to cross the path of another vehicle, would they have time to stop safely? If you are not sure then you should wait at your point of turn for a more convenient gap. Remember 'don't know, don't go.'

You should also remember that an element of rush is an element of risk so if you feel you need to speed up to cross traffic then this is not a safe gap and you should hold back.

It is just as important to assess the road you are turning into as you should not start a manoeuvre you cannot complete. Check for various hazards such as parked vehicles near the mouth of the junction and look carefully for vulnerable road users such as pedestrians who may need to cross the road. Once a pedestrian has stepped into the road they have priority over you.

Selecting the correct point of turn is also important to avoid cutting corners or crossing the centre line of the new road.

Do you have any questions about crossing traffic?'

Overtaking

'Before considering overtaking a moving vehicle or cyclist, you need to ask yourself three important questions: Is it safe? is it legal? and is it necessary? Let us look at each one of these in turn.

Firstly, Is it safe? You should not overtake if your view ahead is blocked such as when you approach a sharp bend, the brow of a hill or a dip in the road which might hide oncoming traffic; when you are approaching junctions or if the road narrows.

Secondly, Is it legal? You must not overtake if you would have to cross double white lines with a solid line nearest to you; the leading motor vehicle within the zigzag lines of a pedestrian crossing; if you would have to enter bus or tram lanes in operation or after you have passed a no overtaking sign.

Lastly, Is it necessary? For example, don't rush to get past someone if you are shortly to turn off.

You should never overtake on the left unless: the vehicle in front is turning right and you can safely pass on the left; you are in a one-way street with two or more lanes and you want to turn left; the traffic is moving in queues, and the vehicles on your right are moving slower than you.

Once you have decided that you are going to overtake, firstly check your interior and right mirrors to make sure no one is overtaking you. Next position your car slightly to the right so you can see the road ahead clearly and then adjust your speed. This will often entail changing down to a lower gear which will give you extra acceleration. Check the road ahead again to ensure it is clear, check your interior and exterior mirrors again and signal right. Carry out the manoeuvre leaving at least a door's width clearance and then check your interior and left mirrors so you can see you are safely past before signalling left. Then return to your safety line and cancel the signal if necessary.

Finally, when overtaking a cyclist, motorcyclist or horse rider, you should give at least the same clearance as you would for a car and more if you have the room. When overtaking a large vehicle, you should firstly drop back to get a better view ahead and then allow more time to complete the manoeuvre.

When assessing a safe gap, ensure you will not cause any oncoming vehicle to change speed or direction as a result of your action. This is often called 'head on speed' which means taking into account both your speed plus the speed of the oncoming vehicle.

Do you have any questions concerning overtaking?'

Allowing Adequate Clearance

'The ideal amount of clearance we need around our vehicle is as follows: In good dry conditions we need to leave a two second gap between us and the car in front for speeds above 30 mph and hopefully the vehicle behind us will do the same. This is called the 2 second rule. As the vehicle in front passes a lamp post or road sign etc. say to yourself 'only a fool breaks the two second rule' and as long as your vehicle hasn't passed the same point before you finish saying this, then you are a safe distance. Secondly, when passing parked cars we should leave about a doors width on the nearside and ideally should have the same clearance on the offside.

For speeds below 30 mph, we should leave about 1 metre clearance for each mile per hour of your speed. Sometimes in slow moving traffic this is not practical. In these situations, you should leave at least the thinking distance, which at 10 mph would be about 3 metres.

In bad conditions such as wet weather you need to leave at least double the distance between you and the vehicle in front and in icy or snowy conditions this can increase by 10 times the normal safety distance.

When stopped in a queue of traffic, leave about half a car length between you and the next vehicle. This is to give you manoeuvring room should the vehicle in front break down for example. We can measure this by being able to see the back wheels of the vehicle in front and a little section of the road - it is called tyres and tarmac. Often a following vehicle will drive too close behind you. The only action we can take is to open up the gap in front to about 3 seconds. This will allow you to brake more gently, which in turn will give the following vehicle more time to react to your brake lights. Even if there is not a vehicle ahead of you, ease off the gas slightly in case a pedestrian were to run out in front of you.

On roads where there are cars parked on both sides of the road, we have less clearance to the sides of our vehicle. In this situation remember the following rule: the narrower the gap, the lower the speed; the lower the speed the lower the gear. This could mean travelling at 20 mph or less in second gear, so that we are able to stop safely if someone was to open a car door for example.

When passing a cyclist on the road, you should give them at least the same clearance as you would a car and more if you have the room, as they tend to swerve round pot holes and drains in the road etc.

Do you have any questions concerning adequate clearance?'

Anticipation

'When looking for hazards on the road we divide them into two groups: Potential Hazards and Developing Hazards. A developing hazard is one that is going to cause you to change speed or direction.

In order to anticipate which potential hazards are likely to become developing ones, we need to look for clues.

For example, when driving down a road where there are parked vehicles you should scan through the windows of these to see if any of them have a person sitting in the driver's seat. This could be a clue that either the vehicle is about to move off or that the driver may open his/her door.

Now imagine you are driving down a road and you see a cyclist on the left riding on the pavement. As you approach, the cyclist starts to look over his/her right shoulder and move closer to the kerb. This is a clue that the cyclist may be about to come onto the road in front of you.

It is hard to see pedestrians when they cross the road between parked vehicles. Sometimes you can see underneath a vehicle such as a van and if you can see feet the other side this is a clue that a pedestrian may be about to walk out in front of you.

To help you anticipate hazards, you should look well ahead and keep your eyes moving as you scan the far, middle and near distance. Check your mirrors frequently so that you always know what is following you and most importantly look for clues as to what may be about to happen.

Do you have any questions concerning anticipation?

Instructor notes: The talkthrough routines for this pre-set test will depend on the elements chosen by the examiner. The examples given below are only examples to show some of the basic routines . The commands should be read from bottom to top.

As you will be dealing with three elements at the same time, you will need to use a mixture of talkthrough and question and answer technique (Q&A). Anticipation can only be dealt with using Q&A as we need to teach the pupil to look for the clues to predict when a potential hazard is likely to become a developing one.

Meeting (parked car on left)

- Move back to your safety line

- Check interior & left mirrors

- Keep a doors width from parked vehicle

- Move off

- Check mirrors and blind spots *(signal?)*

- Handbrake on, prepare the car to move

- Gently brake & stop at the hold back position

  (pupil does not have safe gap)

- Check the gap ahead

- Move slightly to the right

- Check interior & right mirrors

" Parked car ahead"

Meeting (parked vehicles both sides)

- Move back to your safety line

- Check interior & left mirrors

- *(after passing last parked vehicle)*

- Keep this position

- Keep a doors width from parked vehicles

- Move out to the right

- *(no oncoming vehicles)*

- Check the gap ahead

- Check interior & right mirrors

" Parked vehicles ahead"

Crossing
(major to minor)

- Check mirrors on gas

  (pupil enters new road)

- Move off when clear

  (road now clear)

- Prepare car to move

- Wait at your point of turn

  (pedestrian crossing new road)

- Check into road on right

  (no oncoming traffic)

- Look ahead for a safe gap

- Use your MSPSL on approach

" Take the next road on the right"

Overtaking
(main road)

- Resume normal driving position

- Signal left

- Check interior & left mirror
  (after passing vehicle)

- Move out, apply more gas

- Change from 4th to 3rd gear

- Signal right

- Check interior & right mirrors again

- Check the gap ahead

- Move slightly to right

- Check interior & right mirrors

" Slow vehicle ahead"

Clearance
(narrow road/ parked vehicles)

- Look for pedestrians crossing the road

- Scan the parked vehicles for doors opening etc

- Select 2nd gear

- Gently brake

- Position in the centre of the road

- Move out to the right

- Check interior & right mirrors

"Narrow gap ahead"

Clearance
(distance ahead)

- Stop behind so you can see tyres and tarmac

- Gently brake

- Check mirrors

  "Vehicle ahead stopping"

- Leave a gap of 1 metre for each mile an hour

- Gently brake

- Check mirrors

  "Vehicle ahead slowing down"

- As vehicle passes next lamp post, say "only a fool breaks the 2 second rule"

- Keep a 2 second gap

" Vehicle ahead"

Prompting

Instructor notes: The examples given below use two out of a possible six scenarios (refer to the examiner's introduction at the beginning of this chapter). Prompting is where we use selective questions to remind the pupil of the actions they need to carry out. As you are dealing with three elements on the move, the priorities for your prompting questions will depend on the situation ahead.

Meeting, Allowing Adequate Clearance and Anticipation

Instructor:
'Parked car on the left'
'Which mirrors are you going to check?'

Pupil:
'Interior and right door mirrors.'

Instructor:
'Good. Do you have a safe gap ahead?'

Pupil:
'Yes, I can see clearly.'

Instructor:
'Well done. How much clearance will you give this parked vehicle?'

Pupil:
'About a doors width.'

Instructor:
'Yes. What are you looking for in your mirrors before moving back over?'

Pupil:
'To see that I have gone about a car length past the parked vehicle.'

Instructor:
'Vehicles ahead, how much distance will you leave between you and the car in front?'

Pupil:
'About 2 seconds.'

Instructor:
'Scan down this line of parked vehicles. Can you see anyone in the driving seat?'

Pupil:
'Yes. A man just got into the red car ahead.'

Instructor:
'Well spotted. What do you think may happen next?'

Pupil:
'I think he is likely to move off so I've checked my mirrors and I am slowing down.'

Instructor:
'Good anticipation. Keep scanning the road ahead for other hazards.'

Crossing, Overtaking and Anticipation

Instructor:
'Take the next road on the right please.'
'Do you think you have a safe gap in the oncoming traffic?'

Pupil:
'No. I am going to stop at my point of turn.'

Instructor:
'Good. What are you looking for in the new road before crossing the traffic?'

Pupil:
'I need to check for any obstruction such as parked vehicles and pedestrians crossing the road.'

Instructor:
'We have a straight road ahead. If there was a slow moving vehicle, do you think it would be safe to overtake?'

Pupil:
'Yes. It looks clear ahead.'

Instructor:
'What about those junctions on the left and right? Do you think a vehicle could emerge?'

Pupil:
'Oh yes, I didn't think about those.'

Instructor:
'Pedestrian crossing ahead, what do the zig-zag lines tell you about overtaking?'

Pupil:
'I shouldn't overtake the leading motor vehicle within the zigzag line area.'

Instructor:
'Well done. Cyclist ahead riding on the pavement. Do you think he may come onto the road?'

Pupil:
'Yes, he keeps looking over his right shoulder, so I am going to slow down a little, just in case.'

Instructor:
'Excellent. A bus has stopped ahead of us and a number of people have got off. What can you anticipate may happen?'

Pupil:
'Some of the pedestrians may want to cross the road either behind or in front of the bus.'

Instructor:
'Yes, and don't forget that the bus may move off again without signalling.'

> Instructor notes: Prompting questions should elicit either a correct or incorrect response from the pupil. When an incorrect response is given then use fault assessment and appropriate instruction to control the situation.

The examiner will make faults at all stages of the examination. The faults committed will be mainly based around the key points listed at the beginning of this lesson. Each time a fault is committed, you should try to respond with an identification, analysis and rectification. The identification should always be given the moment a fault is committed. The analysis and rectification should be given as soon as it is safe to do so. As you are dealing with three subjects, the fault assessment needs to be kept short and to the point. Some examples are given below.

Meeting, Adequate Clearance And Anticipation

Parked vehicle on the left: Pupil stops too close to the kerb when giving way to an on coming vehicle.

Instructor:
'You have moved too far to the left.'

'The vehicle behind may think you are parking.'

'Remember the position of your car is a signal to other drivers.
You need to position further to your right, so you can see the road ahead, without blocking the oncoming vehicle.'

Pupil is too wide when passing a parked vehicle on the left.

Instructor:
'You are too wide (instructor checks mirrors). Move back to the left.'

'Vehicles behind may think you are about to park on the right.'

'Keep a door's width from the parked car on your left.'

Pupil steers back too early when passing a parked vehicle on the left.

Instructor:
'You have steered back to your safety line too early.'

'This is called shaving and you are in danger of hitting the parked vehicle with the back of your car.'

'Wait until you have passed the parked vehicle and then check your interior and left mirrors so you can see the rear of your car is a car length past the parked vehicle before steering.'

Pupil approaching left turn major to minor as cyclist, riding along pavement, is about to cross the new road without looking behind.

Instructor:
'Slow down. Do you think that cyclist may cross the road you are about to enter?'

'Always scan ahead for clues as to what may happen next.'

'When approaching a junction, always scan for pedestrians and cyclists and act on what you see.'

Crossing, Overtaking, Anticipation

Pupil doesn't look into new road when turning right major to minor.

Instructor:
'You haven't checked the new road is clear.'

'You must not start a manoeuvre you cannot complete.'

'Remember to check ahead and right before turning.'

Tries to overtake a slow moving vehicle when approaching a zebra crossing.

Instructor:
'Hold back! It is illegal to overtake here.'

'The vehicle will block your view of the nearside of the crossing.'

'Never overtake the leading moving or stationary motor vehicle within the zigzag line area of a pedestrian crossing.'

Emerging to go road ahead at crossroads, pupil tries to take an unsafe gap.

Instructor:
'Wait! You do not have a safe gap.'

'You will cause the oncoming vehicle to slow down'.

'Ask yourself: if I were to stall the car when emerging, would the oncoming vehicle be able to stop safely.'

Bus stops ahead and pupil does not anticipate that pedestrians may cross the road from behind the bus.

Instructor:
'Slow down, you are too fast.'

'Do you think that pedestrians may cross from behind the bus?'

'Remember: when a bus stops in front of you, ask yourself what may happen next and scan ahead for pedestrians.'

Part 2

Trained Pupil /
Full Licence Holder

Introduction to Part 2

For the second part of the test, the examiner will portray either a trained (T) pupil or a full licence holder (FLH). Examples of how the examiner will introduce himself as a pupil are given at the beginning of each lesson.

Trained (T) - The examiner should explain that as a pupil, he/she is at the trained stage and has either failed, or is about to take the driving test. Precise experience and source of tuition is at the examiner's discretion. The number of lessons would not normally be stated unless asked, in which case a rough figure may be quoted.

Full Licence Holder (FLH) - Examiners should explain that they are a full licence holder and use one of the suggested scene sets as an introduction:

- Requires development in preparation for a job interview that requires a driving assessment by their potential employer.
- Has been abroad for a couple of years and has now returned to driving in the UK.
- Has not driven regularly for some time and will now be required to commute by car between different urban office locations.
- Has difficulty with reverse parking as they were not taught it and realizes that, with fewer spaces available on-road, there is a need to be able to do so.

All phase 2 PST's could be used for FLH apart from 3&4, where the usual interpretation is, that it would be unreasonable for a FLH not to be able to turn left or right either turning in or out to a satisfactory standard. Frequency of use of FLH is at random on 1 in 3 tests.

Phase 2 lessons start from wherever the phase one lesson ended. The examiner will normally give you a few minutes between phase 1 and phase 2 to prepare yourself for the new pupil. If a Full Licence Holder scenario has been chosen, you will be advised, by the examiner, to take this opportunity to either cover or remove the L plates before the second phase begins. (If the L plates cannot be covered or it is impracticable to remove or stow them away, the examination will still be conducted).

An important point to stress here is that it is essential that you realize that the examiner is now playing a completely different pupil who has much more experience than the pupil you have just been teaching during phase 1, and so your instruction needs to adapt accordingly.

Crossroads

Level: Trained/ Full Licence holder

Key Points

MSM
Speed
Gears
Coasting
Observation
Emerging
Position Right
Position Left
Pedestrians
Cross Approaching Traffic
Right Corner Cut

Lesson Plan

Recap
Objective

Expose gaps in knowledge
Develop/improve skills
Assess general driving
Summary

This exercise may be introduced to the PDI by the examiner saying:

'I would like you to assume I am a pupil at the trained stage with a driving test coming up soon and we haven't met before. You are filling in for my regular instructor and I have had all my training in a car the same as yours. I would like you to assess how I deal with crossroads as I have been told I need to make improvements in this area. That is all aspects to include proceeding ahead, turning right and turning left and correct any faults that may occur. You can call me John.'

Instructor:
'Hello John, I understand you have a driving test coming up soon and you would like to improve your approach and negotiation of Crossroads, so this will be the main area we will practice today. However, I will also assess your general driving and give you any help and guidance you may need. Do you have any questions before we start?'

Recap

Instructor (question suggestions):

'Before we move off, I would like to ask you a few questions to check your current knowledge of Crossroads.

- Imagine you are approaching a crossroads on a minor road to follow the road ahead. Take me through the routine you would use on approach.
- If it was a closed junction and your view of the junction was obscured, how would this affect your speed of approach?
- If you need to pause or stop at the give way line, when would you select first gear?
- What does coasting mean and why should it be avoided?
- If you have stopped at the give way line at a crossroads, where should you be looking and what should you be looking for?
- If your view of the junction was blocked by parked vehicles, explain to me how you would move forward slowly so that you could see it was safe to emerge?
- When turning right form a major road, where do you position the car on approach?
- When emerging left at a crossroads, where should you position the car as you approach the give way line?
- What vulnerable road users do you need to be especially aware of when negotiating crossroads?
- When turning right from a major road to a minor one, how do you assess a safe gap in the oncoming traffic?
- Why is it dangerous to cut a corner when turning right major to minor and do you have a reference point to check your point of turn?'

Note: You should allow approximately 3–4 minutes for recap questions. If time allows, try to ask a question for each key point on the marking sheet, but this is not mandatory. Depending on the answers given, you may wish to ask other questions (e.g. offside and nearside passing, staggered junctions).

Objective

Instructor:

'Our objective today is to be able to recognise, approach and negotiate crossroads safely with due regard for all other road users.'

Driver
Development

Fault
Assessment

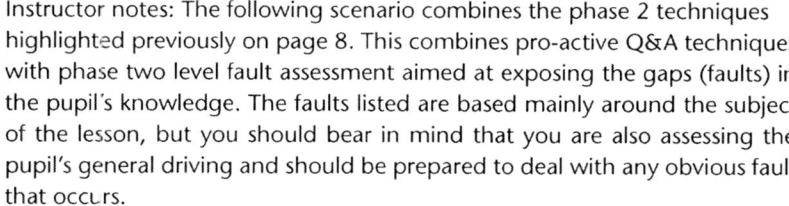

Instructor notes: The following scenario combines the phase 2 techniques highlighted previously on page 8. This combines pro-active Q&A techniques with phase two level fault assessment aimed at exposing the gaps (faults) in the pupil's knowledge. The faults listed are based mainly around the subject of the lesson, but you should bear in mind that you are also assessing the pupil's general driving and should be prepared to deal with any obvious fault that occurs.

For clarity, the examples listed below are split into three sections: major to minor, emerging from a minor road and turning right offside/nearside. In the examination these could occur in any combination.

Cockpit Drill
Move Off

Instructor:
'Before we move off, I would like you to carry out your cockpit drill please.'
(watch for any faults)
'When you are ready, drive on please.'

Pupil doesn't carry out correct observations.

Instructor:
'Stop! You haven't checked your right blind spot.'

'Why is it important to look over your right shoulder before moving off?'

Pupil:
'Oh yes, there could be a pedestrian crossing behind that I cannot see in my mirrors or a vehicle reversing out of a drive opposite.'

Instructor:
'Good. Have you ever heard of the six point check from left to right?'

Pupil:
'Sorry, I just forgot.'

Instructor:
'OK, so please carry out the correct observations and move off when you are ready.'

Crossroads Major To Minor
Following road ahead

Instructor:
'What does that sign on the left mean?'

Pupil:
'There is a crossroads ahead.'

Instructor:
'Good. What is the first thing you should do?'

Pupil:
'Look for emerging vehicles.'

Instructor:
'That's true, but you haven't checked your mirrors.'

'Why is it important to do this first?'

Pupil:
'Oh yes, it may affect my braking.'

Instructor:
'Good, so as soon as you see a crossroads ahead, check your mirrors for following traffic.'

Turning left

Instructor:
'*Take the next road on the left please.* Where should you position the vehicle on approach?'

Pupil:
'On my safety line.'

Instructor:
'Yes, good position. You are too fast, off the gas! At what speed should you approach the turning?'

Pupil:
'About 10–12 mph?'

Instructor:
'Yes, but how far from the junction should you be when you have achieved this speed?'

Pupil:
'Just before I start to steer.'

Instructor:
'No, this is too late. You need time to look and assess the crossroads and ensure you negotiate it at a safe speed. This should be 3–4 car lengths from the junction.'

Turning right

Instructor:
'*Take the next road on the right please.* In what gear are you going to approach the junction?'

Pupil:
'Second gear.'

Instructor:
'Good, but you are coasting, bring the clutch up.'

Why is it not safe to coast up to a junction?'

Pupil:
'You have less control over the vehicle when the engine is disconnected.'

Instructor:
'Yes, remember to bring your clutch all the way up once you have selected second gear.'

Emerging Minor To Major
Turning left

Instructor:
'At the end of the road turn left please. What sort of junction is this?'

Pupil:
'Oh, it is a crossroads because I can see the road ahead.'

Instructor:
'Good. Where are you going to position the vehicle as you come up to the give-way line?'

Pupil:
'I will follow the kerb round to the left.'

Instructor:
'Yes, but you have stopped too early.'

'How does this affect your zone of vision into the new road?'

Pupil:
'I cannot see clearly.'

Instructor:
'That's correct. Let's negotiate the junction and then I will deal with this fault. Is it safe to move off?'

Pupil:
'Yes. I have a safe gap.'

Instructor:
'Good! Carry on. Do you have a reference point to ensure the front of your car is just behind the give-way line?'

Pupil:
'No, not really.'

Instructor:
'OK, try to check, as you are about to stop, that the two give way lines just start to appear under your right exterior door mirror.'

Following road ahead minor to minor

Instructor:
'At the end of the road follow the road ahead please. Look into the new road you are approaching. What do you notice about it?'

Pupil:
'It is slightly staggered to the right.'

Instructor:
'Yes, so how is that going to affect your position on approach?'

Pupil:
'I need to position further to the right.'

Instructor:
'Good, but you are over the centre line. Check your mirrors and move slightly to the left. I will deal with this in a minute. Where should you be looking before emerging?'

Pupil:
'Right and left.'

Instructor:
'Yes, but you are not scanning the road ahead. Can you see there is a pedestrian about to cross the new road you are entering?'

Pupil negotiates junction and enters new road

Instructor:
'Pull in and park on the left please, I just want to deal with the two faults that occurred. Firstly, you were too far to the right on approach, how would this affect any oncoming traffic?'

Pupil:
'Oh yes, I would be in their way.'

Instructor:
'Good! So do you have a reference point to check your position?'

Pupil:
'I was looking at the centre line of the new road I was entering.'

Instructor:
'OK, this explains the problem. As you approach the give-way line, check that the centre line of the road you are in is just visible in the bottom right hand corner of your windscreen.'

Instructor:
'The second fault was that you did not carry out effective observations at the junction. Have you ever heard of the RALAR routine?'

Pupil:
'No, I haven't.'

Instructor:
'This stands for right ahead, left ahead, right and should be carried out several times until you are sure you have a safe gap and have checked for any pedestrian that may be crossing the road you are about to enter.'

Traffic Light Controlled Crossroads - Offside & Nearside

Instructor:
'*At the next crossroads, turn right please.* Do you think this will be either an offside or nearside pass?'

Pupil:
'I am not sure.'

Instructor:
'Can you see any arrows on the tarmac?'

Pupil:
'Oh yes, it is showing nearside to nearside.'

Instructor:
'There are already two vehicles waiting at the point of turn. Is it safe to move forward? '

Pupil:
'Yes, the lights are still green.'

Instructor:
'No. Wait behind the white line.

If you move forward, you will be blocking the area where pedestrians cross and the lights may change to red.'

Instructor notes: For all phase 2 subjects, you will finish by returning to the test centre. Once parked, you should give a summary of the lesson before finishing. This should be given using a positive approach but should include the main problems dealt with as well as the improvements made.

Examiner parks back at driving test centre.

Instructor:
'If you would like to switch off the engine please and relax, I would just like to summarise today's lesson.

At the beginning of today's lesson, you showed you had a good knowledge of crossroads and your general driving today was of a good standard.

However, there were a few faults that we needed to work on. Initially you were approaching junctions from a major road too fast, which wasn't giving you enough time to assess the junction and steer safely. You were also coasting on approach which reduced your control of the vehicle. We also needed to improve your positioning at various junctions.

I felt that you responded well to my instruction and made improvements to most of these areas. If you continue to do this during the weeks leading up to your test, then I think you should be able to reach the standard required.

Do you have any questions before we finish today's lesson?'

This exercise will be ended by the examiner saying:

'Thank you. That is the end of the examination. I will now return to my office to complete the assessment. You are welcome to wait for the result, however if that is not possible I am happy to post the result by first class post at the end of the day.'

Instructor notes: Once the examination is finished, you will normally be asked to wait somewhere convenient and be informed where you will be met to receive the result and debrief.

The examiner will usually give a fairly detailed debrief and try to answer any questions you may have at this time. The debrief usually lasts about 15 minutes and you should allow approximately 30 minutes from the time your examination finishes to complete this part of the examination.

Meeting other traffic, crossing the path of other vehicles, overtaking other vehicles, allowing adequate clearance and anticipation of other road users

Level: Trained/ Full Licence Holder

Lesson Plan

Recap
Objective

Expose gaps in knowledge
Develop/improve skills
Assess general driving
Summary

Key Points

MSM
Meet approaching traffic
Cross other traffic
Overtaking other traffic
Keep a safe distance
Shaving other vehicles
Anticipation of pedestrians
Anticipation of cyclists
Anticipation of drivers

This exercise may be introduced to the PDI by the examiner saying:

'I would like you to assume that I am a qualified driver who has passed a driving test some time ago but needs some further driver development. You have a similar car to mine so I am familiar with all the controls, but I have not driven regularly for some time and will now be required to commute by car between different urban locations. I would like you to instruct me on meeting oncoming traffic, allowing adequate clearance from other road users and anticipation of drivers, cyclists and pedestrians and correct any faults that may occur. You can call me John.'

Instructor:
'Hello John, I understand that you are a qualified driver but haven't been driving regularly for some time so would like to develop your meeting of oncoming traffic, allowing adequate clearance from other road users and your general anticipation skills. I will also assess your general driving and give you any help and guidance you may need. Do you have any questions before we start?'

Recap

Instructor (question suggestions):

'Before we move off, I would like to ask you a few questions to check your current knowledge.

Meeting

- Imagine you are driving down a main road and you see a parked vehicle ahead on your side of the road, what is the first thing you should do?
- How do you assess whether you have a safe gap to proceed or whether you need to hold back?
- If you do not have a safe gap, what would be your normal hold-back position?
- Before moving off again, where would you look and what would you be looking for?
- Why is it important not to steer back too early after passing the parked vehicle, and where should you check to ensure you have left a safe gap?
- If you are driving down a road where there are several parked vehicles with gaps in between, but there are no oncoming vehicles, do you need to move into those gaps or would you wait until you had passed the last parked vehicle?
- Imagine you are approaching a width restriction where the road sign indicates that you have the priority, why is it not always safe to assume that priority?'

Adequate Clearance

- 'At 30mph and above in good driving conditions, what gap should you leave between you and the vehicle in front and how would you assess this?
- In slow traffic moving at 10mph for example, how do you judge a safe gap?
- When stopped in a queue of traffic what distance should you leave from the vehicle in front?
- What distance would you normally leave on your left when passing a parked vehicle and how do you judge this?
- If you had a narrower gap because of parked vehicles on both sides of the road, how would this affect your speed and gear?
- How much clearance should you leave when passing a cyclist?'

Anticipation

- 'There are many hazards on the road which we need to be aware of, but we only need to react to the ones that we think are going to cause us to change speed and direction. As you pass a line of parked vehicles, what clues are you looking for to tell you if a car door is about to open or a vehicle is about to move off?
- You see a cyclist ahead of you riding along the left hand pavement. As you approach, he starts to look over his right shoulder, how should you react to this?
- As you approach a left hand bend you see a warning sign that informs you of a school ahead, how may this affect your speed and gear as you negotiate the bend?
- As you get nearer the school, you notice that children are crossing the road near to a large van parked on the other side of the road. If there was a child about to cross from behind the van, where could you look to anticipate that this was about to happen?
- You are approaching a bridge over the road you are driving on which shows a width restriction. If there was a large vehicle approaching from the opposite direction, where would you expect them to position on the road?'

Note: You should allow approximately 3–4 minutes for recap questions. If time allows, try to ask a question for each key point on the marking sheet, but this is not mandatory. Depending on the answers given, you may wish to ask other questions.

jective

Instructor:

'Our objective today is to be able to meet oncoming traffic safely, allow adequate clearance from other road users and to develop your anticipation of drivers, cyclists and pedestrians.'

Driver Development

Fault Assessment

Cockpit Drill & Move Off

Instructor notes: The following scenario combines the phase 2 techniques highlighted previously on page 8. This combines pro-active Q&A techniques with phase two level fault assessment aimed at exposing the gaps (faults) in the pupil's knowledge. The faults listed are based mainly around the chosen elements for this lesson, but you should bear in mind that you are also assessing the pupil's general driving and should be prepared to deal with any obvious fault that occurs.

Instructor:

'Before we move off, I would like you to carry out your cockpit drill please.'
(watch for any faults)

Pupil is parked on a fairly busy road with parked vehicles both sides.

Instructor:
'Before we move off, look at the road ahead and tell me where you will position your vehicle as we drive down this road?'

Pupil:
'If I position just left of the centre line then that will leave enough room for the oncoming traffic to pass as well.'

Instructor:
'Good. So what do you think would be an appropriate speed as you have reduced clearance?'

Pupil:
'On this road I think about 25mph would be safest.'

Instructor:
'Excellent. When you are ready please drive on.'

Instructor:
'As you pass these parked vehicles, what are you scanning for on the left and right?'

Pupil:
'I am looking for any pedestrians that may be about to cross the road or any vehicles about to move off.'

Pupil approaches a parked vehicle on the left with an oncoming vehicle some distance away.

Instructor:
'Good. Parked vehicle on the left, what mirrors do you need to check?'

Pupil:
'Interior and right?'

Instructor:
'Yes. Do you think you have time to pass this vehicle safely?'

Oncoming vehicle now only about 50 metres away and approaching rapidly.

Pupil:
'Yes, I think if I speed up I will just about make it.'

Instructor:
'No, hold back! You do not have a safe gap.'

'What must you not cause an oncoming vehicle to do by your actions?'

Pupil:
'Oh yes, I shouldn't cause it to change speed or direction.'

Instructor:
'Yes, so by speeding up, how do you think the oncoming driver would have reacted?'

Pupil:
'I think he would have had to slow down.'

Instructor:
'Good. So next time, remember that an element of rush is an element of risk.'

Pupil following a bus some distance ahead which stops at a bus stop.

Instructor:
'Bus has just stopped ahead, how do you assess when it is likely to move off again?'

Pupil:
'I try to look to see how many people are getting on and off as I approach.'

Instructor:
'Well done. There seems to be a lot of people getting on, how should you position your vehicle to assess if you have a safe gap?'

Pupil:
'I need to move out more so I can see ahead. Now I can see it is clear to pass.'

Instructor:
'Good, but you haven't indicated right.'

'Apart from any oncoming vehicles, who else would benefit from this signal?'

Pupil:
'Any pedestrians that may be about to cross the road?'

Instructor:
'Yes, but also the bus driver, if he is about to move off.'

Vehicle ahead stops at a pedestrian crossing.

Instructor:
'How much clearance do you need to leave when you stop behind the vehicle in front?'

Pupil:
'About half a car length?'

Instructor:
'Yes, but you have stopped closer than this.

'If the vehicle had stalled or broken down could you have got round it?'

Pupil:
'No, I would have had to reverse a bit first.'

Instructor:
'Do you have any reference for judging if you are far enough back?'

Pupil:
'No, not really.'

Instructor:
'Remember the phrase 'tyres and tarmac'. If you can see the back tyres of the vehicle in front and about half a metre of the road, then this is usually a sufficient gap.'

Pupil is driving too fast down a minor road with parked cars on both sides.

Instructor:
'Off the gas and gently brake. You are too fast!.'

Pupil:
'But I am only going 25 mph and the speed limit is 30 mph.'

Instructor:
'If a car door was to open just ahead of you, would you have time to stop safely?'

Pupil:
'Oh no, I hadn't thought of this.'

Instructor:
'Remember the phrase 'the narrower the gap the lower the speed, the lower the speed the lower the gear'. On this road, you should be at 20 mph in second gear.'

A cyclist is riding along the left hand pavement ahead and is approaching a zebra crossing.

Instructor:
'Look at that cyclist ahead. Do you think he may suddenly try to cross at the zebra crossing?'

Pupil:
'Yes, sometimes cyclists tend to move first and then look afterwards.'

Instructor:
'Good, so how are you going to approach this situation?'

Pupil:
'Check my mirrors, slow down a little and be prepared to stop.'

Pupil driving down a main road with various parked vehicles on the left and fairly large gaps in between starts weaving in and out unnecessarily.

Instructor:
'You are weaving in and out of these parked vehicles. What do you think the vehicle behind might think you are doing as you move in towards the kerb?'

Pupil:
'I don't know.'

Instructor:
'He may think you are about to park and try to overtake you. If there are no oncoming vehicles where should you position, so you don't mislead the vehicle behind?'

Pupil:
'I should give about a car doors width of clearance and hold this position until I have passed the last vehicle.'

Instructor:
'Good. Make sure you remember to do this next time.'

Pupil steers back too early after passing a parked vehicle.

Instructor:
'You have nearly hit the parked vehicle.'

'This was because you have steered back too early. How far past the parked vehicle should you go before steering back to the left?'

Pupil:
'I am not really sure.'

Instructor:
'You should ensure that the back of your car is at least a car length past before steering back to the left. The best way to check this is to look into your interior and left mirrors where you can see this distance.'

Instructor notes: For all phase 2 subjects, you will finish by returning to the test centre. Once parked you should give a summary of the lesson before finishing. This should be given using a positive approach but should include the main problems dealt with as well as the improvements made.

Examiner parks back at driving test centre.

Instructor:
'If you would like to switch off the engine please and relax, I would just like to summarise today's lesson.

At the beginning of today's lesson, you showed you had a good grasp of the main elements of this lesson and your general driving was of an acceptable standard.

However, there were a few faults that we needed to work on. Initially you tended to approach meeting situations too fast which didn't give you adequate time to assess if you had a safe gap. You also had some problems with weaving in and out of parked vehicles unnecessarily and then steering back to the left too early so that the back of your vehicle was too close to the parked vehicle you were passing.

However, I felt that you responded well to my instruction and made improvements to most of these areas. If you now include these as part of your normal driving, then you should notice the improvements to your overall driving standard.

Do you have any questions before we finish today's lesson?'

This exercise will be ended by the examiner saying:

'Thank you. That is the end of the examination. I will now return to my office to complete the assessment. You are welcome to wait for the result, however if that is not possible I am happy to post the result by first class at the end of the day.'

Instructor notes: Once the examination is finished you will normally be asked to wait somewhere convenient and be informed where you will be met to receive the result and debrief.

The examiner will usually give a fairly detailed debrief and try to answer any questions you may have at this time. The debrief usually lasts about 15 minutes and you should allow approximately 30 minutes from the time your examination finishes to complete this part of the examination.

Approaching Junctions
to turn either right or left

Level: Trained

Lesson Plan

Recap
Objective

Expose gaps in knowledge
Develop/improve skills
Assess general driving
Summary

Key Points

Mirrors
Signal
Brakes
Gears
Coasting
Too fast on approach
Too slow on approach
Position
Pedestrians
Cross Approaching Traffic
Right Corner Cut

This exercise may be introduced to the PDI by the examiner saying:

'I would like you to assume I am a pupil at the trained stage with a driving test coming up soon and we haven't met before. You are filling in for my regular instructor and I have had all my training in a car the same as yours. I would like you to assess how I deal with approaching junctions to turn either right or left as I have been told I need to make improvements in this area. I would also like you to assess my general driving and correct any obvious faults that I may have. You can call me Jill.'

Instructor:
'Hello Jill, I understand you have a driving test coming up soon and you would like to improve approaching junctions to turn either right or left from a major road to a minor road, so this will be the main area we will practice today. However, I will also assess your general driving and give you any help and guidance you may need. Do you have any questions before we start?'

Recap

Instructor (question suggestions):

'Before we move off, I would like to ask you a few questions to check your current knowledge of this subject.

- Imagine you are travelling at 30 mph on a major road and I ask you to take the next road on the left. What is the first thing you should do?
- If you could see the junction clearly ahead, how far from the junction should you start to indicate?
- If you were taking the second road on the right, when would you start to indicate?
- What does progressive braking mean and what speed and gear would normally be suitable to negotiate the junction?
- How far from the junction would you normally be when selecting this gear and why is it important to bring the clutch up once the gear has been selected?
- When turning left from a major road, where do you position the car on approach?
- Imagine you are approaching a junction to turn right but that there is no white centre line, how will you position your vehicle ?
- If a pedestrian steps into the road as you are about to negotiate a junction, who has the priority?
- When turning right from a major road to a minor one, how do you assess a safe gap in the oncoming traffic?
- Why is it dangerous to cut a corner when turning right major to minor and do you have a reference point to check your point of turn?'

Note: You should allow approximately 3–4 minutes for recap questions. If time allows, try to ask a question for each key point on the marking sheet, but this is not mandatory. Depending on the answers given, you may wish to ask other questions

Objective

Instructor:

'Our objective today is to be able to improve your approach and negotiation of both left and right turns from a major road to a minor road safely with due regard for all other road users.'

Driver
Development

Fault
Assessment

Cockpit Drill
Move Off

Instructor notes: The following scenario combines the phase 2 techniques highlighted previously on page 8. This combines pro-active Q&A techniques with phase two level fault assessment aimed at exposing the gaps (faults) in the pupil's knowledge. The faults listed are based mainly around the subject of the lesson, but you should bear in mind that you are also assessing the pupil's general driving and should be prepared to deal with any obvious fault that occurs.

'Before we move off, I would like you to carry out your cockpit drill please.'
(watch for any faults)

Instructor:
'Do you think you need to indicate when you move away from here?'

Pupil:
'Yes, I always indicate when I move away.'

Instructor:
'Who will benefit from your signal?'

Pupil:
'Nobody really.'

Instructor:
'When moving off always base your signal on whether it is of benefit to another road user, rather than by habit. This will ensure that you do not give a misleading or badly timed signal. When you are ready, please drive on.'

Instructor:
'Take the next road on the left, please.'

Pupil checks mirrors in the wrong order.

Instructor:
'You have checked your mirrors in the wrong order.'

'Why is it important to check your interior mirror first?'

Pupil:
'I didn't think it mattered as long as I checked both of them.'

Instructor:
'You should check your interior mirror first as this gives you a true image of what is behind you, then check your left mirror.'

Instructor:
'Take the next road on the right, please.'

Pupil signals too early.

Instructor:
'You have signalled too early.'

'If the driver behind you thinks you are parking, what might he try to do?'

Pupil:
'He may try to overtake me.'

Instructor:
'Yes, that's right. If you can see the junction clearly, how far away would you normally start to indicate?'

Pupil:
'I am not sure, I usually indicate just after I have checked my mirrors.'

Instructor:
'Six to eight car lengths before the junction is normally sufficient.'

Instructor:
'Take the next road on the left please.'

Pupil changes gear before braking on approach.

Instructor:
'You have changed gear before braking.'

'How does the vehicle behind you know that you are slowing down?'

Pupil:
'Oh yes I see. I will not have any brake lights on.'

Instructor:
'That is correct. So next time make sure you use progressive braking first before changing gear.'

Instructor:
'Take the next road on the right, please. There is no white centre line so where are you going to position the car?'

Pupil:
'I can see a join in the tarmac along the centre of the road. I will use this instead.'

Instructor:
'Good. When are you going to select second gear?'

Pupil:
'About three to four car lengths from the junction.'

Instructor:
'Yes, but bring your clutch up, you are coasting.'

'What happens to your control of the car if you approach with the clutch down?'

Pupil:
'I will have less control.'

Instructor:
'So what will you do when we approach the next junction?'

Pupil:
'I will try to bring the clutch up as soon as I have selected second gear.'

Instructor:
'Well done.'

Instructor:
'Take the next road on the left, please. What vulnerable road users are you looking for as you approach the junction?'

Pupil:
'I am looking for any pedestrians who may be about to cross the road.'

Instructor:
'That's correct.'

Pupil steers out to right before steering left into junction.

Instructor:
'You have steered to the right before steering left. Why did you do this?'

Pupil:
'So I could get a better view into the junction as I approached.'

Instructor:
'If the vehicle behind you had started to overtake you what would have happened?'

Pupil:
'Oh, I might have steered into it.'

Instructor:
'Yes, so keep your wheels straight until you reach your point of turn.'

Instructor:
'*Take the next road on the right please.* Do you think you have a safe gap in the oncoming traffic?'

Pupil:
'Yes, I think so.'

Instructor:
'Good, where is your point of turn?'

Pupil:
'When the front of my car is in line with the centre line of the new road.'

Instructor:
'Yes, but you have turned too early and cut the corner.'

'Why is it dangerous to do this?'

Pupil:
'I might drive into a vehicle approaching the junction to emerge.'

Instructor:
'That is correct. Can you see the front of this vehicle clearly?'

Pupil:
'No I just try to guess when it is at the point of turn.'

Instructor:
'Next time I want you to line up your right exterior door mirror with the centre line of the new road. This will ensure you will not cut the corner.'

Instructor:
'Take the next road on the left, please. The warning sign is indicating a turning on the left, but can you see it clearly?'

Pupil:
'No, it must be round the next bend.'

Instructor:
'Off the gas and gently brake. You are approaching too fast.'

'What if a vehicle was emerging from the junction as you came round this bend?'

Pupil:
'I didn't think of this.'

Instructor:
'What should you do if you see triangular warning sign but cannot see the junction?'

Pupil:
'I should slow down earlier.'

Instructor:
'Yes, you should have braked down to a speed of about 10–15 mph and changed into second gear in anticipation of the junction ahead.'

Instructor:
'Take the next road on the right, please.

This time, what reference point are you going to use to ensure you don't cut the corner?'

Pupil:
'I am going to line up my right exterior door mirror with the centre line of the new road I am entering.'

Instructor:
'Good. Do you have a safe gap in the oncoming traffic?'

Pupil:
'Yes, I think if I speed up a bit I should be able to make it.'

Instructor:
'No, wait at the point of turn.'

'What if a pedestrian had started to cross the road as you entered it?'

Pupil:
'I would have had to stop with the rear of my vehicle still in the main road.'

Instructor:
'Yes, remember that an element of rush is an element of risk. How do you assess a safe gap in the oncoming traffic?'

Pupil:
'I usually say that if I can walk into the road then I can drive into the road.'

Instructor:
'That's correct. Next time make sure you give yourself enough time to use this rule properly and look into the new road to make sure you can complete the manoeuvre safely.'

mmary

Instructor notes: For all phase 2 subjects, you will finish by returning to the test centre. Once parked, you should give a summary of the lesson before finishing. This should be given using a positive approach but should include the main problems dealt with as well as the improvements made.

Examiner parks back at driving test centre.

Instructor:
'If you would like to switch off the engine please and relax, I would just like to summarise today's lesson.

At the beginning of today's lesson, you showed you had a good knowledge of approaching junctions to turn either right or left and your general driving today was of an acceptable standard.

However there were a few faults that we needed to work on. Your positioning for both left and right turns needed improvement. For right turns this was mainly when there was no centre line to give you a reference point and for the left turn you were swinging out to the right just prior to turning left. Other areas that we worked on included your reference point for turning right and crossing other traffic safely.

I felt that you responded well to my instruction and made improvements to most of these areas. If you continue to do this during the weeks leading up to your test, then I think you should be able to reach the standard required.

Do you have any questions before we finish today's lesson?'

This exercise will be ended by the examiner saying:

'Thank you. That is the end of the examination. I will now return to my office to complete the assessment. You are welcome to wait for the result, however if that is not possible I am happy to post the result by first class at the end of the day.'

Instructor notes: Once the examination is finished you will normally be asked to wait somewhere convenient and be informed where you will be met to receive the result and debrief.

The examiner will usually give a fairly detailed debrief and try to answer any questions you may have at this time. The debrief usually lasts about 15 minutes and you should allow approximately 30 minutes from the time your examination finishes to complete this part of the examination.

T-Junctions Emerging

Level: Trained

Lesson Plan

Recap
Objective

Expose gaps in knowledge
Develop/improve skills
Assess general driving
Summary

Key Points

MSM
Speed
Gears
Coasting
Observation
Emerging
Position Right
Position Left
Pedestrians

This exercise may be introduced to the PDI by the examiner saying:

'I would like you to assume I am a pupil at the trained stage with a driving test coming up soon and we haven't met before. You are filling in for my regular instructor and I have had all my training in a car the same as yours. I would like you to assess how I deal with my approach and emerging at T-junctions both when turning left and turning right, as I have been told I need to make improvements in this area. I would also like you to assess my general driving and correct any obvious faults that I may have. You can call me Tom.'

Instructor:
'Hello Tom, I understand you have a driving test coming up soon and you would like to improve your approach and emerging at T-junctions when turning left or right, so this will be the main area we will practice today. However, I will also assess your general driving and give you any help and guidance you may need. Do you have any questions before we start?'

Recap

Instructor (question suggestions):

'Before we move off, I would like to ask you a few questions to check your current knowledge of this subject.

- Imagine you are approaching a T-junction to turn right. What is the first thing you should do?
- Bearing in mind you are turning at the end of the road, what would you be looking for ahead to ensure you didn't signal too early?
- How does the difference between an open junction and a closed junction affect your speed of approach?
- At a closed junction, which gear would you need to emerge in and when would you select this gear?
- If you selected this gear earlier than this and kept the clutch down, what is this called and why should it be avoided?
- What are the minimum observations you need to carry out before emerging at a T-junction?
- When turning right, how do you assess a safe gap in the traffic on the main road?
- When turning left, where should you position the car as you approach the give-way line?
- Where would you position the car when turning right?
- What vulnerable road users would you be looking for as you approached the give-way line?'

Note: You should allow approximately 3–4 minutes for recap questions. If time allows, try to ask a question for each key point on the marking sheet, but this is not mandatory. Depending on the answers given, you may wish to ask other questions.

Extra Note: This phase 2 subject follows reversing into a limited opening either to the left or right (phase 1). If the phase 1 finished a safe distance from the junction, the first T-junction to be negotiated for phase 2 would be just a few metres ahead and this should be taken into account when asking the recap questions

Objective

Instructor:

'Our objective today is to be able to improve your approach and emerging at T-junctions both left and right with due regard for all other road users.'

Driver
Development

Fault
Assessment

Cockpit Drill
Move Off

Instructor notes: The following scenario combines the phase 2 techniques highlighted previously on page 8. This combines pro-active Q&A techniques with phase two level fault assessment aimed at exposing the gaps (faults) in the pupil's knowledge. The faults listed are based mainly around the subject of the lesson, but you should bear in mind that you are also assessing the pupil's general driving and should be prepared to deal with any obvious fault that occurs.

Instructor:

'Before we move off, I would like you to carry out your cockpit drill please.'
(watch for any faults)

Instructor:
'In a moment I am going to ask you to move off, but first I want you to look at the T-junction *(see extra note on previous page)* in front of you and tell me whether it is open or closed?'

Pupil:
'It is closed because I cannot see clearly into the new road.'

Instructor:
'Good. So do you think you will need to stop at the give-way line?'

Pupil:
'Yes, because I will need time to assess the new road.'

Instructor:
'Well done. When you are ready, please drive on.'

Instructor:
'*At the end of the road turn left, please.* Where are you going to position as you approach the give-way line?'

Pupil:
'I will need to steer left and follow my safety line.'

Instructor:
'Yes, but you are too far to the right.'

'How will this affect your position when you turn into the new road?'

Pupil:
'I might end up going over the centre line and be in conflict with oncoming traffic.'

Instructor:
'That is correct. Let's emerge from this junction, then I will deal with this fully. As you emerge, you will need to steer more to the left.'

Pupil emerges from the junction safely.

Instructor:
'*Pull in and park on the left.* Do you have a reference point to check your position from the kerb as you approach the give-way line?'

Pupil:
'No, not really I just steer left a bit.'

Instructor:
'As you approach the give way line the left hand curved kerbstones should be in the bottom left hand corner of your front windscreen. Drive on please.'

Instructor:
'*At the end of the road turn right, please.*'

Pupil signals too early.

Instructor:
'Cancel your signal, you have signalled too early.'

'There is another junction on the right before the end of the road. If there was a vehicle waiting to emerge from there what might happen?'

Pupil:
'It may pull out in front of me.'

Instructor:
'Yes, that's right, so as well as checking your mirrors where else should you look before signalling?'

Pupil:
'I need to scan the road ahead to check for other junctions.'

Instructor:
'That is correct.'
Pupil stops at the give-way line where parked vehicles block their view.

Instructor:
'These parked vehicles are blocking your view. How are you going to deal with this situation?'

Pupil:
'I will try to creep forward slowly using clutch control.'

Instructor:
'Good, but how else can you improve your observations?'

Pupil:
'I am not sure.'

Instructor:
'You need to lean forward towards your steering wheel.'

Instructor:
'*At the end of the road turn left please.* Is this an open or closed junction?'

Pupil:
'It is a closed junction.'

Instructor:
'Good, so which gear will you need as you approach the give-way line?'

Pupil:
'I will need first gear.' Pupil selects first gear 3–4 car lengths too early.

Instructor:
'Yes, but you have selected this gear too early.'

'This is causing you to coast up to the give-way line. When should you change into first gear?'

Pupil:
'A bit later?'

Instructor:
'It should be about half a car length before the give-way line, just before you pause or stop.'

Pupil tries to emerge unsafely.

Instructor:
'Stop! You do not have a safe gap.'

'What must you not cause other vehicles to do when emerging?'

Pupil:
'I shouldn't cause them to change speed or direction.'

Instructor:
'That is correct, so how do you measure a safe gap when emerging?'

Pupil:
'I normally say to myself, if I can walk across the road I have a safe gap.'

Instructor:
'This is not enough when emerging, as you need to add more time to get up to the speed of the traffic you are joining, which is travelling at about 30 mph. Say to yourself, can I walk across the road and back again.'

Pupil now emerges safely from the junction.

Instructor:
'Well done. Do you find it easier now to assess a safe gap?'

Pupil:
'Yes. It is much better now I am giving myself more time.'

Instructor:
'*At the end of the road turn right, please.* Where are you going to position your vehicle on approach?'

Pupil:
'Just left of the centre line.'

Instructor:
'Good. But does the centre line stay straight?'

Pupil:
'Oh no, it bends slightly to the left as it reaches the give-way line.'

Instructor:
'How will this affect you as you approach the junction?'

Pupil:
'My other instructor told me to keep my wheels straight on approach to turn right.'

Instructor:
'Steer slightly left. You are now too far to the right. Lets emerge from this junction and then discuss this fault.'

Pupil emerges safely.

Instructor:
'Pull in and park on the left, please. As you approached the last T-junction you positioned correctly just left of the centre line but ended up too far to the right by the time you reached the give-way line. Sometimes T-junctions are positioned at an angle to the main road and when this happens the centre line can curve either to the left or the right. If you don't steer accordingly, what will happen?'

Pupil:
'I will end up by being in the wrong position.'

Instructor:
'That is correct. So next time make sure you assess whether the centre line stays straight or curves. *Drive on when you are ready, please.'*

Instructor:
'*At the end of the road turn left please.* Where are you looking before emerging?'

Pupil:
'Right, left and right.'

Instructor:
'Yes, but you are staring to the right and not looking left.'

'What is that pedestrian about to do on your left?'

Pupil:
'She is about to cross the new road.'

Instructor:
'Good, so what should you do?'

Pupil:
'Wait at the give way line until the road is clear.'

Instructor:
'Next time remember that, as well as checking to the right for a safe gap, you need to check left for pedestrians and any obstructions that could affect when it is safe to emerge before crossing the give-way line.'

Pupil emerges safely. Ahead is a traffic light controlled T-junction.

Instructor:
'*At the end of the road turn right, please.* The lights are green at the moment, do you think they will change to red before you get to them?'

Pupil:
'I think if I speed up a bit I will just make it.'

Instructor:
'Off the gas, you are too fast !'

'The lights have turned amber, what does an amber light mean to you?'

Pupil:
'I thought if I speeded up a bit I could get through before it turned red.'

Instructor:
'No, stop at the junction. An amber light means stop unless it is unsafe to do so.'

Instructor notes: For all phase 2 subjects, you will finish by returning to the test centre. Once parked you should give a summary of the lesson before finishing. This should be given using a positive approach but should include the main problems dealt with as well as the improvements made.

Examiner parks back at driving test centre.

Instructor:
'If you would like to switch off the engine please and relax, I would just like to summarise today's lesson.

At the beginning of today's lesson you showed you had a good knowledge of emerging at T-junctions and your general driving today was of an acceptable standard. However there were a few faults that we needed to work on. Your judgement when choosing a safe gap needed improvement, as did your observations on the approach to ensure a correctly timed signal and before emerging, especially to the left, to ensure you have checked for pedestrians that may be about to cross the road.

I felt that you responded well to my instruction and made improvements to most of these areas. If you continue to do this during the weeks leading up to your test, then I think you should be able to reach the standard required.

Do you have any questions before we finish today's lesson?'

This exercise will be ended by the examiner saying:

'Thank you. That is the end of the examination. I will now return to my office to complete the assessment. You are welcome to wait for the result, however if that is not possible, I am happy to post the result by first class at the end of the day.'

Instructor notes: Once the examination is finished you will normally be asked to wait somewhere convenient and be informed where you will be met to receive the result and debrief.

The examiner will usually give a fairly detailed debrief and try to answer any questions you may have at this time. The debrief usually lasts about 15 minutes and you should allow approximately 30 minutes from the time your examination finishes to complete this part of the examination.

Progress, Hesitancy
& Normal Road Positioning

Level: Trained/ Full Licence Holder

Lesson Plan

Recap
Objective

Expose gaps in knowledge
Develop/improve skills
Assess general driving
Summary

Key Points

Progress too fast
Progress too slow
Hesitancy
Normal position too wide from the left
Normal position too close to the left

Instructor note: The examiner will often play a pupil that is generally too fast or too slow. For this lesson the scenario is for a pupil that is generally too fast, for a pupil that is generally too slow, see lesson 10A.

This exercise may be introduced to the PDI by the examiner saying:

'I would like you to assume that I am a qualified driver who has passed a driving test some time ago but needs some further driver development. You have a similar car to mine so I am familiar with all the controls. I have been living in a rural area but will now be required to commute by car between different urban locations. I would like you to instruct me on my general progress, hesitancy and normal road positioning and correct any faults that may occur. You can call me John.'

Instructor:
'Hello John, I understand that you are a qualified driver who has been living in a rural area but who now is required to drive between different urban locations. Today I will be looking particularly at your general progress, avoiding undue hesitancy and normal road positioning but I will also assess your general driving and give you any help and guidance you may need. Do you have any questions before we start?'

Recap

Instructor (question suggestions):

'Before we move off, I would like to ask you a few questions to check your current knowledge of this subject.

- What is the normal speed limit in an urban location?
- In busy built up areas, what hazards may determine whether it is safe to drive to the speed limit?
- What do you look for when joining a main road from a minor road to tell you if the speed limit has changed?
- On a main road with a speed limit of 30 mph, why is it important that you reach this speed if it is safe to do so and what affect may it have on the vehicles behind you if you were to drive slower than this, say at 25 mph?
- What is your normal driving position (or safety line) from the kerb on a main road?
- Where would you position your vehicle on a narrower road?
- Imagine you are approaching a roundabout to go road ahead, second exit. There are two lanes on approach but no markings such as arrows in them. Which would be the safest lane to choose?
- Now imagine you are waiting at the roundabout for a safe gap, then one appears but you are too slow to take it, how might this affect the traffic behind you?
- Where would you position when negotiating a sharp right hand bend?
- Where would you position when negotiating a sharp left hand bend?
- You are driving down a one-way street which has two lanes. If you were to turn right at the end of the road, where would you position the car?'

Note: You should allow approximately 3–4 minutes for recap questions. If time allows, try to ask a question for each key point on the marking sheet, but this is not mandatory. Depending on the answers given, you may wish to ask other questions.

Objective

'Our objective today is to be able to improve your general progress and observation of speed limits, avoid undue hesitancy at junctions and roundabouts etc, and ensure your normal road positioning is safe and correct.'

Lesson 5a   Progress, Hesitancy & Normal Road Positioning

Driver
Development

Fault
Assessment

Cockpit Drill
& Move Off

Instructor notes: The following scenario combines the phase 2 techniques highlighted previously on page 8. This combines pro-active Q&A techniques with phase two level fault assessment aimed at exposing the gaps (faults) in the pupil's knowledge. The faults listed are based mainly around the subject of the lesson, but you should bear in mind that you are also assessing the pupil's general driving and should be prepared to deal with any obvious fault that occurs.

Instructor:

'Before we move off, I would like you to carry out your cockpit drill please.'
(watch for any faults)

Instructor:
'In a moment I am going to ask you to move off, but first I want you to look at the road ahead and tell me what you think the speed limit is.'

Pupil:
'It is a normal urban road so I think it must be 30 mph.'

Instructor:
'Good and do you think this is a safe speed for this road?'

Pupil:
'No, not really. There are lots of parked cars and some pedestrians about, so I will need to drive about 25 mph instead.'

Instructor:
'Well done. When you are ready, please drive on.'

Pupil approaches a roundabout.

Instructor:
'At the next roundabout, I want you to follow the road ahead, second exit. Which lane are you going to choose on approach?'

Pupil:
'I will choose the left hand lane.'

Instructor:
'Good, but you are stopping unnecessarily.'

'When should you start to look to the right for a safe gap?'

Pupil:
'Just before I get to the give-way line usually.'

Instructor:
'No, this is too late as it does not give you time to assess your gap so is making you hesitate at the junction. Start to look right at least 2–3 car lengths before you reach the give way line.'

Pupil Joins the new road after negotiating the roundabout..

Instructor:
'What is the speed limit of this road?'

Pupil:
'I think it must be 40 mph.'

Instructor:
'No, off the gas, it is still 30 mph, what makes you think it is 40 mph?'

Pupil:
'It looks like it because there are only houses on one side of the road and the road is wider than the previous road.'

Instructor:
'That is true, but did you look for a change of speed limit sign as we approached and exited the roundabout?'

Pupil:
'No, I just thought it looked faster.'

Instructor:
'OK. In future, whenever you approach a junction I want you to look for a change of speed limit sign. If you do not see one then you can assume that the speed limit remains the same as the previous road.'

Instructor:
'What is your normal road positioning on this road?'

Pupil:
'About a metre from the kerb usually.'

Instructor:
'Good. There is a sharp right hand bend ahead, where are you going to position your vehicle?'

Pupil:
'I will move further to the left to get a better view round the bend.'

Instructor:
'No, you are too near the kerb.

Stay on your safety line and slow down. I think you have confused "move to the left" with "keep to the left".

In this situation keep to your safety line and slow down more.'

Instructor:
'*At the end of the road turn left please.* Slow down. You are approaching the junction too fast.'

Pupil:
'It's OK, I am an experienced driver and can stop easily at the end of the road.'

Instructor:
'I am sure you can, but is this a stop junction or a give-way?'

Pupil:
'It is a give-way.'

Instructor:
'If you approached slower, so you could look earlier, do you think you may be able to emerge without stopping?'

Pupil:
'Yes I suppose I could. I had never noticed this about my driving.'

Instructor:
'Remember this phrase 'less speed, more progress'. It is quite common for experienced drivers to approach junctions too fast making needless stops.

If you approach slower and look earlier, you will be less hesitant about whether you have a safe gap.'

Pupil emerges from the junction safely into a narrower road.

Instructor:
'You are weaving about on the road, where should you position your vehicle?'

Pupil:
'I am trying to position about a metre from the kerb but keep finding I am then too close to the centre line.'

Instructor:
'This is because the road is narrower than before. Where should you position when the road is narrower?'

Pupil:
'A bit closer to the kerb?'

Instructor:
'Position in the centre of your lane. The best way to do this is to glance in both exterior mirrors and see that you have the same gap from the kerb to the nearside of your vehicle and from the centre line to your offside.'

Pupil starts to creep over 30 mph.

Instructor:
'Off the gas. You are too fast.'

'Why are you exceeding the speed limit?'

Pupil:
'I was just following the cars in front, so I didn't hold up the vehicles behind me.'

Instructor:
'Remember that about 70% of vehicles regularly exceed the speed limit. If you just follow them without checking your speedometer, you are liable to be breaking the law.'

Pupil:
'Well, as long as there are no speed cameras it doesn't really matter does it?'

Instructor:
'Yes it does. Pull in and park on the left, as I need to deal with this point. Apart from breaking the law, do you know why the speed limit is set at 30 mph in town?'

Pupil:
'Not really, I guess it is so that if you crash into the car in front you don't hurt yourself too much?'

Instructor:
'It is more to do with what would happen if an unseen pedestrian had run out in front of you. At 35 mph it would take you at least an extra 6.5 metres to stop.'

Instructor:
'When you are ready, please drive on. There is a roundabout ahead, what did we say about when to start looking for a gap?'

Pupil:
'Oh yes, I need to start looking at least 2–3 car lengths away.'

Instructor:
'Good. At the next roundabout turn left, first exit, please. Do you have a safe gap?'

Pupil:
'Oh yes, it is much easier to assess if I start looking earlier.'

Instructor:
'Well done. Try to remember to do this in your normal driving as it will help you to be less hesitant.'

Instructor:
'At the end of the road turn right, please. Where are you going to position your vehicle?'

Pupil:
'Just left of the centre line.'

Instructor:
'No, move into the right hand lane.'

'What sort of road is this?'

Pupil:
'Oh sorry, it is a one-way street.'

Instructor:
'Yes, if you happen to miss the signs as you enter the road what else could you look for to tell you the road has become one way?'

Pupil:
'I could look for arrows on the road, I suppose.'

Instructor:
'Yes, also notice that all the parked cars are facing the same way on both sides of the road and also look for further one-way street signs that are often there to remind you.'

Instructor:
'At the next roundabout take the road ahead second exit. Which lane will you choose on approach?'

Pupil:
'Left hand lane.'

Instructor:
'Good, now where are you looking at this time?'

Pupil:
'Right and ahead as well.'

Instructor:
'Well done. Do you have a safe gap?'

Pupil:
'Yes. The car on my right has stopped and the oncoming vehicle is going ahead.'

As pupil negotiates roundabout he crosses from the left lane to the right lane and back again.

Instructor:
'You have just straight lined that roundabout. If there had been a vehicle in the right hand lane what would have happened?'

Pupil:
'I would have cut across his path.'

Instructor:
'That is correct. The reason you did this was because you were staring to the right and not glancing left. Where should you be positioned?'

Pupil:
'I should have stayed in the left hand lane.'

Instructor:
'Good. So next time, as well as checking right for a gap, keep glancing back to the left to ensure you keep the correct position.'

Instructor notes: For all phase 2 subjects, you will finish by returning to the test centre. Once parked you should give a summary of the lesson before finishing. This should be given using a positive approach but should include the main problems dealt with as well as the improvements made.

Examiner parks back at driving test centre.

Instructor:
'If you would like to switch off the engine please and relax, I would just like to summarise today's lesson.

At the beginning of today's lesson, you showed that in your general driving you are quite confident.

However, there were some areas that we needed to improve on. For example, you were approaching junctions too fast with the result that you had less time to assess if you needed to stop or you had a safe gap. This resulted in you being hesitant at both T-junctions and roundabouts. Also your attention to both legal and safe speed limits needed some attention.

I felt that you responded well to my instruction and made improvements to most of these areas. If you include these techniques into your daily driving, I am sure you will feel improvements in both your overall progress and to your general road positioning which we also looked at today.

Do you have any questions before we finish today's lesson?'

This exercise will be ended by the examiner saying:

'Thank you. That is the end of the examination. I will now return to my office to complete the assessment. You are welcome to wait for the result, however if that is not possible, I am happy to post the result by first class at the end of the day.'

Instructor notes: Once the examination is finished, you will normally be asked to wait somewhere convenient and be informed where you will be met to receive the result and debrief.

The examiner will usually give a fairly detailed debrief and try to answer any questions you may have at this time. The debrief usually lasts about 15 minutes and you should allow approximately 30 minutes from the time your examination finishes to complete this part of the examination.

Reverse Parking

Level: Trained/ Full Licence Holder

Key Points

Briefing
Co-ordination of Controls
Observation
Accuracy

Lesson Plan

Recap
Objective
(Briefing)

Expose gaps in knowledge
Develop/improve skills
Assess general driving
Summary

Instructor notes: This is the only phase two topic that may require a full briefing, but since the addition of the Full Licence Holder Scenario into the part 3 examination, this is now less likely. However, three main scenarios are given in this chapter:

1. A trained pupil who has learned other manoeuvres but requires instruction in reverse parking.
2. A trained pupil who has a driving test in a few weeks time and needs improvement in this manoeuvre.
3. A full licence holder who needs improvement in this manoeuvre.

The exercise is designed for parking between vehicles not more than two car lengths apart but, for practical reasons, it is normally performed where there is only one vehicle present. Often the last in a line of parked vehicles.

The examiner will usually try to finish the phase 1 part of this pre-set test, so that you are parked suitably behind the parked vehicle chosen for this phase 2 lesson.

Senario 1

This exercise may be introduced to the PDI by the examiner saying:

'I would like you to assume that I am a trained pupil who has a driving test coming up soon. My usual instructor is on holiday and today he was due to teach me Reverse Parking. I would like you to instruct me on how to perform this manoeuvre and also assess my general driving towards the end of the lesson. You can call me Kate.'

Instructor:
'Hello Kate, I understand that you have a driving test soon and that today you require instruction on how to perform the Reverse Parking manoeuvre. I will start by explaining how to carry out this manoeuvre and then get you to perform this under my control. Then I will reduce my instruction so that you can carry out the manoeuvre independently. Towards the end of the lesson, I will also assess your general driving and give you any help and guidance you may need. Do you have any questions before we start?'

Recap

Instructor (question suggestions):

'Before I brief you on how to carry out this manoeuvre, I would like to ask you a few questions to check your current knowledge.

- What other manoeuvres have you carried out?
  Assume that the pupil answers (as he/she is a trained pupil) that he/she has carried out the turn in the road, left reverse and bay parking.
- When carrying out any manoeuvre, explain to me how you control the speed using clutch, brake and gas and what would you consider to be a safe speed whilst manoeuvring?
- When reversing, where should your main observation be?
- When carrying out the left reverse, where must you look before steering to the left at your point of turn?
- What other road users must you be aware of when carrying out any manoeuvre?
- As with any manoeuvre, we must select a place that is safe, convenient and legal. Give me some examples of where you would consider it unsafe to park.'

Note: You should allow approximately 3–4 minutes for recap questions. If time allows, try to ask a question for each key point on the marking sheet, but this is not mandatory. Depending on the answers given, you may wish to ask other questions.

Instructor:

'Our objective today is to be able to pull up alongside a parked vehicle on the left and then reverse back to park behind it, using clutch control and to finish within two car lengths reasonably close to the kerb. Whilst doing this, we will take into account the action of other road users including vehicles and pedestrians.'

> Instructor notes: It has to be said at this point that there are as many methods of teaching this manoeuvre as there are suitable vehicles for teaching in. The method given below is a generally accepted method which needs to be adapted to whatever vehicle that is used. Also, as with any manoeuvre, reference points will also vary according to the vehicle and the pupil.

'There are two main reasons why it is necessary to learn this manoeuvre. Firstly, because it is a safe method should you need to park your vehicle in between two other vehicles. Secondly, you may be asked to perform the manoeuvre in your driving test so that the examiner can test your control, accuracy and observation skills. For the purposes of the driving test, the examiner will usually choose a location where there is only one vehicle present or choose the last in a line of vehicles. Nevertheless, the manoeuvre should be completed within two car lengths of the chosen parked vehicle.

You should remember, from when you learnt your other manoeuvres, that you should never reverse towards on-coming vehicles and never reverse towards pedestrians. The main skills needed to perform this manoeuvre successfully are the same as for the other manoeuvres - co-ordination of the controls - using gas, clutch and brake to keep the car slow, full and accurate steering and effective all round observation at all times.

From our parked position you should move off in the normal manner and pull up alongside the parked vehicle in front of us, so that you are parallel to it with a space of not more than a doors width on your nearside. I suggest you stop when you can see the front end of the parked vehicle about half way down the front passenger door window. As soon as you stop select reverse gear, as this will light up the reversing lights, which will inform any vehicle behind you that you intend to reverse. Then secure the car by applying the handbrake. Bring your clutch up to the bite point and then check all round from right to left, as you would have done when reversing into a limited opening on the left for example. Because of your position in the road, you need to be aware that you are an obstruction to other traffic. Extra care is essential. Check the road ahead for oncoming traffic. Occasionally it helps to apply a left signal temporarily to emphasise that you are about to carry out a manoeuvre, but cancel this once the oncoming vehicle has realised what you are about to do. Check the road behind and the pavements, being always vigilant that pedestrians may cross the road at this point. Once you have established it is safe, start to reverse slowly under clutch control, remembering that your main observations should be over your left shoulder out through the rear window.

Reverse back slowly until you reach the first point of turn which is when the rear of your car is level with the back end of the parked vehicle. A good reference point for this is when you can see the rear corner of the parked vehicle in your nearside rear quarter-light window (or if no quarter-light, in the bottom left corner of the nearside rear window). At this point I would like you to pause the car because, similar to when you did the left reverse, we need to check forward and to our right blind spot for oncoming vehicles and pedestrians.

As soon as your vehicle starts to move again, steer briskly, one complete turn to the left, whilst remembering to look again through the rear window. When your vehicle has turned approximately 45° your nearside exterior mirror should be approximately in line with the rear offside corner of the parked vehicle. At this point, steer one turn back to the right until your wheels are straight again. At the same time, you should cover the brake and clutch as you will start to go down the camber of the road and you may need to gently brake whilst squeezing the clutch down just slightly. Once the front of your car has cleared the rear end of the parked vehicle, have another scan all round and then steer briskly to full right lock, making sure your car does not come into contact with the parked vehicle. As the front of your car nears the kerbside and you are almost parallel to it, steer briskly to the left once again until your wheels are straight.

You may need to adjust your vehicle's position slightly to ensure that you have sufficient room to move away. Timely correction is allowed in the driving test and you should also make sure that on completion of the manoeuvre you are parallel and close to the kerb, ideally the nearside wheels should be no more than about six inches (15cm) away, and that the front wheels are straight and not protruding out into the road, as this could be a hazard to other road users.
In summary, good co-ordination of the foot controls is essential in order to control the speed of the vehicle. This, in turn, will allow you time for effective all round observation and correct amounts of steering at the various points of turn.

Do you have any questions?'

Instructor notes: When compiling this briefing, it was decided to write it out in full as per the other manoeuvres given in phase 1. However, as you will be dealing with a trained pupil in the examination, it would be appropriate to use more Q&A for the parts where the pupil should already have some prior knowledge. For example, the pupil should have some knowledge of clutch control, where to look when reversing, how the camber of the road may affect the manoeuvre etc.

Reverse Parking: Position 1 to Position 2 -

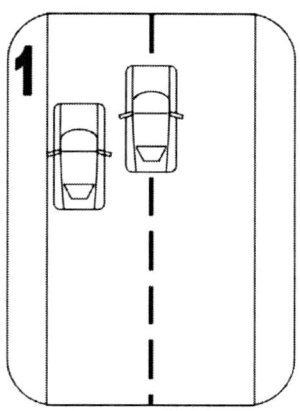 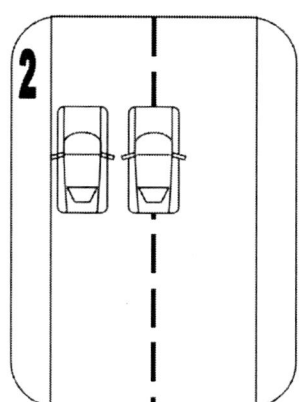

- Start to move and steer one turn left

- Pause, check forward and your right blind spot

- Reverse back to first point of turn

- Check all round right to left *(7 points)*

- Into reverse, handbrake on

- Move off and pull up alongside & parallel to the parked vehicle

" When you are ready, start the engine"

Position 3 to Position 4 -

 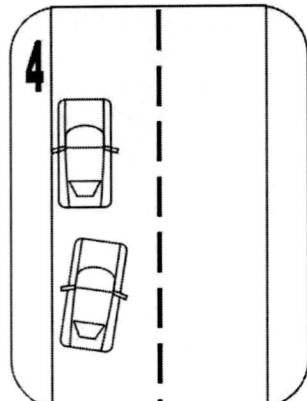

- When almost parallel to kerb, check left exterior mirror (distance from kerb) then steer left until wheels are straight

- When the front of your car clears the rear of the parked vehicle, steer full right lock

- Check your right blind spot again

- When your left exterior mirror lines up with the rear corner of the parked vehicle, steer 1 turn right

- Cover brake & Clutch *(camber)*

Position 5 -

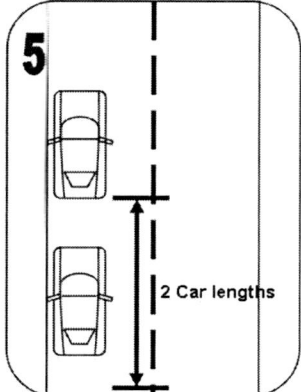

2 Car lengths

- Handbrake on, into neutral

- Stay within two car lengths of the vehicle in front

- Adjust your position *(as necessary)* using clutch control

- Check your position from the kerb in your left exterior mirror

Instructor notes: The talkthrough routines used here are designed to take into account the pupil's previous experience of doing other manoeuvres.

river
lopment

ault
ssment

Instructor notes: This part of the lesson is covered fully in scenario's 2 & 3 on the following pages.

Senario 2

This exercise may be introduced to the PDI by the examiner saying:

'I would like you to assume that I am a trained pupil who has a driving test coming up soon. My usual instructor is on holiday but has said that before my driving test I need to make some improvements to the way I perform the reverse parking exercise. I would like you to assess this manoeuvre today also look at my general driving towards the end of the lesson. You can call me Jim.'

Instructor:
'Hello Jim, I understand that you are a trained pupil with a driving test coming up soon and that today you need to make some improvements to how you perform the Reverse Parking manoeuvre. I will start by asking you some questions about how you carry out this manoeuvre and then get you to show me so that I can assess what improvements we need to make. Towards the end of the lesson, I will also assess your general driving and give you any help and guidance you may need. Do you have any questions before we start?'

Recap

> Instructor notes: This scenario assumes that the pupil has been taught this manoeuvre in a similar way to that explained in scenario 1, so should be able to give fairly knowledgeable answers to the questions below.

Instructor (question suggestions):
'Before I see how you carry out this manoeuvre, I would like to ask you a few questions to check your current knowledge.

- When pulling up alongside the parked vehicle, how much clearance do you give?
- Before starting to reverse, where should you look and what are you looking for?
- Where is your first point of turn and where should you look before steering?
- How much should you steer at this point?
- Explain to me what you do next and where your points of turn are?

- What effect may the camber of the road have on your speed and how would you deal with this?
- Where should your main observations be whilst reversing?
- Once you have straightened the car up, how far should you be from the parked vehicle when you finish?'

Note: You should allow approximately 3–4 minutes for recap questions. If time allows, try to ask a question for each key point on the marking sheet, but this is not mandatory. Depending on the answers given, you may wish to ask other questions.

Objective

Instructor:

'Our objective today is to improve your control, accuracy and observation whilst carrying out the reverse parking manoeuvre. Towards the end of the lesson, I will also take the opportunity to assess your general driving.'

Driver Development

Fault Assessment

Instructor notes: The following scenario combines the phase 2 techniques highlighted previously on page 8. This combines pro-active Q&A techniques with phase two level fault assessment aimed at exposing the gaps (faults) in the pupil's knowledge. The faults listed are based mainly around the subject of the lesson, but you should bear in mind that, towards the end of the lesson, you are also assessing the pupil's general driving and should be prepared to deal with any obvious fault that occurs.

Cockpit Drill Move Off

Instructor:
'OK Jim, you have shown from your answers to my questions that you have a good basic knowledge of this manoeuvre, so what I would like you to do now is to perform one for me so I can assess what improvements need to be made.

Before we move off, I would like you to carry out your cockpit drill please.'
watch for any faults

Instructor:
'When you are ready, start the engine and then pull up alongside the parked vehicle in front and reverse back to park behind it.'

Pupil starts the engine and is about to move off.

Instructor:
'Wait! Your clutch is too high. If you release the handbrake with the clutch in this position, what will happen?'

Pupil:
'The car may stall or move too fast.'

Instructor:
'That is correct. You are not setting any gas before bringing the clutch up. Did your other instructor not tell you to do this?'

Pupil:
'He did mention it but I found the vehicle moved off OK if I didn't bother.'

Instructor:
'It is true that the vehicle, especially if it is a diesel, may move off without gas but you will have more control when you set the gas and can feel the bite point correctly. Do this for me now and then carry on with the manoeuvre.'

Pupil pulls up correctly alongside the vehicle and then starts to reverse.

Instructor:
'Where is your first point of turn?'

Pupil:
'When the back of my car is level with the end of the parked vehicle.'

Instructor:
'Yes, but you have gone back too far. Carry on with the manoeuvre and I will deal with this later.'

Pupil steers too slowly when steering to full right lock.

Instructor:
'You are steering too slowly. You are about to hit the kerb. Move forward again and adjust your position.'

Pupil manages to adjust his position and finish the manoeuvre.

Instructor:
'OK, I just need to deal with a couple of faults that I pointed out. Firstly, your first point of turn is a little too late.'

'Do you have a reference point to check this?'

Pupil:
'No, not really. I just try to judge when the back of my car is level with the rear end of the parked vehicle.'

Instructor:
'Next time I want you to turn when you can see the rear corner of the parked vehicle in the nearside rear quarter-light window *(reference point will depend on vehicle used).*'

Pupil:
'OK, that sounds like that may help me.'

Instructor:
'Secondly, when you are steering to full right lock you are doing this too slowly. What speed have you been told to steer?'

Pupil:
'I have been told to steer briskly, but there is so much to think about with the observations and everything that I tend to forget.'

Instructor:
'OK, well I will remind you next time. It is very important to steer briskly as this will stop you hitting the kerb with your rear nearside wheel. Let us try this again incorporating these improvements.'

Instructor:
'When you are ready, move off again and pull up along side the parked vehicle in front and reverse back to park behind it.'

Pupil pulls up correctly alongside the vehicle and then starts to reverse.

Instructor:
'What reference point are you going to use for your first point of turn?'

Pupil:
'The rear corner of the parked vehicle in the nearside rear quarter-light window.'

Instructor:
'That is correct, but you didn't check forward or your right blind spot before steering. Carry on, I will deal with this in a minute. Now remember to steer briskly to full right lock.'

Pupil:
'Oh, that's better. I am not going to hit the kerb this time.'

Instructor:
'Yes, but now you are straightening up the wheel too late so that the back of your car is starting to come back out into the road.'

Pupil manages to adjust his position and finish the manoeuvre.

Instructor:
'Your points of turn were much better that time, well done. However, there are still a couple of faults we need to deal with. Firstly you did not check forward or your right blind spot before steering at the first point of turn. Why is it important to do this?'

Pupil:
'Because the front of my car will swing out and be an obstruction to other road users.'

Instructor:
'Good, so next time I want you to pause when you get to the point of turn as this will remind you to carry out the correct observations.'

Pupil:
'Yes, I think that pausing will help me to remember this.'

Instructor:
'Secondly, you straightened the wheel too late. What position did your vehicle finish in?'

Pupil:
'It was at a bit of an angle with the back of the car sticking out into the road.'

Instructor:
'Yes and this could be a hazard to other road users. Next time, I want you to check your left exterior mirror and start to straighten just before your vehicle is parallel with the kerb. Let us try this manoeuvre once more.'

Instructor:
'When you are ready, move off again and pull up along side the parked vehicle in front and reverse back to park behind it.'

Pupil pulls up correctly alongside the vehicle and then starts to reverse.

Instructor:
'Now where are you going to look before you start to steer left?'

Pupil:
'I am going to pause and check forward and my right blind spot.'

Instructor:
'Good. Carry on, your accuracy and control are much better this time.'

Pupil is staring in left exterior mirror and not looking behind.

Instructor:
'You are staring into your left exterior mirror.'

'Where do you get the best view of what is behind you?'

Pupil:
'Oh yes, out of the rear window.'

Instructor:
'That is correct, so make sure your main observation is out of the rear window with frequent glances into your left exterior mirror. I felt that overall the last attempt worked very well. How did you feel about it?'

Pupil:
'I feel much more confident about this manoeuvre now and the reference points have certainly helped to ensure I do not hit the kerb.'

Summary

Examiner parks back at driving test centre.

Instructor:
'If you would like to switch off the engine please and relax, I would just like to summarise today's lesson.

At the beginning of today's lesson, you showed that you had some experience of this manoeuvre which you tried to carry out to a structured method.

However, there were some areas that we needed to improve on. To start with, your clutch was too high when moving off but, when this was identified, you managed to rectify this straight away. Secondly, some of your points of turn needed improvement, which we did by adding in some new reference points. Lastly, and just as importantly, we improved your overall observation during the manoeuvre.

I felt that you responded well to my instruction and made improvements to most of these areas. Your last attempt at the manoeuvre was very good and if you continue to practice the manoeuvre with these improvements, then you should not have any problems with this for your driving test.

Do you have any questions before we finish today's lesson?'

This exercise will be ended by the examiner saying:

'Thank you. That is the end of the examination. I will now return to my office to complete the assessment. You are welcome to wait for the result. However, if that is not possible, I am happy to post the result by first class post at the end of the day.'

Instructor notes: Once the examination is finished, you will normally be asked to wait somewhere convenient and be informed where you will be met to receive the result and debrief.

The examiner will usually give a fairly detailed debrief and try to answer any questions you may have at this time. The debrief usually lasts about 15 minutes and you should allow approximately 30 minutes from the time your examination finishes to complete this part of the examination.

Senario 3

This exercise may be introduced to the PDI by the examiner saying:

'I would like you to assume that I am a qualified driver who has passed a driving test some time ago but was not taught the Reverse Parking manoeuvre. You have a similar car to mine so I am familiar with all the controls. I have recently moved to this area and have to park on a busy street in between other parked vehicles. I realize that, with fewer spaces on the road, I will need to use this manoeuvre frequently and feel that I could improve with some instruction from a professional such as yourself. I would like you to assess what I am doing and suggest any improvements you think are necessary. You can call me David.'

Instructor:
'Hello David, I understand that you are a full licence holder and need to make some improvements to how you perform the Reverse Parking manoeuvre. I will start by asking you some questions about how you carry out this manoeuvre at present and then get you to show me so that I can assess what improvements we need to make. Towards the end of the lesson, I will also assess your general driving and give you any help and guidance you may need. Do you have any questions before we start?'

Recap

Question suggestions:

Instructor:
'Before I see how you carry out this manoeuvre, I would like to ask you a few questions to get an idea of how you currently do it.'

Instructor:
'How slow do you keep the car whilst performing this manoeuvre?'

Pupil:
'Quite slow I suppose, but not too slow as it just holds up other vehicles that may be waiting to get passed me.'

Instructor:
'I will look at how you control the speed of the car, to see if I need to suggest any improvements that will help your overall control. When pulling up alongside the parked vehicle, how much clearance do you give?'

Pupil:
'I am not sure really, I suppose about a door's width?'

Instructor:
'This seems OK. Where are your main observations whilst reversing?'

Pupil:
'To the rear, but I do try to keep an eye around me as well.'

Instructor:
'Good. When do you start to steer left usually?'

Pupil:
'I just sort of know really but it is about when the back of my car is level with the end of the parked vehicle.'

Instructor:
'This seems OK. Explain to me how you finish the rest of the manoeuvre.'

Pupil:
'Once the car gets to about 45° I start to steer back the other way and then use my left exterior mirror to check how far I am from the kerb. Sometimes, I need to move forwards to adjust my position.'

Instructor:
'OK. Do you use any reference points for when to steer back to the left?'

Pupil:
'Not really, I just try to use my judgement of how close to the kerb I am.'

Instructor:
'Well, I think the best thing is for you to show me how you carry out this manoeuvre so that I can assess what improvements we need to make.'

Note: You should allow approximately 3–4 minutes for recap questions. If time allows, try to ask a question for each key point on the marking sheet, but this is not mandatory. Depending on the answers given, you may wish to ask other questions.

Objective

Instructor:

'Our objective today is to improve your control, accuracy and observation whilst carrying out the reverse parking manoeuvre. Towards the end of the lesson, I will also take the opportunity to assess your general driving.'

Driver
Development

Fault
Assessment

Instructor notes: The following scenario combines the phase 2 techniques highlighted previously on page 8. This combines pro-active Q&A techniques with phase two level fault assessment aimed at exposing the gaps (faults) in the pupil's knowledge. The faults listed are based mainly around the subject of the lesson, but you should bear in mind that, towards the end of the lesson, you are also assessing the pupil's general driving and should be prepared to deal with any obvious fault that occurs.

**Cockpit Drill
& Move Off**

Instructor:

'OK David, you have shown from your answers to my questions that you have a good basic knowledge of this manoeuvre, so what I would like you to do now is to perform one for me so I can assess what improvements need to be made.
Before we move off, I would like you to prepare your car in the normal manner ready for safe driving.' *(watch for any faults)*

Instructor:
'When you are ready, start the engine and then pull up alongside the parked vehicle in front and reverse back to park behind it.'

Pupil starts the engine and moves off.

Instructor:
'You are using brake and clutch together to control the speed of the car. I will deal with this once you have completed the manoeuvre.'

Pupil reverses too fast.

Instructor:
'You are too fast, slow down!'

Pupil:
'Well, there is no point in taking too long to complete the manoeuvre as it just holds up other traffic.' *Pupil completes the manoeuvre but is wide of the kerb.*

Instructor:
'OK, please secure the car and turn the engine off for a moment. I pointed out two faults as you were carrying out the manoeuvre and they are both linked. Firstly you are trying to use brake whilst the clutch is engaged to try to control the speed of your vehicle. Can you feel that each time you take your foot off the brake the car moves quickly and jerkily?'

Pupil:
'Yes, I must admit that I did seem to move off a bit fast.'

Instructor:
'This is because, with your foot on the brake, you cannot feel the bite point so you are lifting the clutch too high. Can I ask you, have you been driving an automatic recently?'

Pupil:
'Yes, I used to have a company car and this was automatic.'

Instructor:
'OK, this could explain why you are doing this, because with an automatic you would use the brake much more when carrying out manoeuvres. Next time use gas and clutch together to move slowly and then brake and squeeze the clutch to slow the car.'

Pupil:
'Yes, I can see I have developed some bad habits driving an automatic car.'

Instructor:
'OK, the second problem was that you were too fast when reversing. Do you think you would have had time to react quickly enough if a pedestrian had walked out from behind the parked vehicle?'

Pupil:
'I see what you mean. I was so anxious to get out of the way of other traffic that I forgot to look for pedestrians.'

Instructor:
'Let us try the manoeuvre again and this time try to combine good clutch control, which should keep your car at a snail's pace, with all round observation of other road users. This may also help your final position from the kerb.'

Instructor:
'When you are ready, move off again and pull up alongside the parked vehicle In front and reverse back to park behind it.'

Pupil pulls up correctly alongside the vehicle and then starts to reverse.

Instructor:
'Your speed is much better this time, but you are using your interior mirror instead of looking out the rear window.'

Pupil steers too early when turning to full right lock and ends up too far from kerb again.

Instructor:
'OK, your speed and clutch control was much better that time but you were using your mirrors too much when reversing and once again you have finished too wide from the kerb.'

'Lets deal with the mirrors first. Look into your interior mirror and then look over your left shoulder out through the rear window. Which one gives you the best view of what is happening immediately behind you?'

Pupil:
'Definitely the rear window, I get a much wider view.'

Instructor:
'Good, so next time make sure your main observations are over your left shoulder out through the rear window.'

'Now once again you have finished too wide from the kerb. Do you use a reference point to know when to steer to full right lock?'

Pupil:
'No, I just guess it really and I am trying not to hit the kerb.'

Instructor:
'Next time I want you to look for when your left exterior mirror is in line with the rear corner of the parked vehicle and then steer to full right lock *(reference point may vary depending on the vehicle used).*'

Pupil:
'Right, I will try to look for this.'

Instructor:
'When you are ready move off again and pull up alongside the parked vehicle in front and reverse back to park behind it.'

Pupil pulls up correctly alongside the vehicle and then starts to reverse.

Instructor:
'Now where are your main observations going to be?'

Pupil:
'Out through the rear window.'

Instructor:
'Good. Where do you need to look before steering left.'

Pupil:
'Ahead and over to my right blind spot.'

Instructor:
'That is correct, now remember the reference point for steering to full right lock.'

Pupil:
'Oh yes, I need to line up the left exterior mirror with the rear corner of the parked vehicle.'

Instructor:
'Well done. Now do you find this helps you to get closer to the kerb?'

Pupil:
'Yes, using a reference point gives me a bit more confidence that I am going to end up in the right place.'

Instructor:
'This manoeuvre now seems to be working well for you. Do you have any further questions or concerns?'

Pupil:
'When I move off again after parking like this, do I need to indicate?'

Instructor:
'That is a good question. Normally, when moving off we would only indicate if it was of use to another road user. However, after reverse parking, we need to move off at an angle. Also as your view is limited, I recommend that you use a precautionary right indicator signal after you have determined it is safe to move off.'

Instructor notes: After about 20 minutes of the lesson has passed, the examiner will tell you to drive off (as you will need to get back to the driving test centre by the end of the examination). Remember that the examiner will remain in role during this drive and so you should treat this as an assessment of the pupil's general driving. Once again use a combination of pro-active Q&A and phase 2 fault assessment techniques to rectify any obvious faults that may occur.

Summary

Instructor notes: For all phase 2 subjects, you will finish by returning to the test centre. Once parked, you should give a summary of the lesson before finishing. This should be given using a positive approach but should include the main problems dealt with as well as the improvements made.

Examiner parks back at driving test centre.

Instructor:
'If you would like to switch off the engine please and relax. I would just like to summarise today's lesson.

At the beginning of today's lesson, we discussed how you currently performed this manoeuvre and then you demonstrated this to me.

Your basic method was OK but needed some improvements to gain more control and accuracy. The main areas we looked at were firstly the way you were using the foot controls to keep the car slow, namely brake and clutch engaged together, and secondly improving your second point of turn to full right lock by introducing a new reference point.

I think you will agree that these small changes to the way you carry out the manoeuvre certainly improved your accuracy and control. If you continue to practice the manoeuvre with these improvements, then you should be confident this should work in most street parking situations.

Do you have any questions before we finish today's lesson?'

Instructor notes: Once the examination is finished, you will normally be asked to wait somewhere convenient and be informed where you will be met to receive the result and debrief.

The examiner will usually give a fairly detailed debrief and try to answer any questions you may have at this time. The debrief usually lasts about 15 minutes and you should allow approximately 30 minutes from the time your examination finishes to complete this part of the examination.

This exercise will be ended by the examiner saying:

'Thank you. That is the end of the examination. I will now return to my office to complete the assessment. You are welcome to wait for the result, however if that is not possible I am happy to post the result by first class post at the end of the day.'

Pedestrian Crossings and Use of Signals

Level: Trained/ Full Licence Holder

Lesson Plan

Recap
Objective

Expose gaps in knowledge
Develop/improve skills
Assess general driving
Summary

Key Points

MSM
Speed on approach
Stop when necessary
Overtaking on approach
Inviting pedestrians to cross
Signals by indicator
Signals by arm
Signals - timing
Unnecessary signals

This exercise may be introduced to the PDI by the examiner saying:

'I would like you to assume I am a pupil at the trained stage with a driving test coming up soon and we haven't met before. You are filling in for my regular instructor and I have had all my training in a car the same as yours. I would like you to assess how I deal with pedestrian crossings and my use of signals, especially by indicator and by arm. I would also like you to assess my general driving and correct any obvious faults that I may have committed. You can call me Jill.'

Instructor:
'Hello Jill, I understand you have a driving test coming up soon and you would like to improve your approach and negotiation of pedestrian crossings and your use of signals, so this will be the main area we will practice today. However, I will also assess your general driving and give you any help and guidance you may need. Do you have any questions before we start?'

Recap

Instructor (question suggestions):

'Before we move off, I would like to ask you a few questions to check your current knowledge of this subject.

- Imagine you see a zebra crossing ahead. What is the first thing you should do?
- At the zebra crossing there are some people already on the crossing, how will this affect your speed of approach?
- As you get near to the zebra crossing, you see that there is another pedestrian waiting to cross. What should you do?
- What is your stop position at a zebra crossing and do you need to apply the handbrake?
- If you are stopped at a single zebra crossing and pedestrians are crossing from left to right, when is it safe to move off again?
- If a pedestrian seems unsure of whether to cross, is it permissible to wave him/her across?
- What do the zigzag lines mean?
- At a pelican crossing, what does a flashing amber light mean?
- Do you always need to indicate when you move off from the side of the road?
- If I told you to take the second road on the right, when would you start to indicate?
- Imagine you are approaching a roundabout to take the road ahead, second exit. When would you indicate?'

Note: You should allow approximately 3–4 minutes for recap questions. If time allows, try to ask a question for each key point on the marking sheet, but this is not mandatory. Depending on the answers given, you may wish to ask other questions.

Extra Note: Rather than ask questions regarding arm signals, it is suggested that you should get the pupil to demonstrate these before moving off. See Cockpit drill and move off on next page. You should also aim to cover arm signals on the move if it is safe to do so.

Objective

Instructor:

'Our objective today is to improve your approach and negotiation of all types of pedestrian crossings and your use of signals both by indicator and by arm.'

**Driver
Development**

**Fault
Assessment**

**Cockpit Drill
Move Off**

Instructor notes: The following scenario combines the phase 2 techniques highlighted previously on page 8. This combines pro-active Q&A techniques with phase two level fault assessment aimed at exposing the gaps (faults) in the pupil's knowledge. The faults listed are based mainly around the subject of the lesson, but you should bear in mind that you are also assessing the pupil's general driving and should be prepared to deal with any obvious fault that occurs.

Instructor:

'I would like you to carry out your cockpit drill please.'
(watch for any faults)

Instructor:
'Before we move off, I would like to deal with arm signals. Please open your driver's door window and then check that it is safe to put your right arm out.'

Pupil checks his right exterior door mirror and over his shoulder.

Instructor:
'Good. Firstly demonstrate the arm signal for turning right.'

Pupil does this correctly.

Instructor:
'OK. Now the arm signal for turning left.'

Pupil gives the arm signal for slowing down instead.

Instructor:
'This is the arm signal for slowing down.'

'The arm signal for turning left is to rotate your arm in an anti-clockwise direction.'

Pupil:
'Oh yes. I have got these two mixed up.'

Instructor:
'Try to remember this in future as the slowing down signal is occasionally used on approach to a pedestrian crossing when you feel you need to emphasise this.'

Instructor:
'When you are ready, I would like you to drive on please.'

Pupil signals unnecessarily.

Instructor:
'Cancel your signal, it is unnecessary.'

'What road user is benefiting from this?'

Pupil:
'Nobody really. I usually signal when I move off so I will not forget in my driving test.'

Instructor:
'When moving off you should base your signal on who will benefit, so it is effective all round observation that is important.'

Pupil approaches a zebra crossing.

Instructor:
'Zebra crossing ahead, what is the first thing you should do?'

Pupil:
'Come off the gas and start to slow down.'

Instructor:
'No, check your mirrors first. Why is it important to do this? '

Pupil:
'Oh yes, I need to know what is behind me and how close any following traffic is.'

Instructor:
'Good. So remember to check your mirrors first. Now where are you looking?'

Pupil:
'Both sides of the road to see if any pedestrians are crossing.'

Instructor:
'That's correct. The crossing is clear so how should you proceed?'

Pupil:
'I can start to accelerate again.'

Instructor:
'No, you are too fast. Off the gas.

'What if another pedestrian was to approach the crossing and may be rushing as he/she is in a hurry? Would you be able to stop safely?'

Pupil:
'No, I didn't think of this.'

Instructor:
'Always approach pedestrian crossings at a speed where you can stop safely if you need to.'

Pupil approaches a bus stopped at a bus stop.

Instructor:
'Is it safe to overtake this bus ahead?'

Pupil:
'Yes, there is no oncoming traffic at the moment.'

Instructor:
'OK, do you need to signal right?'

Pupil:
'No, I think the traffic behind me knows that I will go past the bus.'

Instructor:
'You need to indicate right.'

'What about the bus driver, do you think he would benefit from seeing a signal?'

Pupil:
'Oh, yes, he may be assessing when to move off again.'

Instructor:
'Good. Remember to consider all other road users when deciding on whether to signal and not just those behind you. '

Instructor:
'Tell me when you can see the next pedestrian crossing.'

Pupil:
'I can see a zebra crossing just ahead of those parked vehicles on the left.'

Instructor:
'Good. Can you see clearly on the nearside if there are any pedestrians waiting to cross?'

Pupil:
'No. The vehicles are blocking my view.'

Instructor:
'How will this affect your speed of approach?'

Pupil:
'I need to slow down until I can see if it is clear. Now I can see there is a pedestrian waiting to cross.'

Instructor:
'Well done. Where are you going to stop?'

Pupil:
'With the front of the car just behind the broken white line.'

Instructor:
'Good, but you haven't applied the handbrake. Why is this important?'

Pupil:
'I thought that if I just kept my foot on the footbrake it would be quicker when moving off again.'

Instructor:
'What if your foot slipped off the clutch, what would happen then?'

Pupil:
'Oh, the car could jump forward and maybe hit the pedestrian.'

Instructor:
'Good. So always apply the handbrake once you have stopped to let pedestrians cross the road. It is a single zebra crossing, when is it safe to move off again?'

Pupil:
'Once the pedestrian has cleared my side of the road.'

Instructor:
'No! Wait!

What if the pedestrian changed his/her mind and turned round and walked back again?'

Pupil:
'That's true, I didn't think of this possibility.'

Instructor:
'OK, at a single zebra crossing you must wait until all pedestrians are on the pavement before moving off again. Drive on once this has happened.'

Instructor:
'At the end of the road turn left please.'

Pupil signals too early as there is another left turn before the end of the road.

Instructor:
'Cancel your signal, it is too early.

There is another road on the left so what will the driver waiting to emerge think?'

Pupil:
'Oh yes, he will think I am turning left and may pull out in front of me.'

Instructor:
'Good, so as well as checking your mirrors, where else should you be looking?'

Pupil:
'I should be scanning down the road to see if there are any other roads before the one I need to take and then signal after I have passed.'

Pupil approaches the end of a one-way street where there is a round blue mandatory sign showing that he must turn right.

Instructor:
'Do you need to indicate right here?'

Pupil:
'No because following vehicles will know I have to turn right.'

Instructor:
'You should indicate right.'

'Would pedestrians in the new road have seen the road sign?'

Pupil:
'No, I guess not.'

Instructor:
'Remember that you should indicate if this would be of benefit to another road user and this includes pedestrians.'

Pupil stops at split zebra crossing (one with an island in the middle) with a pedestrian crossing from left to right.

Instructor:
'When are you going to move off again?'

Pupil:
'Once the pedestrian is on the opposite pavement.'

Instructor:
'No, if it is safe move off when the pedestrian reaches the central island. This can be treated as two crossings.'

Pupil stops at a traffic light controlled crossroads where the lights are red

Instructor:
'What are you looking for as you wait here?'

Pupil:
'I am checking to see when the lights go green.'

Instructor:
'Scan the crossroads, can you see pedestrians crossings?'

Pupil:
'Oh yes, which type are these. Pelicans, puffins or Toucans?'

Instructor:
'They are none of these. Most major junctions have controlled pedestrian crossings. I call them 'junction crossings'. Treat them the same as any other controlled crossing and scan for pedestrians that may still be crossing the road. Where should you be looking as you move off?'

Pupil:
'Ahead for pedestrians.'

Instructor:
'Yes, but don't forget your left and right blind spot.'

'It is important to check for any pedestrian who may make a last minute dash to cross the road.'

Summary

Examiner parks back at driving test centre.

Instructor:
'If you would like to switch off the engine please and relax. I would just like to summarise today's lesson.

At the beginning of today's lesson, you showed that you have a good basic knowledge of both pedestrian crossings and use of signals

However, there were some areas that you needed to improve on. For example, when moving off or passing parked cars, you were generally signalling more by habit rather than basing this on observation of who would benefit.

Your approach to pedestrian crossings was generally too fast and sometimes you were trying to move off before it was safe to do so.

I felt that you responded well to my instruction and made improvements to most of these areas. If you include these techniques into your regular driving, I am sure this will help you with your forthcoming driving test.

Do you have any questions before we finish today's lesson?'

This exercise will be ended by the examiner saying:

'Thank you. That is the end of the examination. I will now return to my office to complete the assessment. You are welcome to wait for the result, however if that is not possible I am happy to post the result by first class post at the end of the day.'

Instructor notes: Once the examination is finished you will normally be asked to wait somewhere convenient and be informed where you will be met to receive the result and debrief.

The examiner will usually give a fairly detailed debrief and try to answer any questions you may have at this time. The debrief usually lasts about 15 minutes and you should allow approximately 30 minutes from the time your examination finishes to complete this part of the examination.

Meeting other traffic, crossing the path of other vehicles, overtaking other vehicles, allowing adequate clearance and anticipation of other road users

Level: Trained/ Full Licence Holder

Lesson Plan

Recap
Objective

Expose gaps in knowledge
Develop/improve skills
Assess general driving
Summary

Key Points

MSM
Meet approaching traffic
Cross other traffic
Overtake other traffic
Keep a safe distance
Shaving other vehicles
Anticipation of pedestrians
Anticipation of cyclists
Anticipation of drivers

This exercise may be introduced to the PDI by the examiner saying:

'I would like you to assume I am a pupil at the trained stage with a driving test coming up soon and we haven't met before. You are filling in for my regular instructor and I have had all my training in a car the same as yours. I would like you to assess how I deal with crossing the path of approaching traffic, overtaking other vehicles and also in anticipating the actions of other road users and correct any faults that may occur. You can call me John.'

Instructor:
'Hello John, I understand you have a driving test coming up soon and you would like to improve your crossing of traffic, overtaking and your general anticipation skills. I will also assess your general driving and give you any help and guidance you may need. Do you have any questions before we start?'

Recap

Instructor (question suggestions):

'Before we move off, I would like to ask you a few questions to check your current knowledge.'

Crossing
- 'When turning right from a major road to a minor road, how do you choose a safe gap in the oncoming traffic?
- What are you looking for in the new road you are about to enter, before making the turn?
- If you saw a pedestrian about to cross the road you are entering, how would you deal with this?
- When emerging from a crossroads to go road ahead across the main road, where are you looking and what are you looking for?
- Imagine you are emerging right from a T-junction and there are some cars parked in the main road opposite you. How will this affect your position as you emerge and the gap you will need to emerge safely?'

Overtaking
- 'You are on a long straight road and there is a slow moving vehicle in front of you which you are considering overtaking. There are no on-coming vehicles but there are various minor roads ahead on both the left and the right. Do you think it would be safe to overtake?
- Give me some examples of when it would be illegal to overtake?
- Why is it useful to ask yourself if it is necessary to overtake a slow moving vehicle?
- Take me through the basic routine you would use for overtaking a slow moving vehicle ahead of you.
- When is it permissible to overtake on the left instead of the right?

Anticipation
- 'There are many hazards on the road which we need to be aware of, but we only need to react to the ones that we think are going to cause us to change speed and/or direction. As you pass a line of parked vehicles, what clues are you looking for to tell you if a car door is about to open or a vehicle is about to move off?
- You see a cyclist ahead of you riding along the left hand pavement. As you approach, he starts to look over his right shoulder. How should you react to this?
- As you approach a left hand bend you see a warning sign that informs you of a school ahead. How may this affect your speed and gear before you negotiate the bend?

- As you get nearer the school you notice that children are crossing the road near to a large van parked on the other side of the road. If there was a child about to cross from behind the van, where could you look to anticipate that this was about to happen?
- You are approaching a bridge over the road you are driving on which shows a width restriction. If there was a large vehicle approaching from the opposite direction, where would you expect them to position on the road?'

Note: You should allow approximately 3–4 minutes for recap questions. If time allows, try to ask a question for each key point on the marking sheet, but this is not mandatory. Depending on the answers given, you may wish to ask other questions.

jective

Instructor:

'Our objective today is to be able to cross the path of approaching vehicles safely, overtake other vehicles and to develop your anticipation of drivers, cyclists and pedestrians.'

river
lopment

ault
ssment

Instructor notes: The following scenario combines the phase 2 techniques highlighted previously on page 8. This combines pro-active Q&A techniques with phase two level fault assessment aimed at exposing the gaps (faults) in the pupil's knowledge. The faults listed are based mainly around the chosen elements for this lesson, but you should bear in mind that you are also assessing the pupil's general driving and should be prepared to deal with any obvious fault that occurs.

Extra note: Overtaking - there may be few opportunities to overtake other vehicles during the 30 minutes allowed for phase 2. In these circumstances the examiner will often test this aspect by asking suitable questions to assess your knowledge. However, it is suggested that you pre-empt this by asking the examiner (pupil) pro-active questions as the opportunity arises. Some examples of how this can be achieved are included in the driver development and fault assessment section of this chapter.

**Cockpit Drill
& Move Off**

Instructor:

'Before we move off, I would like you to carry out your cockpit drill please.'
(watch for any faults)

Pupil is parked on a fairly busy road with parked vehicles both sides.

Instructor:
'Before we move off, I would like you to assess the road ahead and tell me what hazards you need to anticipate.'

Pupil:
'I need to be looking for any pedestrians that may cross the road between the parked vehicles and any of the parked vehicles that may be about to move off.'

Instructor:
'Good. So what clues are you looking for with regards to the parked vehicles?'

Pupil:
'Any drivers sat in their vehicles, brake lights on or someone indicating right.'

Instructor:
'Excellent. When you are ready, please drive on.'

Ahead of the pupil someone gets into a vehicle on the left.

Instructor:
'Did you see that person just get into the blue car ahead?'

Pupil:
'Yes, they seemed to be in a bit of a hurry.'

Instructor:
'What do you think may happen next?'

Pupil:
'I think they may move away, so I had better slow down.'

Instructor:
'Well done. Keep scanning ahead so that you can anticipate other hazards.'

Instructor:
'*Take the next road on the right, please.* Do you think you have a safe gap in the oncoming traffic?'

Pupil:
'Yes, I think if I speed up I should just be able to make it.'

Pupil starts to accelerate towards the junction.

Instructor:
'Off the gas! You are too fast.'

'Have you had time to check the road you are entering?'

Pupil:
'No, I was concentrating on the oncoming vehicle.'

Instructor:
'Remember that an element of rush is an element of risk and so if you feel you need to accelerate to cross traffic then the gap is not safe.'

Pupil approaches a slow moving road sweeping lorry on a straight road.

Instructor:
'Do you think you have time to overtake this vehicle safely?'

Pupil:
'Yes, there are no oncoming vehicles so I should have plenty of time.'

Pupil has not seen a crossroads warning triangle.

Instructor:
'Look at the crossroads sign. Do you think a vehicle could emerge from the minor road as you are trying to overtake?'

Pupil:
'Oh yes, I didn't see the road sign. I will wait until I have passed the junction.'

Instructor:
'Good. So, next time, remember that, as well as checking for oncoming traffic, you need to assess the road ahead for other hazards such as junctions or exits to factories for example.'

Pupil passes the junction and it is now safe to overtake.

Instructor:
'Talk me through your actions as you overtake this vehicle.'

Pupil:
'I will check my interior and right mirrors first and then move slightly to the right so I can see clearly ahead. It is still clear so I am going to start to accelerate.'

Pupil starts to accelerate in 4th gear.

Instructor:
'You are in the wrong gear.'

'Change back to 3rd as this will give you better acceleration.'

Pupil:
'OK. Now I am checking my mirrors again and signalling right so the driver I am overtaking knows what I am doing.'

Instructor:
'Good. Now, when is it safe to move back over?'

Pupil:
'As soon as I pass the vehicle I am overtaking.'

Instructor:
'You are turning back too early.'

'What could happen to the back of your car if you do this?'

Pupil:
'It could be too close to the front of the vehicle I am overtaking.'

Instructor:
'Yes, so wait until you can see in your interior and left mirrors that you are at least two car lengths past.'

Pupil approaches a crossroads from the minor road.

Instructor:
'At the next crossroads, take the road ahead. Is it safe to cross the main road?'

Pupil:
'Yes, I have a safe gap both left and right.'

Instructor:
'Wait! You haven't checked the new road you are entering, what can you see?'

Pupil:
'There is a lorry blocking the entrance to the junction and vehicles waiting to emerge.'

Instructor:
'Yes. So remember, it is just as important to check the road you are entering as well as looking for a safe gap. Never start a manoeuvre you cannot complete.'

Pupil approaches a zebra crossing with a cyclist ahead.

Instructor:
'What do those zigzag lines mean?'

Pupil:
'I think they mean no overtaking.'

Instructor:
'That's right, but can you overtake the cyclist?'

Pupil:
'No I don't think so.'

Instructor:
'Yes, you can, if it is safe to do so, as the rule only applies to motor vehicles.'

'Do you think it is safe? '

Pupil:
'Yes, there are no pedestrians anywhere near the crossing.'

Instructor:
'OK, but keep scanning both sides of the road.'

Pupil now driving down a main road with double white lines and a solid line nearest him.

Instructor:
'Are you allowed to cross the solid white line to overtake another moving vehicle?'

Pupil:
'No, not if the solid line is nearest to me.'

Instructor:
'That's correct. Now look ahead. That pedestrian on the left is waving at someone on the other side of the road. What do you think may happen next?'

Pupil:
'I think the pedestrian on the right may cross the road.'

Instructor:
'Good. How will you deal with this situation?'

Pupil:
'Check my mirrors, come off the gas and cover the brake.'

Instructor:
'Well done, that was good anticipation.'

Pupil stops at the give way line of a T-junction to emerge right.

Instructor:
'You have steered right too early.'

'As you enter the main road, how will this affect your road position as you cross the traffic on your right?'

Pupil:
'I am not really sure.'

Instructor:
'You will end up too far to the right and be in conflict with any oncoming traffic. When should you normally start to steer right when emerging?'

Pupil:
'Just as I approach the give way line, I think.'

Instructor:
'No, if the centre line is straight as you approach the T-junction, wait until your front wheels have passed over the give way line before you start to steer right.'

Instructor notes: For all phase 2 subjects, you will finish by returning to the test centre. Once parked, you should give a summary of the lesson before finishing. This should be given using a positive approach but should include the main problems dealt with as well as the improvements made.

Examiner parks back at driving test centre.

Instructor:
'If you would like to switch off the engine please and relax. I would just like to summarise today's lesson.

At the beginning of today's lesson, you showed you had a good grasp of the main elements of this lesson and your general driving was of an acceptable standard.

However there were a few faults that we needed to work on. Initially when turning right across traffic you tended to rush your gaps. One way to improve your assessment of this in most situations is to say to yourself, if, as I cross traffic, I were to stall my vehicle, would the oncoming traffic be able to stop safely. If the answer is yes, you have a safe gap. If the answer is no, then you need to hold back. When overtaking you needed to assess other hazards as well as looking for a safe gap.

However, I felt that you responded well to my instruction and made improvements to most of these areas. If you now include these as part of your normal driving, then you should notice the improvements to your overall driving standard.

Do you have any questions before we finish today's lesson?'

This exercise will be ended by the examiner saying:

'Thank you. That is the end of the examination. I will now return to my office to complete the assessment. You are welcome to wait for the result, however if that is not possible I am happy to post the result by first class post at the end of the day.'

Instructor notes: Once the examination is finished, you will normally be asked to wait somewhere convenient and be informed where you will be met to receive the result and debrief.

The examiner will usually give a fairly detailed debrief and try to answer any questions you may have at this time. The debrief usually lasts about 15 minutes and you should allow approximately 30 minutes from the time your examination finishes to complete this part of the examination.

Pedestrian Crossings and Use of Signals

Level: Trained/ Full Licence Holder

Lesson Plan

Recap
Objective

Expose gaps in knowledge
Develop/improve skills
Assess general driving
Summary

Key Points

MSM
Speed on approach
Stop when necessary
Overtaking on approach
Inviting pedestrians to cross
Signals by indicator
Signals by arm
Signals - timing
Unnecessary signals

This exercise may be introduced to the PDI by the examiner saying:

'I would like you to assume I am a pupil at the trained stage with a driving test coming up soon and we haven't met before. You are filling in for my regular instructor and I have had all my training in a car the same as yours. I would like you to assess how I deal with pedestrian crossings and my use of signals, especially by indicator and by arm. I would also like you to assess my general driving and correct any obvious faults that I may have. You can call me Tom.'

Instructor:
'Hello Tom, I understand you have a driving test coming up soon and you would like to improve your approach and negotiation of pedestrian crossings and your use of signals, so this will be the main area we will practice today. However, I will also assess your general driving and give you any help and guidance you may need. Do you have any questions before we start?'

Recap

Instructor (question suggestions):

'Before we move off, I would like to ask you a few questions to check your current knowledge of this subject.

- Imagine you see a zebra crossing ahead. What is the first thing you should do?
- At the zebra crossing there are some people already on the crossing. How will this affect your speed of approach?
- As you get near to the zebra crossing, you see that there is another pedestrian waiting to cross. What should you do?
- What is your stop position at a zebra crossing and do you need to apply the handbrake?
- If you are stopped at a single zebra crossing and pedestrians are crossing from left to right, when is it safe to move off again?
- If a pedestrian seems unsure of whether to cross, is it permissible to wave him/ her across?
- What do the zigzag lines mean?
- At a pelican crossing, what does a flashing amber light mean?
- Do you always need to indicate when you move off from the side of the road?
- If I told you to take the second road on the right, when would you start to indicate?
- Imagine you are approaching a roundabout to take the road ahead second exit. When would you indicate?'

Note: You should allow approximately 3–4 minutes for recap questions. If time allows, try to ask a question for each key point on the marking sheet, but this is not mandatory. Depending on the answers given, you may wish to ask other questions.

Extra Note: Rather than ask questions regarding arm signals, it is suggested that you should get the pupil to demonstrate these before moving off. See Cockpit drill and move off on next page. You should also aim to cover arm signals on the move if it is safe to do so.

Objective

Instructor:

'Our objective today is to improve your approach and negotiation of all types of pedestrian crossings and your use of signals both by indicator and by arm.'

Driver Development

Fault Assessment

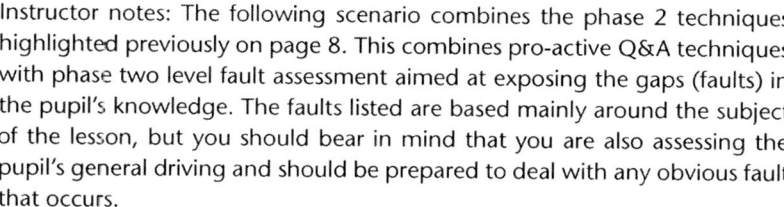

Instructor notes: The following scenario combines the phase 2 techniques highlighted previously on page 8. This combines pro-active Q&A techniques with phase two level fault assessment aimed at exposing the gaps (faults) in the pupil's knowledge. The faults listed are based mainly around the subject of the lesson, but you should bear in mind that you are also assessing the pupil's general driving and should be prepared to deal with any obvious fault that occurs.

Cockpit Drill / Move Off

Instructor:
'I would like you to carry out your cockpit drill please.' *(watch for any faults)*

Instructor:
'Before we move off, I would like to deal with arm signals. Please open your drivers door window and then check that it is safe to put your right arm out.'

Pupil checks his right exterior door mirror and over his shoulder.

Instructor:
'Good. Firstly demonstrate the arm signal for turning right.'

Pupil does this correctly.

Instructor:
'OK. Now the arm signal for turning left.'

Pupil gives the arm signal for slowing down instead.

Instructor:
'This is the arm signal for slowing down.'

'The arm signal for turning left is to rotate your arm in an anti-clockwise direction.'

Pupil:
'Oh yes. I have got these two mixed up.'

Instructor:
'Try to remember this in future as the slowing down signal is occasionally used on approach to a pedestrian crossing when you feel you need to emphasise this.'

Instructor:
'When you are ready I would like you to drive on please.'

Pupil signals unnecessarily.

Instructor:
'Cancel your signal, it is unnecessary.'

'What road user is benefiting from this?'

Pupil:
'Nobody really. I usually signal when I move off so I will not forget in my driving test.'

Instructor:
'When moving off you should base your signal on who will benefit, so it is effective all round observation that is important.'

Pupil Approaches a zebra crossing.

Instructor:
'Zebra crossing ahead, what is the first thing you should do?'

Pupil:
'Come off the gas and start to slow down.'

Instructor:
'No, check your mirrors first.'

'Why is it important to do this?'

Pupil:
'Oh yes, I need to know what is behind me and how close any following traffic is.'

Instructor:
'Good. So remember to check your mirrors first. Now where are you looking?'

Pupil:
'Both sides of the road to see if any pedestrians are crossing.'

Instructor:
'That's correct. The crossing is clear so how should you proceed.'

Pupil:
'I can start to accelerate again.'

Instructor:
'No, you are too fast. Off the gas.'

'What if another pedestrian was to approach the crossing and maybe rushing as he/
she is in a hurry? Would you be able to stop safely?'

Pupil:
'No, I didn't think of this.'

Instructor:
'Always approach pedestrian crossings at a speed where you can stop safely if you
need to.'

Pupil approacnes a bus stopped at a bus stop.

Instructor:
'Is it safe to overtake this bus ahead?'

Pupil:
'Yes, there is no oncoming traffic at the moment.'

Instructor:
'OK, do you need to signal right?'

Pupil:
'No, I think the traffic behind me knows that I will go past the bus.'

Instructor:
'You need to indicate right.'

'What about the bus driver, do you think he would benefit from seeing a signal?'

Pupil:
'Oh, yes, he may be assessing when to move off again.'

Instructor:
'Good. Remember to consider all other road users when deciding on whether to
signal and not just those behind you.'

Instructor:
'Tell me when you can see the next pedestrian crossing.'

Pupil:
'I can see a zebra crossing just ahead of those parked vehicles on the left.'

Instructor:
'Good. Can you see clearly on the nearside if there are any pedestrians waiting to cross?'

Pupil:
'No. The vehicles are blocking my view.'

Instructor:
'How will this affect your speed of approach?'

Pupil:
'I need to slow down until I can see if it is clear.

Instructor:
'Open your window, check your exterior mirror and blindspot and give a slowing down arm signal to the driver behind.'

Pupil gives incorrect arm signal.

Instructor:
'That is the signal for turning left. What is the signal for slowing down?'

Pupil:
'Oh sorry, I should move my hand and arm up and down like this.'

Instructor:
'That is correct. What might the driver behind do if he thinks you are turning left instead of slowing down?'

Pupil:
'He might try to overtake me.'

Instructor:
'Yes. Remember, the arm signal for slowing down is to move your hand and arm up and down with your palm facing downwards. The arm signal for turning left is to rotate your hand and arm anticlockwise with your palm facing forwards. There is a pedestrian waiting to cross. Where are you going to stop?'

Pupil:
'With the front of the car just behind the broken white line.'

Instructor:
'Good, but you haven't applied the handbrake. Why is this important?'

Pupil:
'I thought that if I just kept my foot on the footbrake it would be quicker when moving off again.'

Instructor:
'What if your foot slipped off the clutch, what would happen then?'

Pupil:
'Oh, the car could jump forward and maybe hit the pedestrian.'

Instructor:
'Good. So always apply the handbrake once you have stopped to let pedestrians cross the road. It is a single zebra crossing, when is it safe to move off again?'

Pupil:
'Once the pedestrian has cleared my side of the road.'

Instructor:
'No! Wait!'

'What if the pedestrian changed their mind and turned round and walked back again?'

Pupil:
'That's true. I didn't think of this possibility.'

Instructor:
'OK, at a single zebra crossing you must wait until all pedestrians are on the pavement before moving off again. Drive on once this has happened.'

Pupil approaches a right turn obscured by parked vehicles on the right hand side of the road.

Instructor:
'As well as a right indicator signal, I want you to give a right arm signal'
Pupil gives correct arm signal but then keeps arm out when changing back to second gear.

Instructor:
'You have no hands on the steering wheel when changing gear.'

'Is it safe to keep your right hand out whilst changing gear with your left?'

Pupil:
'No. I don't have full control of the vehicle.'

Instructor:
'You should have at least one hand on the steering wheel at all times whilst driving. When using an arm signal on approach to a junction, bring your right arm in and hold the steering wheel with your right hand whilst changing gear.'

Pupil stops at split zebra crossing (one with an island in the middle) with a pedestrian crossing from left to right.

Instructor:
'When are you going to move off again?'

Pupil:
'Once the pedestrian is on the opposite pavement.'

Instructor:
'No, if it is safe move off when the pedestrian reaches the central island. This can be treated as two crossings.'

Pupil stops at a traffic light controlled crossroads where the lights are red.

Instructor:
'What are you looking for as you wait here?'

Pupil:
'I am checking to see when the lights go green.'

Instructor:
'Scan the crossroads. Can you see pedestrian crossings?'

Pupil:
'Oh yes, which type are these. Pelicans, puffins or Toucans?'

Instructor:
'They are none of these. Most major junctions have controlled pedestrians crossings. I call them 'junction crossings'. Treat them the same as any other controlled crossing and scan for any pedestrians that may still be crossing the road. Where should you be looking as you move off?'

Pupil:
'Ahead for any pedestrians.'

Instructor:
'Yes, but don't forget your left and right blind spot.'

'It is important to check for any pedestrian who may make a last minute dash to cross the road.'

Summary

Examiner parks back at driving test centre.

Instructor:
'If you would like to switch off the engine please and relax. I would just like to summarise today's lesson.

At the beginning of today's lesson, you showed that you have a good basic knowledge of both pedestrian crossings and use of signals.

However there were some areas that we needed to improve on. For example, when   moving off or passing parked cars, you were generally signalling more by habit rather than basing this on observation of who would benefit.

Your approach to pedestrian crossings was generally too fast and sometimes you were trying to move off before it was safe to do so.
I felt that you responded well to my instruction and made improvements to most of these areas. If you include these techniques into your regular driving, I am sure this will help you with your forthcoming driving test.

Do you have any questions before we finish today's lesson?'

This exercise will be ended by the examiner saying:

'Thank you. That is the end of the examination. I will now return to my office to complete the assessment. You are welcome to wait for the result, however if that is not possible I am happy to post the result by first class post at the end of the day.'

> Instructor notes: Once the examination is finished you will normally be asked to wait somewhere convenient and be informed where you will be met to receive the result and debrief.
>
> The examiner will usually give a fairly detailed debrief and try to answer any questions you may have at this time. The debrief usually lasts about 15 minutes and you should allow approximately 30 minutes from the time your examination finishes to complete this part of the examination.

Progress, Hesitancy & Normal Road Positioning

Level: Trained/ Full Licence Holder

Key Points

Progress too fast
Progress too slow
Hesitancy
Normal position too wide from the left
Normal position too close to the left

Lesson Plan

Recap
Objective

Expose gaps in knowledge
Develop/improve skills
Assess general driving
Summary

This exercise may be introduced to the PDI by the examiner saying:

'I would like you to assume I am a pupil at the trained stage with a driving test coming up soon and we haven't met before. You are filling in for my regular instructor and I have had all my training in a car the same as yours. I would like you to instruct me on my general progress, hesitancy and normal road positioning and correct any faults that may occur. You can call me John.'

Instructor:
'Hello John, I understand you have a driving test coming up soon and you would like to improve your general progress, avoiding undue hesitancy and normal road positioning but I will also assess your general driving and give you any help and guidance you may need. Do you have any questions before we start?'

Recap

Instructor (question suggestions):

'Before we move off, I would like to ask you a few questions to check your current knowledge of this subject.

- What is the normal speed limit in an urban location?
- In busy built up areas, what hazards may determine whether it is safe to drive to the speed limit?
- What do you look for when joining a main road from a minor road to tell you if the speed limit has changed?
- On a main road with a speed limit of 30 mph, why is it important that you reach this speed if it is safe to do so and what effect may it have on the vehicles behind you if you were to drive slower than this, say at 25 mph?
- What is your normal driving position (or safety line) from the kerb on a main road?
- Where would you position your vehicle on a narrower road?
- Imagine you are approaching a roundabout to go road ahead, second exit. There are two lanes on approach but no markings such as arrows in them. Which would be the safest lane to choose?
- Now imagine you are waiting at the roundabout for a safe gap, then one appears but you are too slow to take it, how would this affect the traffic behind you?
- Where would you position when negotiating a sharp right hand bend?
- Where would you position when negotiating a sharp left hand bend?
- You are driving down a one-way street which has two lanes. If you were to turn right at the end of the road, where would you position the car?'

Note: You should allow approximately 3–4 minutes for recap questions. If time allows, try to ask a question for each key point on the marking sheet, but this is not mandatory. Depending on the answers given, you may wish to ask other questions.

Objective

Instructor:

'Our objective today is to be able to improve your general progress and observation of speed limits, avoid undue hesitancy at junctions and roundabouts etc, and ensure your normal road positioning is safe and correct.'

**Driver
Development**

**Fault
Assessment**

**Cockpit Drill
& Move Off**

Instructor:

'Before we move off, I would like you to carry out your cockpit drill please.'
(watch for any faults)

Instructor:
'When you are ready, I would like you to move off please.'

Pupil now driving at 25 mph down a clear main road with a speed limit of 30 mph.

Instructor:
'You are driving too slowly. What is the speed limit on this road?'

Pupil:
'It is 30 mph, but that is a maximum speed and not a target. I feel a bit safer driving at this speed.'

Instructor:
'You are holding up the traffic behind you.'

'Give some more gas and then change from 3rd to 4th gear.'

Pupil:
'It's not me that is the problem, it's the other drivers driving too close and trying to overtake me. Why don't they drive a bit slower and then we would all be safer.'

Instructor:
'OK John, pull in and park on the left as I need to deal with your comments.'

Pupil parks on the left.

Instructor:
'Now, the reason you are giving me for not reaching the speed limit on this road is that you feel safer. However, what you haven't realised is that actually you are less safe because you have become the hazard. Was the road clear ahead of you?'

Pupil:
'Yes it was.'

Instructor:
'Do you think that if you had reached the speed limit the cars would have been so close behind you?'

Pupil:
'No, I suppose they wouldn't.'

Instructor:
'Good. So remember that if the road conditions are safe to do so you need to make good progress.'

Pupil approaches a roundabout.

Instructor:
'At the next roundabout, I want you to follow the road ahead, second exit. Which lane are you going to choose on approach?'

Pupil:
'I will choose the left hand lane.'

Instructor:
'Good, but you are stopping unnecessarily.'

'What are you looking for on your right?'

Pupil:
'I am looking at that car approaching.'

Instructor:
'Yes but look ahead, the car opposite you is entering the roundabout, how will this affect the car on your right?'

Pupil:
'Oh, it looks like it is stopping.'

Instructor:
'Yes, so off the brake and keep going, you have a safe gap.'

Pupil joins the new road after negotiating the roundabout.'

Instructor:
'You are too slow. What is the speed limit of this road?'

Pupil:
'I think it is still 30 mph.'

Instructor:
'No, it is 40 mph. Didn't you see the change of speed limit sign as you exited the roundabout?'

Pupil:
'No. I was looking on approach but not on exit.

Instructor:
'Remember that at roundabouts you can have different speed limits depending on which exit you take so you must check again as you leave the roundabout.'

Pupil:
'OK, I will try to remember this in future.'

Instructor:
'You are too close to the left on this road.'

'How far from the kerb should you be?'

Pupil:
'About a metre from the kerb usually.'

Instructor:
'Good. Do you have a reference point to check this?'

Pupil:
'No, not really. I just try to estimate it.'

Instructor:
'OK. Firstly you can use a reference point of where the kerb appears along the bottom of your front windscreen *(Instructor note: this will vary depending on the vehicle)*. Also you can check your left mirror and see you are about a doors width from the kerb.'

Instructor:
'At the end of the road turn left please.'

Pupil stops at the give way line as cars pass on the main road and then misses a safe gap.

Instructor:
'You have missed that gap. How do you choose a safe gap when emerging?'

Pupil:
'I usually say to myself if I could walk across the road and back again I would have time to emerge safely and get up to the speed of the traffic I am joining.'

Instructor:
'Good, but have you noticed that you are not ready to move? Your right foot is still on the brake and the clutch is down. What effect does this have?'

Pupil:
'It means I cannot move straight away and so I become hesitant.'

Instructor:
'Yes, so in future once you have stopped at a junction make sure you are ready to move off with your clutch at the bite point and your right foot over the gas.'

Pupil emerges from the junction safely into a narrower road.

Instructor:
'You are weaving about on the road. Where should you position your vehicle?'

Pupil:
'I am trying to position about a metre from the kerb but keep finding I am then too close to the centre line.'

Instructor:
'This is because the road is narrower than before. Where should you position when the road is narrower?'

Pupil:
'A bit closer to the kerb?'

Instructor:
'Position in the centre of your lane. The best way to do this is to glance in both exterior mirrors and see that you have the same gap from the kerb to the nearside of your vehicle and from the centre line to your offside.'

Pupil emerges into a new road but takes too long to reach the speed limit.

Instructor:
'You are taking too long to reach the speed limit.'

'What should you not cause other cars to do once you have emerged into a new road?'

Pupil:
I shouldn't cause them to slow down.'

Instructor:
'Yes, so you need to use more gas and check your mirrors to ensure you do not do this.'

Instructor:
'At the next roundabout, take the road ahead second exit. Which lane will you choose on approach?'

Pupil:
'Left hand lane.'

Instructor:
'Good. Now where are you looking this time?'

Pupil:
'Right and ahead as well.'

Instructor:
'Well done. Do you have a safe gap?'

Pupil:
'Yes, the car on my right has stopped and the oncoming vehicle is going ahead.'

As pupil negotiates roundabout, he crosses from left lane to right lane and back again

Instructor:
'You have just straight lined that roundabout. If there had been a vehicle in the right hand lane, what would have happened?'

Pupil:
'I would have cut across his path.'

Instructor:
'That is correct. The reason you did this was because you were staring to the right and not glancing left. Where should you have positioned?'

Pupil:
'I should have stayed in the left hand lane.'

Instructor:
'Good. So next time, as well as checking right for a gap, keep glancing back to the left to ensure you keep the correct position.'

Instructor:
'*At the end of the road, turn right please.* Where are you going to position your vehicle?'

Pupil:
'Just left of the centre line.'

Instructor:
'No. Move into the right hand lane.'

'What sort of road is this?'

Pupil:
'Oh sorry, it is a one-way street.'

Instructor:
'Yes, if you happen to miss the signs as you enter the road what else could you look for to tell you the road has become one way?'

Pupil:
'I could look for arrows on the road I suppose.'

Instructor:
'Yes, also notice that all the parked cars are facing the same way on both sides of the road and also look for further one-way street signs that are often there to remind you.'

Lesson 10a   Progress, Hesitancy & Normal Road Positioning

Instructor notes: For all phase 2 subjects, you will finish by returning to the test centre. Once parked you should give a summary of the lesson before finishing. This should be given using a positive approach but should include the main problems dealt with as well as the improvements made.

Examiner parks back at driving test centre.

Instructor:
'If you would like to switch off the engine please and relax. I would just like to summarise today's lesson.

At the beginning of today's lesson. you were trying very hard to drive in a safe and responsible way.

However this resulted in you sometimes being too slow on clear main roads where you had become a hazard by holding up following traffic. At some junctions, you were not getting the car ready to move and this was causing you to miss safe gaps. Also your positioning needed some attention, especially when negotiating roundabouts

I felt that you made improvements to most of these areas today. If you include these techniques into your driving lessons, I am sure you will feel improvements in both your overall progress and to your general road positioning. Also you will gain confidence in taking safe gaps and so become less hesitant.

Do you have any questions before we finish today's lesson?'

This exercise will be ended by the examiner saying:

'Thank you, that is the end of the examination. I will now return to my office to complete the assessment. You are welcome to wait for the result, however if that is not possible I am happy to post the result by first class at the end of the day.'

Instructor notes: Once the examination is finished, you will normally be asked to wait somewhere convenient and be informed where you will be met to receive the result and debrief.

The examiner will usually give a fairly detailed debrief and try to answer any questions you may have at this time. The debrief usually lasts about 15 minutes and you should allow approximately 30 minutes from the time your examination finishes to complete this part of the examination.

Part 3

Instructional Techniques / The Core Competencies

Example: Part 3 Examination Sheet (ADI 26) -side 1

Candidate's Declaration

I certify that

- The vehicle I have provided for the test is properly insured under the Road Traffic Act of 1988 and
- I do/do not have to wear seat belts under the Motor Vehicles (Wearing of Seat Belts) Regulations 1982.

Signed

Date

Centre

Date

Make & Model

Reg Mark

Dual Controls   Fitted   Not Fitted

Candidate's Name

Ref. No

Column A

PST 7 No.7 Exercises 7P and 12T
Phase 1 - 7P Partly trained-Approaching junctions to turn either right or left

	Not Covered	Inadequately Covered	Adequately Covered
Briefing	☐	☐	☐
Mirrors	☐	☐	☐
Signal	☐	☐	☐
Brakes	☐	☐	☐
Gears	☐	☐	☐
Coasting	☐	☐	☐
Too fast on approach	☐	☐	☐
Too slow on approach	☐	☐	☐
Position	☐	☐	☐
Pedestrians	☐	☐	☐
Cross Approaching Traffic	☐	☐	☐
Right Corner Cut	☐	☐	☐

Phase 2 - 12T Trained/FLH-Pedestrian crossings and the use of signals

	Not Covered	Inadequately Covered	Adequately Covered
MSM	☐	☐	☐
Speed on approach	☐	☐	☐
Stop when necessary	☐	☐	☐
Overtaking on approach	☐	☐	☐
Inviting pedestrians to cross	☐	☐	☐
Signals by indicator	☐	☐	☐
Signals by arm	☐	☐	☐
Signals - timing	☐	☐	☐
Unnecessary signals	☐	☐	☐

The results of your test are:

Phase I Grade   Phase II Grade

Supervising Examiners Name

Location   Section No.

S E Signature

Column B

In this column the top line of boxes refer to phase I and the bottom line of boxes refer to phase II

1/2/3 = Unsatisfactory   4/5/6 = Satisfactory

Core Competencies

	1	2	3	4	5	6
Fault identification						
Fault analysis						
Remedial action						

Instructional Techniques

	1	2	3	4	5	6
Level of instruction						
Planning						
Control of lesson						
Communication						
Q/A Techniques						
Feedback/ Encouragement						
Instructor use of controls						

Instructor Characteristics

	1	2	3	4	5	6
Attitude and Approach to Pupil						

Assessment Notes

The examiner has assessed your overall performance based on the markings shown in the columns A and B. Using this measurement a final assessment for each phase has been made against the criteria below and these grades are shown at the foot of column A.

Criteria for Grading

6. Overall performance to a very high standard with no significant instructional weaknesses.

5. A good overall standard of instruction with some minor weaknesses in the instructional technique.

4. A competent overall performance with some minor deficiencies in instructional technique.

3. An inadequate overall performance with some deficiencies in instructional technique.

2. A poor overall performance with numerous deficiencies in instructional technique.

1. Overall standard of instruction extremely poor or dangerous with incorrect or even dangerous instruction.

The minimum level for a PASS is a grade 4 in each phase. You must achieve a satisfactory grade in each phase on the same occasion to obtain an overall pass in the examination.

Recommended Reading

There are some books available which may help you. In particular we recommend the following publications:

"Instructional Techniques and Practice for Driving Instructors" by Les Walklin published by Nelson Thornes Ltd.

"The Driving Instructor's Handbook" by J Miller and Margaret Stacey published by Kogan Page .

The Agency's Driving Manual and "Your Driving Test'. These can be obtained from HMSO and most bookshops.

Appeals

You have no grounds to appeal against the examiner's decision because you don't agree with it. But if you consider that your test was not properly conducted in accordance with the Regulations, you may apply to a Magistrates Court in the area in which you reside (in Scotland to the Sheriff within whose jurisdiction you reside) which has power to determine this point. Should the Court find that the test was not properly conducted, they may order a refund of the fee. (See Road Traffic Act1988, Section 133).

You should note, however, that your right of appeal to the Court under section 133 is strictly limited to the question of whether the test was properly conducted in accordance with the Regulations.

Before you consider making any appeal, you may wish to seek legal advice.

The Part 3 examination sheet explained

Note: The numbers used in the following explanation refer to those used to highlight the various sections on side 1 of the marking sheet.

Sections 1–2

1. Insurance
Part of the candidate's declaration requires you to sign that your vehicle is properly insured for use during the test which should include provision for the examiner to drive it. This should include any liability that the examiner may have for all third party and damage risks and for liability to any passenger, including any official passenger. The insurance cover should not name a specific examiner as the driver as DSA cannot guarantee that a particular examiner will conduct the test.

It is vital that you check with your insurance company to ensure that your vehicle is properly insured for the test. Some insurance companies do not cover this.

If planning to use a hire car for the test, you should check with the hire car company that the vehicle is properly insured. Most hire car companies do not cover this.

For more information, refer to the relevant section of the DSA publication "Your Road to Becoming an Approved Driving Instructor" or contact the DSA.

2. Vehicle details
In this section, the examiner will record details of the vehicle you use for the examination and your name.

For vehicle requirements, refer to the relevant section of the DSA publication "Your Road to Becoming an Approved Driving Instructor" or contact the DSA.

You do not have to have dual controls fitted.

Column A - Section 3–4

3. (Phase 1) & 4. (Phase 2): The key points
The main content for the lesson is listed here as a series of key points both for phase 1 and for phase 2. There is a separate list of key points for each subject heading. These are laid out at the start of each lesson in this manual.

Next to each key point are three columns: not covered, inadequately covered and adequately covered. The examiner will record the instruction given to each key point as follows:

Not Covered
Subject not covered or grossly incorrect or dangerous instruction given.

Inadequately Covered
Subject attempted, but the guidance and/or the training offered was incomplete or not fully satisfactory.

Adequately Covered
Subject was covered satisfactorily or better.

It is very important that you learn the key points for each subject as they can be used in a number of different ways as follows:

- They should be explained in the briefing for phase 1.
- You should ensure they are covered during the 'on the move' part of both phases (for example 'pedestrians' is a key point on pst 7 phase 1: Approaching junctions to turn either right or left. Even if you do not see a pedestrian approaching or crossing the road the pupil is turning into during the lesson, it can still be covered by pointing out to the pupil what he is looking for when scanning the road they are about to enter.

- They should be used to form the basis of your recap questions at phase 2 where the pupil should have prior knowledge of the subject. If you look at the recap questions at the start of each phase 2 lesson, you will see they are based around the key points.
- They should be used as a 'mental checklist' of faults to look for and faults covered.

> Note: If an examiner chooses not to cover a key point then this will be reflected on the marking sheet by drawing a line through it. For example, on pst 7 phase 1: Approaching junctions to turn either right or left, if the examiner plays a pupil who is generally too fast on approach then he may decide not to cover too slow on approach. Also, for subjects where only certain elements are chosen such as Meeting, Crossing, Overtaking, Adequate clearance and Anticipation, the elements not chosen will once again have a line drawn through them.

Column B- Sections 5–7

After marking Column A, the examiner will usually start at the bottom of column B with Instructor Characteristics and then work up through the Instructional Techniques (apart from Level of Instruction) to the Core Competencies. Level of Instruction will usually be marked last as this is directly related to the result in the core competencies.

For each topic there is an upper and lower marking box which corresponds to phase 1 (top row) and phase 2 (bottom row). The marking boxes are split into 6 columns marked 1–6.

To pass the examination, you must obtain a minimum mark of 4 in each of the three Core Competencies at both phases. The lowest mark in each phase will be used for the grade. So, for example, if at phase 2 you obtained a 5 for fault identification, a 3 for fault analysis and a 4 for remedial action, this would result in a failure and a grade 3 would be recorded.

The Instructor Characteristics and Instructional Techniques should reflect the marks of the Core Competencies, so your aim is to obtain a mark of 4 and above in as many of these elements as possible.

Section 5- Instructor Characteristics

Attitude and approach to pupil

This is an overall assessment of how you create a relaxed and supportive learning environment for the lesson, how effective you are at creating a good rapport with 'the pupil' and the right atmosphere for learning to take place. You should display a relaxed, outgoing and confident, patient and tactful manner whilst avoiding any undue familiarity. You should also avoid any unnecessary physical contact with 'the pupil' as this can be reflected in the marking of this section.

Section 6- Instructional Techniques

Instructor's use of controls
This refers to all driver operated controls (Steering, indicators, brakes etc.), not just the dual foot controls. They should only be used to maintain the safety of you and the pupil or as part of a demonstration. The pupil should be told when and why they have been used. You must not be controlling the pupil all or most of the time through use of dual controls as this would be viewed as a lack of, or failure of, your verbal instruction.

It is permissible to take the instructional ability test in a vehicle without dual pedals. A dual interior mirror should be fitted.

Feedback and encouragement
Encouraging the pupil is part of any lesson. The pupil needs to know when he/she has done something well. Feedback is linked to both the level of instruction and the Core Competencies. With fault assessment you are telling the pupil what they are doing wrong and how to correct it. It is vital that we balance this by providing feedback and encouragement when the pupil is doing something right or improving. Praise, confirmation, reinforcement for effort, progress and achievement are all areas where feedback and encouragement can be an effective instructional technique. Also, use of appropriate feedback in response to pupil's questions.

Question and answer techniques
This is covered fully with a separate chapter of this manual.

Communication

Here the examiner will assess how well he thinks a pupil would understand your instruction. Using clear, easy to understand language without too much use of jargon (with or without explanation) and also avoiding over-technical and complex explanations.

Control of lesson

In its basic form, this includes directions which should be clear and given at the correct time and instruction (such as talkthroughs) which should be given in good time to allow the pupil to respond to the situation at hand. While this element is closely linked with level of instruction it should not be confused with it. Control is about controlling and/or stopping any unsafe driving practices that may occur during the lesson. For example, if the pupil is about to emerge from a junction unsafely then you should control the situation with some timely instruction such as 'Wait! You do not have a safe gap'.

Planning

This concerns how both the structure and content of your lesson is used to achieve the lesson objectives within the time limit. With only 30 minutes for each phase, good planning is essential. This manual contains, at the beginning of each lesson, a basic lesson plan including approximate timings.

The example below shows how you might plan Emerging at T-junctions phase 1:

Recap questions at the beginning and setting the objective
2–3 minutes

Briefing
8–10 minutes

Full Talkthrough (approximately 3–4 junctions)
8–10 minutes

Prompting -less instruction with Q&A (approximately 2–3 junctions)
3–4 minutes

Independence from instruction (depends on progress of pupil)
3–4 minutes

Summary
1 minute

Level of Instruction

This is where the examiner will compare the level of instruction given against the ability of the pupil for each phase of the examination. The two areas to avoid are:

Under instruction: A typical example at phase 1, where you are teaching a new subject such as turn in the road, would be to omit to give a full talkthrough to the pupil after the briefing (see lesson 3 for appropriate talkthrough).

Over instruction: A typical example at phase 2, where you are reviewing an area of a pupil's driving such crossroads, would be to resort to a full talkthrough routine to correct an error such as right corner cut when fault assessment of that error would suffice.

The grade given for level of instruction is normally the same as the overall grade for each phase.

Section 7- Core Competencies

This is an assessment of how you dealt with all faults the examiner/pupil made over the whole lesson and not individual faults. The rating given will reflect the balance between correct and incorrect fault assessment. This is the most important part of the examination and will ultimately determine your final grade, so your aim should always be to deal fully with the majority of faults.

Fault identification
This is an assessment of your ability to clearly identify all the important faults committed by the pupil during the lesson. The faults will be based mainly around the key points for each PST, but you should deal fully with any obvious fault that you identify.

Fault analysis
This is an assessment of how accurately you analyse the cause of the fault. The analysis should be based around the reason why you think the fault has happened and/or what has been caused (consequences) by the fault.

Remedial Action (Fault rectification)
This is an assessment of your ability to cure each fault that you have identified and analysed. This often includes instruction and advice such as reference points with the objective that the pupil can eventually remedy the fault independently of you.

A full and detailed explanation of the Core Competencies is covered in a separate section of this manual.

Section 8- The results of the test.

1. Criteria for grading

See part 3 examination sheet (side 2) in this manual for an explanation of the criteria for grading.

2. Overall assessment mark

To pass the examination you must achieve a minimum competency of a grade 4 in each of the two phases. The lowest rating of the core competencies in each phase will reflect the grading given. This means for example, if at phase one you were given a 4 for fault identification, a 3 for fault analysis and a 4 for remedial action, your overall grade for phase one would be a 3. You must achieve a grade of 4 or higher in each phase to pass the examination.

Question and Answer Technique

Introduction

Question and answer technique is used in a number of different ways in both phase 1 and phase 2 lessons. Numerous examples are given throughout this manual and it is worth studying their construction and wording. The aim of this section is to look in detail at how to construct effective questions.

A breakdown of the times when Q&A can be used effectively are:

Recap

Beginner or partly trained (phase 1) - As you are teaching a new subject the questions are focused on checking the pupil's previous knowledge.

Trained or Full Licence Holder (phase 2) - Here you are reviewing a subject, so the questions are aimed at assessing the pupil's current knowledge and understanding of that subject.

Prompting

This is used mostly at phase 1 as a technique for moving the pupil from full talkthrough towards independence.

Pro-active

During the recap we are trying to assess the pupil's current knowledge. Pro-active Q&A is used to expose gaps in the pupil's knowledge and can be an extremely effective technique on the move at phase 2.

Fault assessment

This is used mainly during a phase 2 lesson where, once a fault has been identified, we need to find suitable questions for the analysis and/or rectification to determine why the pupil (who has previous experience of the subject) has committed the fault.

Recap

Nearly every driving lesson starts with a Recap Q&A session and this would normally include questions to check the pupil's knowledge of their previous lesson with you. In the examination however, you are meeting the pupil for the first time and are required to teach a certain subject chosen by the examiner. Time allowed for the Recap is very short and the introductory description of the pupil given by the examiner tells you very little about their previous experience.

Phase 1: This is particularly relevant at phase one, where apart from the Controls lesson (where you are usually told this is the first ever driving lesson) and Moving Off and Stopping (where you are usually told the pupil has had one previous lesson which was Controls), the only information given is that the pupil has had several previous driving lessons. If you ask the pupil/examiner how many lessons he has had, the reply is normally 'I cannot remember exactly how many' and even if he did tell you, this is of little value as some pupils learn quickly and some slowly. You could also ask what the pupil did on his last lesson and this could be more relevant depending on the response. If, for example, you are teaching crossroads and the pupil informed you that on his last lesson he learnt about emerging at T-junctions, then you would want to find out more about his knowledge of MSPSL etc. However, if, for example, you are required to teach Turn in the Road and the pupil covered Pedestrian Crossings and Use of Signals on his last lesson, then this information is of limited value.

What you are really trying to find out with the phase 1 Recap is what skills does the pupil have already which you can use and develop within the new topic you are about to instruct. To help you assess this, the following diagram shows a 'Hierarchy of Learning' which sets out, in a visual way, what lessons the pupil may have already done before.

Hierarchy of Learning

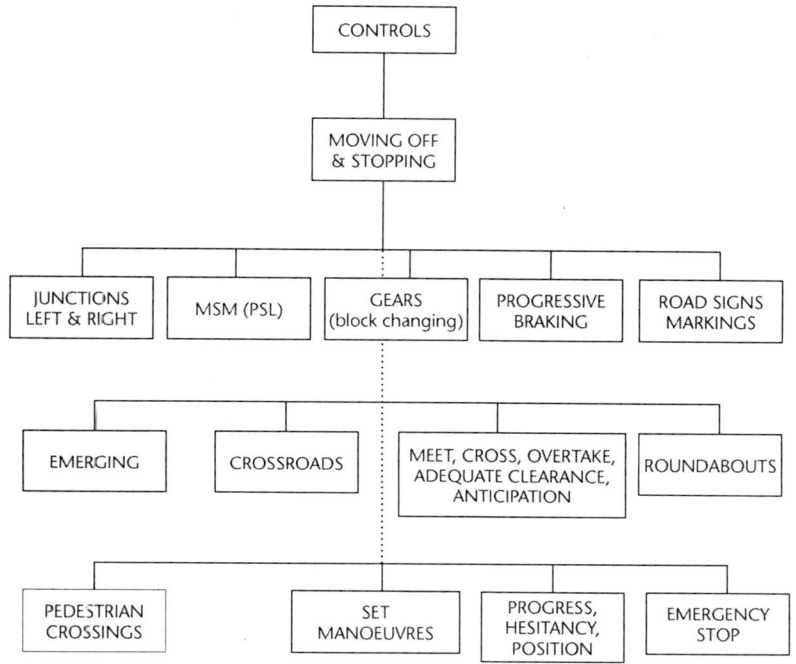

How to use this diagram: If, for example you are about to teach Crossroads as a new subject then the pupil should have previous experience of all the lessons above this such as Junctions left and right, MSPSL, Moving Off and Stopping etc. The pupil may also have done some or all of the lessons on the same line as Crossroads such as Emerging.

Manoeuvres can be taught at any time after the pupil has learnt the basics of Moving Off and Stopping and turning at junctions, so this is shown as a broken line.

The examiner usually goes into role as a pupil at the driving test centre and, for all the phase 1 pre-set tests, apart from controls and moving off and stopping, he will start in the driving seat. Depending on what the first few junctions are as you leave the driving test centre, this can sometimes add to the confusion as to the pupil's previous experience. For example, if you are required to teach Approaching junctions to turn either right or left (pst 7 phase 1) then this would normally be done before teaching Emerging. However, if the first junction outside the driving test centre is a T junction and the second a roundabout, then how is the pupil going to be able to manage this? The examiner usually gets over this problem by saying that all his previous driving lessons started from the driving test centre and so he is hinting that he has driven out of the test centre before (see lesson 7 where a full scenario is given).

How you ask the question will ultimately determine what answer you get. Your aim when constructing your questions is that there are only two possible replies: either the answer you are looking for, or the pupil says they don't know. If you have to ask two or three questions to obtain the answer, then usually the original question was not constructed well enough. Also you should avoid questions where the pupil can respond with a simple "yes" or "no".

As an initial example, lets presume that you want to know if the pupil knows how to use progressive braking.
You could say:
How do you use the brake? But the pupil could say: *With my right foot.*
Or you could say:
Do you know what progressive braking is? But here the pupil could reply simply: *Yes.*
But if you said:
What does progressive braking mean? Then the pupil will either give you the answer or say they don't know.

A good way to start a question is to use What? Why? Which? Where? When? or How? For example:

- *Which mirrors do you check before signalling right?*
- *Why is it important to bring the clutch up slowly when moving off?*
- *Where should you position your vehicle when turning right at a T-junction?*
- *When should you signal if you were taking the second road on the left?*
- *How do you assess a safe gap in the oncoming traffic when turning right (major to minor)?*

Another useful technique is to try to amalgamate several questions into one. For example, if you were checking a pupil's knowledge of the MSPSL routine when turning right from a major road, you could ask a question on each element such as:

- *When turning right from a major road to a minor road, which mirrors would you check?*
- *When would you signal?*
- *Where would you position your vehicle?*

However, this could all be amalgamated as follows:

- *Take me through the routine you would use when turning right from a major road to a minor road?*

Here, with one question the pupil has to describe the whole routine to you. You could then ask supplementary questions to clarify any particular point. For example, if the pupil starts by saying: 'I would check my mirrors' you could then ask: *'which mirrors and in what order?'* Or if he said: 'I would position my vehicle just left of the centre line' You could ask: *'What reference point do you have to check this?'*

As mentioned earlier the aim of the Recap at phase 1 is to check what skills the pupil has already which you can use and develop within the new topic you are about to instruct. For some lessons, this is more obvious than others. For example, if you were teaching Emerging (Lesson 8), then you would ask questions based around Approaching Junctions to Turn either Right or Left (Lesson 7) and if you were teaching Crossroads then some of your questions would be based on Emerging at T-junctions.

As a contrast, let's look at recap questions for Pedestrian Crossings (Lesson 6) as a new subject. Here you need to take a wider look at what you think may be the pupil's previous experience both as a driver and as a pedestrian. For example:

- *As you are about to turn left from a major road to a minor road, a pedestrian starts to cross the road in front of you, who has the priority?*
- *As a pedestrian, as you approach a zebra crossing to cross the road, what does the traffic usually do?*
- *When a vehicle lets you cross, whereabout does it stop?*

Another useful technique is to start a question with a short description to ensure that the mental picture in the pupil's mind is the same as yours. For example:

- *Imagine you are driving down a major road at 30 mph in 4th gear and I ask you to take the next road on the left, take me through the routine you would use on approach.*

This descriptive approach can then continue as you ask further questions. For example:

- *Ahead of you is a pedestrian on the left hand pavement who looks as if he/she is about to cross the road, how will this affect your speed of approach?*

Phase 2: Here we are reviewing a subject of which the pupil has previous experience, apart from one scenario with reverse parking (see lesson 6A). Our main aim with the recap is to assess the pupil's current knowledge of the chosen subject.

Base the questions on the key points listed under column A on the examination marking sheet. These are also listed at the beginning of each phase 2 lesson in this manual.

Your aim should be to ask a question for each of the key points during the few minutes available at the beginning of the lesson. This is easier with some subjects than others. For example, for Progress, Hesitancy and Normal Road Positioning (lessons 5A & 10A) we have 5 key points, but for Approaching Junctions to Turn either Right or Left (lesson 3A) we have 11 key points. You should normally allow 3–4 minutes for the phase 2 recap questions so any questions that cannot be asked during this time can be covered on the move.

When constructing your questions, you should remember that you are dealing with either a trained pupil or full licence holder who should have a good knowledge of the chosen subject. Your questions should seek to find out the extent of this knowledge. For example, if you were covering Emerging at phase 2 (lesson 4A) and you wanted to check the pupil's approach routine with regards to signalling, compare the following questions:

- *After checking your mirrors, what do you need to do next?*

This tells you very little other than if the pupil is familiar with the MSM routine.

- *After checking your mirrors, how far from the junction would you usually signal?*

This question will give you a little more information about the pupil's knowledge, but consider the following question:

- *After checking your mirrors, what do you look for ahead of you to ensure that your signal is properly timed?*

This last question really tests the pupil's knowledge. It takes into account the fact that your command for emerging is 'at the end of the road, turn left/right,' and so there could be a minor left or right turn before the end of the road which would alter the timing of the signal.

With some of the key point lists it is fairly obvious which questions to ask. If we take Approaching Junctions to Turn Right or Left (lesson 3A) we have a list that includes the following: Mirrors, signal, brakes, gears, coasting etc. With other lessons this is not so obvious. If we take Meeting, Adequate clearance and Anticipation (lesson 2A) the relevant key points are:

MSM, meet approaching traffic, keep a safe distance, shaving other vehicles and anticipation of pedestrians, drivers and cyclists.

Take the first key point MSM, what is it you want to find out as the pupil uses this routine in numerous different situations? However, if you link it to the next key point of meeting approaching traffic, now you can ask the following:

- *Imagine you are driving down a main road and you see a parked vehicle ahead of you on your side of the road, what is the first thing you should do?*
- *If the road is clear ahead of you do you usually need to signal right, before passing the parked vehicle?*

After these initial two questions you could introduce the meeting element by asking:

- *Now imagine that as you approach the parked vehicle there is an oncoming vehicle, how do you assess if you have a safe gap to pass or you need to hold back?*

Then you can develop this as follows:

- *If you need to hold back, what is your ideal hold back position?*
- *Before moving off again, why is it important to check your mirrors?*

Study the Recap questions for lesson 2A for further examples.

Prompting Q&A

This is a form of Q&A which is used mostly with a beginner or partly trained pupil and is used to bridge the gap between full control and independence. Let's use Moving off and stopping as an example. After the briefing you will be controlling the pupil on the move using full talkthrough (see lesson 2). After the pupil can perform this exercise under your control, then you need to reduce your instruction. However, to expect a pupil to move from being under your full control to suddenly doing the exercise on their own is too big a leap, so we need a bridge to lead them from one to the other and this is called 'prompting'.

Full talkthrough ————————> Prompting Q&A ————————> Independence

The best way to do this is to take selected commands from the talkthrough and change them into questions putting what, why, which, when, where or how at the beginning. Compare the following:

Moving Off

Talkthrough	Prompting
• Check mirrors, clutch gently up, gently on gas.	*What is your normal driving position?*
• Steer ¼ turn to right, ½ turn left, ¼ turn to right.	*How much do you need to steer?*
• Clutch gently up until car starts to move, keep feet still. • Release the handbrake. • Check interior, right mirror & right blind spot again.	*Move off when you are ready*
• Indicate up right.	*Do you need to indicate?*
• Check your left blind spot, left exterior mirror, interior mirror, forward, right exterior mirror & right blind spot.	*Where are you looking before you move off?*
• Gently clutch up until engine note dips slightly, keep both feet still. • Set gas with your right foot, keep foot still. • Hand back on steering wheel. • Push lever left and forward to select 1st gear. • Left hand on gear lever palm towards me. • Clutch down hold it down. • Left foot cover clutch. • Both hands on steering wheel at 10–2 position.	*Prepare the car to move*
• Start the engine. • Check the handbrake is on and the gear lever is in neutral.	*Carry out your safety precautions and start the engine*

Pro-active Q&A

This form of Q&A is most effective when used with either a trained pupil or a full licence holder (phase 2), where you are assessing a subject in which the pupil has previous knowledge.

There are two basic approaches with this type of pupil: Reactive or Pro-active.

The Reactive approach is to sit quietly and watch the pupil as he drives, wait for the faults to happen and then try to deal with them. This approach often leads to a feeling of the pupil being more in control than the instructor.

The Pro-active approach is to use early targeted questions to try to expose gaps in the pupil's knowledge in order to expose some of these faults. The result is that you either stop faults before they happen or reduce their effect. To illustrate this, look at the following examples for approaching and emerging at a closed T-junction to turn right:

Instructor:
'Is this an open or closed junction?'

Pupil:
'Closed.'

Instructor:
'How will that affect your speed of approach?'

Pupil:
'I will need to slow down more and pause at the give-way line.'

Instructor:
'Where are you going to position the car?'

Pupil:
'Just left of the centre line.'

Instructor:
'Does the centre line stay straight?'

Pupil:
'No, it curves to the right.'

Instructor:
'How will you deal with this?'

Pupil:
My other instructor told me to keep my wheels straight on approach to turn right.'

Instructor:
'Steer slightly to the right as you approach the give-way line.'

Here the pro-active Q&A managed to expose a potential positioning fault before it happened and so give the opportunity for the instructor to control it.

The secret to effective pro-active Q&A is to make an early assessment of the road ahead in relation to the subject. In the example given above, the instructor noticed that the centre line curved to the right just before the give-way line and wanted to know how the pupil would react to this.

Numerous examples of pro-active Q&A are given throughout the phase 2 lessons.

Fault Assesment Q&A

Once again this form of Q&A is used mostly with a trained pupil or full licence holder. The pupil should usually have a good knowledge and previous experience of the subject to be covered, so if a fault is committed you need to find out why it has happened.

Fault assessment is dealt with fully in a separate chapter but the first thing to say here is: ***Never ask a question to identify a fault.*** This should always be a statement of what the pupil has done wrong. However, once the fault has been identified then we need to find the gap in the pupil's knowledge and the best way to do this is to ask a question to cover the analysis and a question to cover the rectification (remedial action). As an example, consider the following:

Pupil stops too early as he approaches a give-way line.

Instructor:
'You have stopped too early (identification statement). *How does this affect your vision into the new road? (analysis question)*'

Pupil:
'My view is partially blocked.'

Instructor:
'What reference point do you use to ensure you have stopped at the give -way line?'

Pupil:
'I try to get the front of the car just behind the double white line.'

Instructor:
'Can you see the end of the bonnet on this car? (rectification question)'

Pupil:
'No, I just try to guess where it is.'

Instructor:
'Next time look for the give-way lines to appear just under your right exterior mirror before stopping.'

The Core Competencies

As the name suggests, the Core Competencies or Fault Assessment, are the most important part of the instructional ability examination and will ultimately decide whether you pass or fail. The three areas that make up the Core Competencies are as follows:

- Fault identification
- Fault analysis
- Remedial action (Rectification)

This can be translated into three basic questions:

- What did the pupil do wrong?
- Why did it happen and/or what were the consequences?
- How do you put it right in a way that will enable the pupil to rectify the fault independently of you?

Your overall grading in both the instructional ability test and subsequent check tests is usually based on the lowest core competency mark. For this reason it is vital that full and timely fault assessment is given for each fault the pupil commits.

Fault Identification

Identifying faults is probably the easiest part of the core competencies as, if you are looking for it, you can observe the mistake. The following check list will help you to achieve this:

- For each subject (PST), have a mental check list of possible faults; in the examination this will be based on the key points for the lesson.
- Observe the pupil.
- Observe the road ahead for early warning of possible hazards that could lead to faults.
- Be pro-active: don't wait for faults to happen: try to predict them.

Once a fault has been committed, it should be identified straight away. This should be done with a clear statement of what is wrong – don't use questions to identify a fault. This applies for all types of pupil (beginner, partly trained, trained etc). The following example highlights this:

Fault:
Pupil doesn't check right exterior mirror before signalling right.

Instructor could say:
What mirror should you check before signalling right?

However, this does not tell the pupil what he has done wrong. He may even answer the question correctly as he may be unaware that he has made a mistake.

Instructor should say:
'You didn't check your right exterior mirror before signalling'. Here the fault is clearly identified with a short statement of what was wrong.

Avoid retrospective fault identification. This is where a pupil has committed a fault but you do not identify it straight away. For example:

> A pupil approaches a closed T-junction but stops too early before the give way line. The instructor notes this but doesn't say anything until the pupil has negotiated the junction. He then tells the pupil 'You stopped too early at the last T-junction'. The pupil could say 'No, I didn't, I thought I stopped in the right place', as he may not be aware of the fault. If the instructor had clearly identified the fault when it happened, then the pupil could see the mistake and even if the analysis and rectification were done later to avoid holding up any following traffic at the junction, the pupil would still recall the fault.

The phase 1 and phase 2 lessons in this manual contain numerous examples of clear fault identification.

Fault Analysis

Fault analysis is often the most difficult part of the Core Competencies because you have to work out why the fault happened - was it a lack of knowledge of the correct procedure or was there something else that the pupil was doing which caused the fault?

Let us take the example given on the previous page: A pupil approaches a closed T-junction but stops too early before the give way line. Any one of the following could be the analysis:

1.   The pupil could simply not have a reference point (or forgotten it) for stopping.
2.   He/she does not realise the consequences of stopping too early (cuts zone of vision) and thought it was safer to stop early than late.
3.   The reference point could be wrong or not work well - the pupil could be trying to stop with the front of the car just behind the give-way line, but on most modern cars the front of the car is not visible from the driver's seat so a certain amount of guess work is involved.
4.   It could be that just as the pupil reaches the give way line and they change back into 1st gear, they are looking down at the gear lever instead of the give-way line.
5.   It could be that as they put the clutch down just before stopping it causes a reaction with the right foot of braking harder.
6.   It could be that they have experienced drivers turning right from the main road cutting the corner and so they feel it is safer to stop early, even though they know the correct reference point.

Here I have given six possible causes of the fault and there could be others. Your job as an instructor is to work out which one applies to the pupil. Sometimes this is done simply by observing the pupil such as in 4 above, or you could feel what has happened as in 5 above. For the other examples it is often a process of elimination using some Q&A. For example, you could start by asking the pupil if he is aware of the consequences of stopping early, then if this is answered correctly, follow this by asking what reference point the pupil uses. If this is answered correctly and you have not observed any other reason why this could have happened, then you have eliminated two possible causes. Your next question would then logically be to ask the pupil why he stopped early and this is when you would discover an answer such as in example 6.

In the examination the faults will be based around the key points for the lesson and it is useful to have a 'mental database' of potential causes as in the example above.

For a beginner or partly trained pupil where we are teaching a new subject we use more telling than questioning for the analysis as we are developing the pupil's knowledge. For a trained pupil or full licence holder where you are reviewing a subject, then we use more Q&A to answer the question why has the pupil done this wrong (where is the gap in their knowledge)?

Study the phase 1 and phase 2 lessons in this manual which contain numerous examples of fault analysis.

Remedial action

This is often known as Fault Rectification. The objective is to give a solution to the fault that will enable the pupil to overcome the error and avoid repeating it and to be able to do this independently of you. Let us once again take the example of a pupil who approaches a closed T-junction but stops too early before the give way line.

Our rectification could be: *'Move up a bit - a bit more- right stop there. This is where I want you to stop next time.'* However, this will not cure the fault as the pupil is only in the right place because you have placed him there and has no reference of how to do this on his own.

However if the rectification was: *'I want you to move forward until you can see the give-way lines just appear under your right exterior door mirror.'* Now the pupil has a reference point which he can use next time on his own to help position correctly.

Your remedy should be precise, clear and concise. Use doing words such as: start; check; keep; select; use; look; turn; straighten; steer; and then qualify these doing words with specific actions. For example if you are trying to rectify the point where a pupil should steer left when turning major to minor: *steer left three quarters of a turn,* or *steer left when the front of your car reaches the last straight kerb stone before the bend,* or this can be developed further by using reference points such as *'steer left when you can see the curved kerbstones are in the bottom left hand corner of your front windscreen.'*

For a beginner or partly trained pupil where you are teaching a new subject, use more telling than questioning for the remedial action in the early stages of the lesson.

For a trained pupil or full licence holder use questioning to establish if the pupil has a rectification such as a reference point and if, in your opinion it would work. For example, let's once again take the fault of a pupil who approaches a closed

T-junction but stops too early before the give way line. It is established, using Q&A, that the pupil is using a reference point of trying to position the front of the car just behind the give-way line. However you assess that the front of the car is not visible from the drivers seat so a certain amount of guess work must be involved which is why the pupil's reference point is not working. Now you can instruct by giving the pupil a more effective reference point: *'I want you to stop when you see the give-way lines just appear under your right exterior door mirror.'*

Study the phase 1 and phase 2 lessons in this manual which contain numerous examples of fault rectification.

> Instructor notes: All reference points given in this manual are examples only and may need to be changed or adapted to whichever tuition vehicle you are using.

Fault Assessment Development

A good way to develop a 'mental database' for effective fault assessment is to make a list of the key points for each of the lessons contained in this manual. Next to each key point, list the faults that you think could be made, then a clear identification of the fault. Next to this, list what the analysis could be and finally a rectification for each fault.

Key Point	Fault	Identification	Analysis	Remedy

As an example, the following table uses the key points from lesson 8 - Emerging at T-junctions. This is not an exhaustive list but serves to highlight the value of developing a 'mental database' of what faults could occur and just as importantly, a vocabulary of words and phrases that will allow you to deliver the identification, analysis and remedy in a concise and effective manner.

Fault Assessment Table Example: Emerging at T-Junctions

Key Point	Fault	Identification	Analysis	Remedy
MSM	Doesn't check mirrors before signalling	You didn't check your mirrors before signalling	You need to check the speed and proximity of the vehicles behind you before signalling	Remember MSM, Mirrors, Signal, Manoeuvre
	Checks mirrors in wrong order	You have checked your mirrors in the wrong order	You need to check your interior mirror first as this gives you a true picture of the vehicles behind you	Remember 'Inside to outside' and check interior mirror followed by exterior mirror
	Checks wrong exterior mirror when turning right	You have checked the wrong exterior mirror	You need to check your right exterior mirror for any overtaking vehicles such as a motorbike	Always check the exterior mirror for the direction you intend to take
Speed	Approach speed too fast (closed junction)	You are too fast, slow down (or more brake)	You are not braking early enough OR this is a closed junction and you need to pause at the end of the road	By the time you are 1 to 2 car lengths from the junction your speed should be reduced to only 5 mph
	Approach speed too slow (open junction)	You have slowed down too early OR too much	There are no approaching vehicles in the new road and you have a safe gap	At an open junction, if you have a safe gap, approach in 2nd gear at about 10–12 mph
Gears	Uses gears to slow vehicle instead of brakes (3rd–2nd–1st)	Don't use the gears to slow the car down	If you do not brake the driver behind you will not see any brake lights and cannot judge your speed	Remember, 'brakes to slow - gears to go'. You can block change from 3rd to 1st as you approach the give-way line
	Stops at the give-way line in 2nd gear	You are in the wrong gear	If you try to emerge in 2nd gear you may stall the vehicle	Change into 1st gear between 1 & ½ a car length from the give-way line before you stop
Coasting	Changes into 1st gear too early (closed junction) and keeps clutch down	You are coasting	This is because you have changed gear too early	Only change into 1st gear between 1 & ½ a car length from the give-way line
Observation	Pupil staring to the right at the give way line	You are not looking left	You need to check for obstructions and pedestrians on your left	Look right, left and right as many times as it takes before crossing the give-way line to ensure it is safe to emerge - glance don't stare
Emerging	Pupil tries to emerge unsafely	Stop! You do not have a safe gap	You will cause the vehicle on your right to slow down	To assess a safe gap ask yourself 'can I walk across the road and back again safely'
Position Right	Offside wheels are over the centre line	You are too far to the right	You will be in conflict with oncoming vehicles	Check that the centre line is visible in the bottom right hand corner of your windscreen and, if the centre line is straight, keep your wheels straight
Position Left	Doesn't steer enough to the left when approaching the give-way line	You are too far from the left kerb	You are looking right for a gap but not looking left on approach	Glance to the left on approach and make sure the left hand kerb is visible in the left hand corner of your front windscreen as you approach the give-way line
Pedestrains	Doesn't slow down enough as pedestrian walks across end of road	Slow down there is a pedestrian crossing the road	The end of the road is a common place for pedestrians to cross the road and you need to anticipate this may happen	At a closed junction you need to approach at a speed where you can stop safely if a pedestrian crosses the road near the give-way line

Part 4

Check Test Preparation

The Check Test

Introduction

Once you have qualified as an Approved Driving Instructor (ADI) you will be inspected periodically, by a DSA examiner, to ensure that you retain and display the competence to give instruction that you demonstrated during your part 3 instructional ability examination.

Under the Road Traffic Act the full name for these inspections is: 'tests of continued ability and fitness to give instruction in the driving of motor cars' but is more commonly known as 'check tests'.

The regulations state that you will be assessed on your instructional ability and in particular the following:
*   Method, clarity, adequacy and correctness of instruction
*   Observation and proper correction of the pupil's errors
*   Manner, patience and tact in dealing with the pupil
*   Ability to inspire confidence

The Frequency of Tests

This depends on your grade. For newly qualified ADIs, the Supervising Examiner will try to arrange an 'educational check test' within the first year to help you prepare for the 'real thing' which should take place soon after this first year is up. As this is at the discretion of the Supervising Examiner, it is in your interest that you contact him/her to ensure that you receive this valuable feedback.

To stay on the register, all ADIs must achieve at least a grade 4. Grade 4 instructors are usually check tested every two years and grade 5 or 6 instructors every four years.

The Appointment

You will be contacted by the DSA ADI Check Test Booking Office informing you of the place (usually your local test centre), date and time of your check test. This is usually between 4–6 weeks prior to the appointment. All appointments will be confirmed by post and you should ensure you return the completed appointment slip confirmation within 10 days of receiving it.

You must attend the check test on this date unless exceptional circumstances prevent you from doing so.

Occasionally, you may also be contacted to see if you would be available to attend a check test at short notice if your local test centre has a cancellation date to be filled.

You should ensure that you are displaying your valid ADI registration (green badge) in your vehicle. If you are unable to produce and display this, the test will not be conducted.

The Vehicle

Basically the vehicle used for the check test should meet the minimum driving test standards and be roadworthy, safe and reliable. If you have any doubts about the suitability of your vehicle, you should contact DSA ADI Check Test Booking Office or your local examiner.

Pupil or Role Play

The purpose of the check test is for the examiner to observe what you do on a normal lesson with a learner pupil. However, if you do not have a learner pupil available for the check test, you can give a lesson to a full license holder (but not another ADI) or the examiner can offer a 'role play' check test where he/she will portray a trained pupil (more details of this are given in the next section).

> Instructor note: The points highlighted above are general guidelines. For more detailed instructions, you should contact the DSA ADI Check Test Booking Office. **This section does not deal with Fleet Driver Trainer check tests.**

Check Test Preparation

Selecting a pupil

This should be given careful consideration. Do not select your 'star pupil'. The examiner wants to see a lesson tailored to the pupil's needs. Remember they are assessing your ability to instruct, not your pupil's ability to drive so choose a pupil who needs to learn something rather than just practice something already learnt.

The standard of the pupil can range from a total novice to an experienced driver or even a full licence holder.

Subject of the lesson

If you are using a pupil, then you choose whatever subject(s) you feel that best meet the criteria of your pupil's needs and enable the examiner to accurately assess your instructional ability.

Role Play

If you cannot supply a pupil and request a 'role play' check test, then you will be asked to choose a subject from a predetermined list (subject to change by DSA). This list will be sent to you in advance so you can prepare your lesson and you tell the examiner on the day which subject you have chosen. The current list of subjects is as follows:

- A remedial lesson - the subject matter is chosen by the examiner who will provide a driving test report (DL25) on which there will be 2 serious faults recorded and a few driver (minor) faults
- MSM & pedestrian crossings
- MSM & a manoeuvre
- Junctions - the examiner will usually specify whether it is emerging, crossroads or roundabouts
- Meeting, crossing, overtaking, anticipation and pedestrian crossings - a general driving lesson that should include 2 subjects plus anticipation
- Pass Plus module - you must be Pass Plus registered to choose this option. Only modules 2, 3, 5, & 6
- Dual carriageways and open roads
- A disqualified driver needing to take an extended test
- A full licence holder

Unlike the part 3 examination, you choose the route and direct the examiner who will stay in role for the whole of the lesson.

Prepare your car

Make sure your vehicle is clean and tidy inside and out and that the back seat is clear as this is where the examiner will sit if you are using a pupil.

Prepare yourself

Dress smartly but comfortably. First impressions count and the examiner will be asking themselves, does this person look professional?

Don't be late

Make sure you arrive and park at the test centre between 5–10 minutes before your check test is due to start.

Meeting the examiner

Leave your pupil in the car if possible (take the car keys with you) as the examiner will wish to speak to you privately for a few minutes. Be confident when you exchange greetings and, if you do not already know the examiner, make sure you remember his/her name when he/she introduce himself/herself.

Introduction: The examiner will want to ask various questions about the pupil's progress to-date. This should include the number of hours tuition received from you, whether the pupil has received any tuition from another source, any strengths and areas for development of which you are aware and your lesson plan for the check test. It is a good idea to have this information typed out and a copy available for the examiner. If you have kept a Drivers Record of the lessons undertaken, this should also be made available for the examiner to see.

Example of introductory briefing for the examiner

Pupil: Joe Smith

Joe is 17 years old and lives in the local area. He is attending courses at the Adult Education College with the aim of joining the Police.

Joe started with me as a beginner in September and has currently had 12 hours of training. He does, however, drive a motorbike/scooter and so has some useful road experience and also does occasional private practice with his father. He passed his theory examination in October and is a very focused and enthusiastic pupil.

The main objective of today's lesson is to train Joe in all aspects of Crossroads including proceeding ahead, turning left and turning right both approaching on major roads and emerging from minor roads. Depending on the progress made, I may move on to a secondary objective of developing Joe's ability to cross traffic safely at other types of junctions.

I intend to achieve my objectives as follows:
- *Review Joe's existing knowledge of approaching and emerging from other junctions*
- *Develop this knowledge by briefing him on the similarities and differences at crossroads*
- *Carry out some controlled practice through talkthrough*
- *Reduce my instruction using pro-active Q&A techniques to encourage learning to take place*
- *Deal with any faults that occur*

By the end of the lesson, Joe should be able to recognise crossroads early, approach at a safe speed using MSPSL and negotiate safely with due regard for other road users.

The walk to your car

Once the above introductions have been completed the examiner will ask you to take him to your car. During this time, he will normally tell you where he wants to sit and remind you to introduce him to your pupil. Other things he may mention include the duration of the test, where to park at the end and what to do with the pupil while he gives you the debrief.

The lesson

Once you are both in the car, introduce the examiner to your pupil properly and remind the pupil that the examiner is there to assess you and not the pupil. It is also worth mentioning to the pupil that, as there is now an extra person, the car will be heavier and this may affect the braking slightly.

With the introductions over, try to forget that the examiner is there and relax. Concentrate on giving the pupil the lesson he/she needs.

The standard of the pupil chosen will determine what lesson you choose to give. If you choose a beginner or partly trained student and you are teaching something new, then you should construct your lesson using the techniques in part 1 (phase 1) of this manual. A suggested basic structure of the lesson would be as follows:

Recap
Aims and Objectives
Briefing

Talkthrough
Prompting   } The Core Competencies
Independence   Fault Assessment

Recap (summary) at the end

If the pupil is trained, and you are trying to improve an area that the pupil already had some previous experience of, then you should use the techniques shown in part 2 (phase 2). A suggested basic structure would be as follows:

Recap (previous lesson)
Q&A session (check pupil's existing knowledge of subject)
Aims and objectives
Driver development and fault assessment (Core competencies)
Recap (summary) at the end

The most important thing is to give a lesson that the pupil needs and, as stressed previously, that by the end of the lesson the pupil has learnt something.

Example: Check Test Marking Sheet (ADI 26CT) - side 1

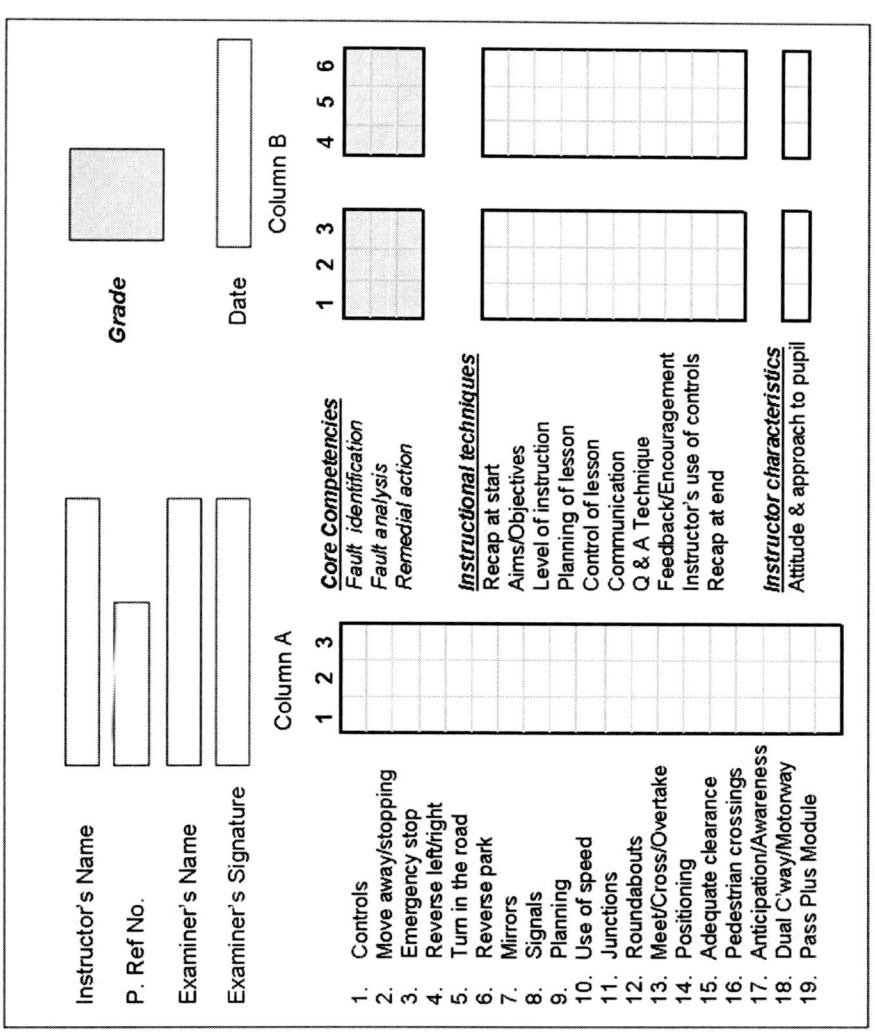

Assessment notes

This form is designed to identify the strengths in your instruction and to highlight the areas which need to be improved upon. It is given in conjunction with the de-briefing at the end of your check test with the aim of improving your teaching skills.

Column A

BOX 1 Subject not covered/incorrect or dangerous instruction.
BOX 2 Subject covered unsatisfactorily.
BOX 3 Subject covered satisfactorily in all respects.

Column B

The marking in this column reflects your performance in relation to the core competencies, the instructional techniques that you employed and your attitude and approach to the pupil and the lesson. Each heading is broken down into a six point rating scale. The closer to the right the mark is, the better you performed.

A majority of the marks placed to the right does not necessarily reflect a high grade as some aspects marked to the left may have played a more significant part in the lesson and therefore have an effect on the overall grading

The criteria for grading are as follows:
6. Overall performance to a very high standard with no significant instructional weaknesses.

5. A good overall standard of instruction with some minor weaknesses in instructional technique.

4. A competent overall performance with some minor deficiencies in instructional technique.

3. An inadequate overall performance with some deficiencies in instructional technique.

2. A poor overall performance with numerous deficiencies in instructional technique.

1. Overall standard of instruction extremely poor or dangerous with incorrect or even dangerous instruction.

The check test examination sheet explained

The content of the boxes on the check test marking sheet is similar to those on the forms for the part 3 instructional ability test and a similar system and standard of marking applies (see section on part 3 examination sheet explained).

Column A

The examiner will record the main content of your lesson by circling appropriate numbers next to column A. This will reflect the lesson given and will include the subject and any other main areas of the pupil's driving that you deal with. For example, if your main aim was to teach a partly trained pupil crossroads as a new subject, then the examiner would record: 11. Junctions. He may record other areas such as 7. Mirrors & 17. Anticipation/Awareness. Also if during the lesson you dealt with a fault at a roundabout and also had to deal with an adequate clearance problem then the examiner may also circle 12. Roundabouts and 15. Adequate clearance.

> Instructor note: The examiner will use a similar marking system to the instructional ability test (part 3) by marking down column A and then start at the bottom of column B with Instructional Characteristics and then work up through the Instructional Techniques (apart from Level of Instruction) to the Core Competencies. Level of Instruction will usually be marked after the core compentencies as this is directly related to the result in the core compentencies. Finally, your grade will be given.

The three columns headed 1, 2 & 3 record your response to the pupil's progress, in other words, the instruction given on each individual item relevant to the subject heading. Each item has three possible marks:

Box 1 - Not covered - subject not covered or grossly incorrect or dangerous instruction given.

Box 2 - Unsatisfactory - subject attempted, but guidance and/or training offered was unsatisfactory or incomplete.

Box 3 - Satisfactory - subject covered satisfactorily or better.

Column B

> Instructor note: You should also refer to the previous sections: Part 3 marking sheet explained; Q&A technique and Fault assessment and use them in conjunction with the following notes.

Core Competencies

This is an assessment of all faults over the whole lesson, both major and minor. It takes into account some explanations you give may be correct, some incorrect and the grade will depend on the balance of correct to incorrect.

As this area will ultimately determine your grade, it is a good idea to have your ability at delivering the core competencies assessed by an ORDIT qualified instructor trainer. If you are not seeing some of the faults, you may not be aware of it and this could seriously affect your final grading.

Fault identification
This covers your ability to clearly identify all the important faults committed by the pupil during the lesson, whether these are within the subject(s) chosen or any other aspect of the pupils driving, that will require correction as part of the effective instructional process. This ability is expected to cover all aspects of control of the car and procedure on the road at all times and covers faults that occur inside (gear, clutch etc.) and outside the car (awareness and anticipation etc.).

Fault analysis
This covers how accurately you analyse the cause of the fault. This is often the area that ADIs find the most difficult and should be based around the reason why you think the fault has happened and/ or what has been caused (consequences) by the fault. If you do not correctly analyse the fault then your remedial action is unlikely to be effective in curing the problem.

Remedial Action (Fault rectification)
This is an assessment of how fully you have explained to the pupil what they need to do to avoid repeating the fault. This may not be immediate if this would be inappropriate at the time, but it should be given at the first opportunity and may include use of visual aids and or reference points etc.

A full and detailed explanation of the Core Competencies is covered in a separate section of this manual.

Instructional Techniques

1. Recap at the start

Beginner or partly trained pupil - If you are teaching a new subject to a pupil then your recap should be based around what was covered during the previous lesson and how what was learnt will help in achieving the aims and objectives of the lesson you are about to begin.

Trained pupil - Where you are trying to improve an area of a pupil's driving of which he/she has some previous experience then, as well as reviewing the previous lesson, you should check the pupil's existing knowledge of the chosen subject.

Role Play - If you have chosen a role play check test then your recap at the start should be an assessment of the pupil's current knowledge of the chosen subject. The lessons in part 2 of this manual contain a wide range of suitable recap scenarios.

2. Aims/Objectives

These should obviously be the same as those given to the examiner prior to the start of the lesson. It is a good idea to have one main subject and then a back-up secondary one in case the pupil achieves the first one earlier than you expected (see the example of introductory briefing for the examiner). The pupil should clearly understand what the aims & objectives of the lesson are and how you intend to achieve them.

3. Level of instruction

You must match your level of instruction to the level of the pupil so that the pupil can, with your guidance achieve the aims/objectives you have set (also see relevant section of Part 3 marking sheet explained). The mark given in this section will normally match your final grade.

4. Planning of lesson

The test lasts about one hour and within this time limit you need to achieve the aims/objectives you have chosen, so it is vitally important that you plan your lesson carefully. Planning should include the following elements:

- The allocation of time between theory (briefing) and practice (talkthrough, prompting etc)
- How the actual sequence of your instruction aids the progress of the pupil towards achieving the aims/objectives
- Ensuring that the route chosen is commensurate with the pupil's ability to cope with the various traffic conditions. If for example you are teaching crossroads then make sure that your route allows the pupil to attempt the same junction from the same direction several times. This will give the pupil the opportunity, once a fault has been committed, to be able to correct this firstly under your guidance and then independently before moving on to other areas of the lesson. Plan your route carefully prior to the test and it is a good idea to drive it several times yourself to ensure it is the right route for your pupil and to achieve the aims/objectives

5. Control of lesson

It is important that you stay in control throughout the lesson. You should ensure that:

- You use correct and timely route directions: *At the next roundabout take the road ahead second exit* - Not - *Go straight on at the next roundabout*; Or *At the end of the road turn left* - Not - *Take a left at the end of the road*
- Instruction needs to be flexible to take into account any road or traffic conditions experienced during the lesson
- Your instruction takes into account your pupil's ability to respond.

Control should not be confused with level of instruction. Think of control as stopping or correcting any unsafe driving practices committed by your pupil and you need to use the appropriate amount of instruction to ensure you remain in control throughout the lesson. In some cases, this may even mean diverting from your original aims/objectives to deal with a serious or persistent fault that has occurred. For example: Say you have chosen to teach a partly trained pupil emerging at T-junctions. However, during the lesson you find that your pupil has a persistent adequate clearance problem of being too close when passing parked vehicles. This needs to be dealt with as the examiner makes an assessment of all faults observed during the lesson. The main criteria is that the lesson meets the needs of the pupil.

6. Communication

Your pupil needs to be able to clearly understand your instruction. Make sure you use appropriate language and be careful in your use of jargon and terminology, explaining any terms that may not be understood – for example, if you are dealing with crossroads and you are telling the pupil about offside and nearside when turning right, does the pupil know what the offside or nearside of the vehicle is? Avoid complex explanations where possible.

7. Q&A technique

Use Q&A technique at appropriate points where this will contribute towards realizing the objectives of your lesson. The separate section in this manual on Q&A technique should be studied carefully. As well as asking questions to the pupil you should consider provoking questions from the pupil when appropriate. Be careful not to ask too many questions that could overwhelm or distract the pupil when on the move.

8. Feedback and encouragement

A vital part of any lesson is to ensure you tell the pupil when they are improving or doing something well. This should be continuous in the form of praise, confirmation, encouragement for effort, acknowledging progress and when a task is achieved. Remember that, when asking a pupil questions, it is very important to listen carefully to the answer so that you can respond with appropriate feedback and encouragement.

9. Instructor's use of controls

This refers to all driver operated controls (Steering, indicators, brakes etc.), not just the dual foot controls. They should only be used to maintain the safety of you, other road users and the pupil or as part of a demonstration. The pupil should be told when and why they have been used and when you hand back control. You must not be controlling the pupil all or most of the time through use of dual controls as this would be viewed as a lack of or failure of your verbal instruction.

10. Recap at end

At the end of the lesson, you should summarise the main points covered during the lesson. The summary should highlight how well the pupil has achieved the aims/ objectives and should normally include a plan for the next lesson. Praise should be given for tasks well done and areas for improvement should be identified. The summaries at the end of each lesson in section 2 of this manual give some good examples of how to construct an end of lesson recap.

Instructor characteristics - Attitude and approach to pupil

This covers your ability to create a relaxed and supportive learning environment and maintaining the right atmosphere for learning to take place. You should be self-confident, patient, relaxed and enthusiastic. Avoid any unnecessary physical contact with the pupil.

The result

The examiner will endeavour to discuss the check test result in a place where this cannot be heard by other people. This will usually be in a suitable room in the test centre and in this case you should ask your pupil to wait in your vehicle. Occasionally, when a suitable place cannot be found, the examiner may ask the pupil to wait in the main waiting room and carry out the de-brief in your car.

If you have passed, the examiner will tell you whether you have obtained a Grade 4 (competent), Grade 5 (Good) or a Grade 6 (Very Good). This is usually done after the examiner offers some advice on the lesson just seen. There will also be an opportunity for you to ask questions about any driving instruction matters.

If a grade 3 or 2 is awarded then this means that the ADI's performance did not reach an acceptable standard. In addition to the advice and guidance given during the de-brief, the examiner will also send a detailed written report. The ADI will usually be given a further two attempts to meet the required standard. The second check test will normally be in 12 weeks for a grade 3 or 8 weeks for a grade 2. It is strongly advised that, during this period, professional training and guidance is taken, preferably from an ORDIT approved instructor trainer.

If the second check test is also considered to be sub-standard, then the final one will usually be conducted by a more senior examiner to ensure transparency and fairness. If a grade 4 or higher is not achieved on this final check test, then the Registrar will usually decide to remove the ADI from the Register of Approved Driving Instructors.

A check test marked as grade 1 is considered to be dangerous instruction and the examiner may need to intervene and stop the check test if it is felt that to continue could endanger the pupil, the ADI and the examiner. An ADI will usually only be given one further attempt with a more senior examiner to demonstrate they can meet the minimum standards before action is taken to remove them from the Register.

Educational check test

On the first check test after entering the register (if this is within 2 or 3 months after qualifying), the examiner has the discretion to enter an 'E' as the grade if he feels the lesson is not up to standard and improvements need to be made. Faults will be clearly outlined during the de-brief and confirmed in writing. A second check test is usually carried out six months later. If however, the first check test is more than 12 months after qualification, then it is assumed that the ADI will have gained sufficient experience for a normal check test to be carried out.

Important Note: Fleet Driver Trainer Check Tests: ***This manual does not deal with Fleet Driver Trainer check tests.***

Part 5

Appendix

Appendix 1
Abbreviations used in this manual

ABC   accelerator, brake, clutch

ABS   anti-lock braking system

ADI   approved driving instructor

COD   (extra) care, (extra) observation, (extra) danger

DSA   driving standards authority

DSSSM   doors, seat, steering, seat belt, mirrors

FLH   full licence holder

IAN   identify, approach, negotiate

LADA   look, assess, decide, act

MOT   ministry of transport test

MPH   miles per hour

MSM   mirror, signal, manoeuvre

MSPSL   mirror, signal, position, speed, look

PDI   potential driving instructor

POM   preparation, observation, manoeuvre

PST   pre-set test

Q&A   question and answer

RALAR   right ahead, left ahead, right

SCALP   safe, legal and convenient position

SE   senior examiner

Appendix 2
Useful phrases

The following list contains some useful and memorable phrases that can be used with pupils. A brief explanation is given where appropriate.

An element of rush is an element of risk *choosing safe gaps*

Back to front *safety precautions (handbrake, gears)*

Brakes to slow - gears to go

Clutch it - gear it - clutch it - steer it *used to avoid coasting*

Don't know - don't go *choosing safe gaps*

Gears are for going - brakes are for slowing

Inside out *order of checking mirrors*

More paint more danger *refers to road markings*

Never start a manoeuvre you cannot complete *crossing traffic*

Only a fool breaks the 2 second rule *safe separation distance*

Straight and clear - into 4th gear

Slow car - quick wheel *turn in the road*

Tyres and tarmac *safe distance behind stationary vehicle*

When a pause becomes a wait -
apply the handbrake *waiting at junctions*

Where there's a bus there's a fuss

Instructor note: If you have any useful or memorable phrases that you would like to submit for possible inclusion in future additions, please send them to: info@instructordoctors.co.uk

Appendix 3
Voluntary code of practice

Personal conduct
- The instructor will at all times behave in a professional manner towards clients
- Clients will be treated with respect and consideration
- The instructor will try to avoid physical contact with a client except in an emergency or in the normal course of greeting
- Whilst reserving the right to decide against giving tuition, the instructor will not act in any way which contravenes legislation on discrimination.

Business dealings
- The instructor will safeguard and account for any monies paid in advance by the client in respect of driving lessons, test fees or for any other purpose and will make the details available to the client on request
- The instructor on or before the first lesson should provide clients with a written copy of his/her terms of business to include:

    - legal identity of the school/instructor with full address and telephone number at which the instructor or his/her representative can be contacted the price and duration of lessons
    - the price and conditions for use of a driving school car for the practical driving test
    - the terms under which cancellation by either party may take place
    - procedure for complaints

- The instructor should check a client's entitlement to drive the vehicle and his or her ability to read a number plate at the statutory distance on the first lesson. When presenting a client for the practical driving test, the instructor should ensure that the client has all the necessary documentation to enable the client to take the test and that the vehicle is roadworthy.
- Instructors will advise clients when to apply for their theory and practical driving tests, taking into account local waiting times and forecast of clients' potential for achieving the driving test pass standard. The instructor will not cancel or re-arrange a driving test without the client's agreement. In the event of the instructor's decision to withhold the use of the school car for the driving test, sufficient notice should be given to the client to avoid loss of the DSA test fee.
- The instructor should at all times, to the best of his or her ability, endeavour to teach the client correct driving skills according to DSA's recommended syllabus.

Advertising

- The advertising of driving tuition shall be honest; claims made shall be capable of verification and comply with codes of practice set down by the Advertising Standards Authority.
- Advertising that refers to clients' pass rates should not be open to misinterpretation and the basis on which the calculation is made should be made clear.

Conciliation

- Complaints by clients should be made in the first instance to the driving instructor/driving school/contractor following the complaints procedure issued.
- Failing agreement or settlement of a dispute, reference may be made to DSA's Registrar of Approved Driving Instructors who will consider the matter and advise accordingly.
- Should the Registrar not be able to settle the dispute he or she may set up a panel, with representatives from the ADI industry, to consider the matter further or advise that the matter should be referred to the Courts or other statutory body to be determined.

Index

Lightning Source UK Ltd.
Milton Keynes UK
20 August 2010

158729UK00007B/5/P